EAST COAST PILOT

Great Yarmouth to Ramsgate

Garth Cooper & Dick Holness

Imray Laurie Norie & Wilson

Published by
Imray Laurie Norie & Wilson Ltd
Wych House St Ives
Cambridgeshire PE27 5BT England
℡ +44 (0)1480 462114
Email ilnw@imray.com
www.imray.com
2019

1st edition 2005
2nd edition 2008
3rd edition 2011
4th edition 2015
5th edition 2019

ISBN 978 184623 953 3

British Library Cataloguing in Publication Data.
A catalogue record for this book is available from the British Library.

PLANS

The plans in this guide are not to be used for navigation. They are designed to support the text and should at all times be used with up to date navigational charts.

CAUTION

SUPPLEMENTS AND UPDATES

This pilot book will be amended as and when necessary through corrections and updates published on www.eastcoastpilot.com. These may be read and downloaded free of charge. Printed copies are also available on request from the publishers at the above address.

EAST COAST PILOT

Introduction	iv
Acknowledgements	v
Symbols used on charts	vi
Abbreviations	vii
Supporting website	viii
General information	1
Tidal stream diagrams	4

1	GREAT YARMOUTH	8
2	LOWESTOFT	12
3	SOUTHWOLD	18
4	RIVERS ORE AND ALDE	22
5	RIVER DEBEN	30
6	HARWICH HARBOUR	38
7	RIVER STOUR	44
8	RIVER ORWELL	48
9	WALTON BACKWATERS	58
10	RIVER COLNE	66
11	RIVER BLACKWATER	76
12	RIVER CROUCH	92
13	RIVER ROACH	102
14	CANVEY AND LEIGH	110
15	RIVER THAMES	116
16	RIVER MEDWAY	134
17	THE SWALE	154
18	NORTH KENT COAST	170
19	RAMSGATE	178
20	THAMES ESTUARY PASSAGES	182

Index	188

Norwich

Great Yarmouth

Yare

Norfolk

Lowestoft

Benacre Ness

Southwold

Suffolk

Aldeburgh

Alde

Ore

Orford Ness

Woodbridge

Orford

Deben

North Sea

Ipswich

Orwell

Stour

Harwich

Felixstowe

Walton Backwaters

Colchester

Walton

Colne

Brightlingsea

Mersea I

Clacton

Essex

Blackwater

Maldon

Crouch

Burnham

Roach

Havengore I

Southend

River Thames

Holehaven

LONDON

Thames Estuary

I of Sheppey

Herne Bay

Margate

North Foreland

Medway

Rochester

Swale

Whitstable

Ramsgate

Faversham

Sandwich

Kent

Deal

Dover

South Foreland

THE EAST COAST CHAPTER COVERAGE

INTRODUCTION

FULLY REVISED FIFTH EDITION

Welcome to the fifth edition of *East Coast Pilot*. We've had a busy time pounding up and down the East Coast to collect the data and check the huge number of updates and changes that have made this new edition essential.

We've been out and about visiting just about every port, creek and potential mooring hole on the East Coast and in the process, we've met many interesting people, who've helped make putting this new edition together a real joy. Thank you.

Large numbers of you regularly visit our dedicated website at www.eastcoastpilot.com to download updates. By incorporating these into your copy of the book, you will keep it current and ensure that you get full benefit from it as you pilot your boat around the East Coast and Thames Estuary. However, when we fully research the area afresh, as we have for this new edition, we always find even more changes, and these are incorporated now, but may not have been published on the website.

ECP is an evolving project, in previous issues we have extended the area of coverage to include Great Yarmouth in the North, we've expanded the tidal stream diagrams to give more information on each one and have used larger photographs with more overlaid tracks and annotations to make it easier for the pilot approaching a strange port or harbour. In this edition we've added the tidal data for Sheerness as many readers tell us it is more relevant to local sailing than Dover.

Shoal draught

We occasionally use the description 'shoal draught' and it's as well to understand what we mean by the term. For us a shoal draught lies between 3ft 6in and 4ft or 1–1·2m. This is important, because boat sizes (and draughts) are commonly increasing, but many creeks and anchorages are becoming shallower. Beware!

Accuracy and updates

The East Anglian coast and Thames Estuary is an area of huge and frequent change. We have done our best to ensure accuracy at the time of writing, but even by the

The Clyde cruiser *Nixi* dwarfed by the Trinity Quay containers

time of publication there will have been changes, particularly to the entrance channels in river mouths like the Ore and Deben. We must, therefore, caution you to watch for changes and alterations, particularly those shown on www.eastcoastpilot.com and to exercise seamanlike common sense, always referring to the most up-to-date charts and published corrections.

The advice and guidance in ECP is given in good faith and is as accurate as we can make it but neither the authors nor the publisher can accept responsibility for any errors or omissions in the published material.

Electronic chart plotter displays

Chart plotters are widely used, but the temptation to rely on them not only for position fixing but also for pilotage is a bit risky, especially if the power goes down.

The authors base their navigation on paper charts, updated at regular intervals, but find that a modern plotter is a valuable aid to pilotage. However, if you are using paper charts in parallel with either a chart plotter or the Imray Navigator app, it is quite possible for the two systems to be at odds if you have not kept a perfect record of all updates and Notices to Mariners (NtMs).

It is appealing to think you can perhaps find the way up an unmarked creek by following the dotted line on the plotter display that indicates where the deepest water was when the survey was last done but remember that gutways move and many such creeks won't have been surveyed in detail for many years.

Before plotters, we might have approached such a shallow creek challenge by gently weaving from side to side and watching the echo sounder – and that is still a sensible method.

The plotter can be a valuable aid, but it is just that – an aid.

Chart plotters are a useful tool

Honorary Port Pilots

With the second edition of ECP we introduced Honorary Port Pilots (HPPs) who helped us gather updates and offered local, on-the-spot advice to readers who contacted them. Some of these have now stepped down, having perhaps moved away or even given up boating, and we took this opportunity to review the concept. In some places we know that the harbour staff or their equivalent are helpful and friendly, making HPPs less needed than they once were, so we now have a shorter list — Phillip Attwood (Orford and Ore/Alde entrance), John White (Deben), Alec Moss (Walton Backwaters), Nigel Harmer (Blackwater), Rob Scriven (Canvey), and Simon Smedley (Conyer and Swale).

The contact details of these HPPs are listed in the relevant information boxes at the beginning of each chapter and are also listed at www.eastcoastpilot.com.

QR codes

In the fourth edition we introduced QR codes – the black and white chequerboard patterns printed in some of the information boxes. If you use a smartphone or a tablet (with the appropriate free app on it), you can scan these QR codes and link directly to the website wherever you have internet access. It's easier and quicker than trying to type in the web addresses, particularly when butting into a Wallet chop!

ACKNOWLEDGEMENTS

Within Imray Laurie Norie & Wilson, we are indebted to both Willie and Lucy Wilson for their continued enthusiastic support for the ECP project. We're also grateful for the help provided by Jane Russell and the editorial and production team at Imray, without whose patience the development of this fifth edition of *East Coast Pilot* would have been so much more painful.

We would like to say a special thank you to Roger Gaspar, Tim Thomas, Rob Scriven, Tony Lavelle, John Ranson, Adrian Munnings, Peter Hytch, John Langrick – all of whom joined us in the research process.

Finally, we must not forget the many readers who have kept us sailing a good course with a clean wake and provided a steady flow of pilotage updates for our companion website www.eastcoastpilot.com.

Garth Cooper, Dick Holness
June 2019

This is what cruising on the East Coast is all about – a fair wind and well balanced boat

Garth Cooper

Dick Holness

DEDICATION

To the late Colin Jarman who had the original idea and entrusted the project to Garth and Dick to take forward. His quiet wisdom and knowledge are much missed.

SYMBOLS USED ON CHARTS

ABBREVIATIONS

Bn	Beacon	NCM	North Cardinal Mark (eg beacon)
By	Buoy	NE	Northeast or Northeastwards
CC	Cruising Club	NEly	Northeasterly
CG	Coastguard	NW	Northwest, Northwestwards
Ch	Channel	NWly	Northwesterly
Conspic	Conspicuous	Oc	Occulting light
DSC	Digital Selective Calling	ODAS	Ocean Data Acquisition System
E	East, Eastwards, Easterly	PAYG	Pay As You Go
ECB	East Cardinal Buoy	PH	Port Hand
ECM	East Cardinal Mark (eg beacon)	PHB	Port Hand Buoy
F	Fixed light	PHM	Port Hand Mark (eg beacon)
Fl	Flashing light	PLA	Port of London Authority
ft	Foot, feet	Pt	Point
G	Green	PWC	Personal Water Craft (jet ski)
H	Hour, eg H+15 is 15 minutes past the hour	Q	Quick flashing light
hr	Hour, hours	R	Red
HW	High Water	S	South, Southwards, Southerly
HWN	High Water Neaps	s	second(s)
HWS	High Water Springs	SC	Sailing Club
IDM	Isolated Danger Mark	SCB	South Cardinal Buoy
IQ	Interrupted Quick flashing light	SCM	South Cardinal Mark (eg beacon)
Iso	Isophase light	SH	Starboard Hand
kn	Knot, knots	SHB	Starboard Hand Buoy
L.Fl	Long flash	SHM	Starboard Hand Mark (eg beacon)
LNG	Liquefied Natural Gas	S'ly	Southerly
LOA	Length Overall	SW	Southwest,Southwestwards
LPG	Liquefied Petroleum Gas	SWB	Safe Water Buoy
LW	Low Water	SWly	Southwesterly
LWN	Low Water Neaps	SWM	Safe Water Mark
LWS	Low Water Springs	TSS	Traffic Separation Scheme
M	Mile (nautical mile)	UKHO	United Kingdom Hydrographic Office (the Admiralty)
m	metre	UTC	Universal Time Corrected (same as GMT – Greenwich MeanTime)
MHWS	Mean High Water springs	vert	vertical
min	Minute	VQ	Very Quick flashing light
mins	Minutes	VTS	Vessel Traffic Service
MLWS	Mean Low Water Springs	W	West, Westwards, Westerly; White
MMSI	Maritime Mobile Service Identity	WCB	West Cardinal Buoy
MSI	Maritime Safety Information incl. inshore waters forecast, gale warnings and navigational warnings	WCM	West Cardinal Mark (eg beacon)
Mo	Morse	Y	Yellow
N	North, Northwards, Northerly	YC	Yacht Club
NCB	North Cardinal Buoy		

SMALL CRAFT SYMBOLS

The following symbols are used on larger scale charts and plans, and are shown in magenta

- Visitors' moorings
- Visitors' berths
- Yacht marina
- Public landing
- Slipway for small craft
- Water tap
- Fuel
- Pump-out facilities
- Customs
- Public house, inn, bar
- Restaurant
- Yacht or sailing club
- Toilets
- Public car park
- Hard standing for boats
- Launderette
- Caravan site
- Camping site
- Nature reserve
- Harbourmaster
- Travel hoist
- Public telephone
- Post office
- Building
- Airport
- Flagpole/flagstaff
- Castle/Fort
- Hospital
- Notice Board
- Wooded
- Beacon (with various topmarks)
- Mooring buoy
- Crane
- Chimney
- Radio/TV Mast
- Water tower
- Tower
- Monument
- Wind turbine
- Tilting bridge

LIFE-SAVING SIGNALS

SOLAS CHAPTER V REGULATION 29
To be used by Ships, Aircraft or Persons in Distress when communicating with life-saving stations, maritime rescue units and aircraft engaged in search and rescue operations.

Note: All Morse Code signals by light (below).

1. SEARCH AND RESCUE UNIT REPLIES
YOU HAVE BEEN SEEN. ASSISTANCE WILL BE GIVEN AS SOON AS POSSIBLE

Orange smoke flare

Three white star signals or three light and sound rockets fired at approximately 1 minute intervals

2. SURFACE TO AIR SIGNALS

Note: Use International Code of Signals by means of light or flags or by laying out the symbol on the deck or ground with items that have a high contrast background.

Message	International Code of Signals		ICAO
I require assistance	V	· · · —	V
I require medical assistance	W	· — —	X
No or negative	N	— ·	N
Yes or affirmative	C	— · — ·	Y
Proceeding in this direction			↑

3. AIR TO SURFACE REPLIES
MESSAGE UNDERSTOOD
Drop a message. Rocking wings. Flashing landing or navigation lights on and off twice. OR T— OR R · — ·
MESSAGE NOT UNDERSTOOD
Straight and level flight. OR Circling OR R · — · P · — — · T —
Note: Use signals most appropriate to prevailing conditions.

4. AIR TO SURFACE DIRECTION SIGNALS
SEQUENCE OF 3 MANOEUVRES MEANING PROCEED IN THIS DIRECTION
Circle vessel at least once. Cross low, ahead of vessel rocking wings. Overfly vessel and head in required direction.
YOUR ASSISTANCE IS NO LONGER REQUIRED
Cross low, astern of vessel rocking wings.
Note: As a non preferred alternative to rocking wings, varying engine tone or volume may be used.

5. SURFACE TO AIR REPLIES
MESSAGE UNDERSTOOD - I WILL COMPLY
Change course to required direction. OR T— OR Code & answering pendant "Close Up".
I AM UNABLE TO COMPLY
International flag "N". OR N — ·

6. SHORE TO SHIP SIGNALS
SAFE TO LAND HERE
Vertical waving of both arms,white flag, light or flare
Horizontal waving white flag, light or flare. Putting one flare/ flag on ground and moving off with a second indicates direction of safer landing.
K — · —
LANDING HERE IS DANGEROUS ADDITIONAL SIGNALS MEAN SAFER LANDING IN DIRECTION INDICATED
S · · · Landing here is dangerous.
R · — · Land to right of your current heading.
L · — · · Land to left of your current heading.

VHF Channels
VHF Ch 37 is often listed in *ECP* as the calling channel for services such as harbour ferries. We have used this outdated designation, because VHF radios variously show the channel as 37A, M1, N1 or P1. Correctly it is now known as M1 but manufacturers have not yet standardised radio displays.

Keeping your East Coast Pilot up to date

We believe that East Coast Pilot remains unique among pilot books in having its own dedicated website, www.eastcoastpilot.com, created and maintained by the authors, as the primary vehicle for providing updates.

Generally, we show changes on the website soon after learning of them, although we sometimes take a few days to verify the information if we are unsure of the source.

By using a website to provide this information, we can afford to be generous with words, chartlets and pictures – we can give full descriptions of the changes and provide visual evidence as well, for example a photo of a new approach buoy or changes to a marina entrance.

Apart from pilotage changes and updates, we also aim to keep you abreast of other information that may affect you as you cruise the area. This we do through a 'News' section where items are left available to read until they are no longer current. Everything else is left on the website until the next edition is published.

We also offer 'e-newsletters' – distributed by email, approximately monthly in summer, but less often in winter – designed to call your attention to Updates and News that we have put on the website. These are completely free, just part of the service, and you can easily sign up for them via the button on the website. There are many hundreds of subscribers and the considerable feedback tells us how useful these emails are to ECP readers.

You can also 'follow' us on Twitter @eastcoastpilot, where we also broadcast news of changes.

We are delighted when readers get in touch and we do encourage you to tell us if you find that features we have described have changed. You can contact us by email through the website and you will usually get a quick response if we're not away sailing.

Incidentally, something we do not do on the website is provide Notices to Mariners or chart changes that are readily available from the UKHO or other publishers, although we will bring them to your attention if they are important. (Relevant NtMs can quickly be found at www.crossingthethamesestuary.com.)

For those without ready access to the internet, updates for this fifth edition are also available in paper form on request from the publisher. This is an abbreviated version of the fuller descriptions published on the website and without any photos, but will still be right up to date, because it will be printed from the website at the time of the request. Again, we believe this to be a unique feature of ECP.

We do urge you to use these facilities, via the internet or by requesting regular updates from Imray, to keep your East Coast Pilot up to date.

Through the website we can even supply you with an ECP 'community' burgee, so stand up and be counted – join the ECP Users' Community!

ECP 'Rolling Roads'

Most chapters in this book have at least one 'rolling road' diagram to assist pilotage.

Read each rolling road from the bottom upwards.

The long blue arrow through the middle of the diagram shows which buoys are to be left to port and which to starboard.

Distances between buoys/waypoints are also given.
The angled short blue arrows tell the helmsman the general direction to take when passing a particular buoy, until the navigator works out the exact new course.

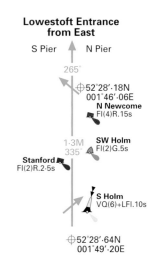

Lowestoft Entrance from East

S Pier N Pier

265°

⊕ 52°28'·18N
001°46'·06E
N Newcome
Fl(4)R.15s

1·3M **SW Holm**
335° Fl(2)G.5s

Stanford
Fl(2)R.2·5s

S Holm
VQ(6)+LFl.10s

⊕ 52°28'·64N
001°49'·20E

GENERAL INFORMATION

Chart datum

The charts are based on UK Hydrographic Office (Admiralty) data and, therefore, drawn to Lowest Astronomical Tide (LAT). This means, that they show a 'worst case scenario' and that there will normally be more water in an area than is shown.

The horizontal datum is WGS84, which complies with modern GPS equipment.

Courses and bearings

We have applied the general pilot book convention of providing courses and bearings in degrees True but have used the qualifiers 'about' or 'approximately'. This is because it is the skipper/navigator's responsibility to confirm such courses and bearings regarding tide, wind and sea conditions as well as applying corrections unique to the boat. We also believe that to steer a course in a seaway to within ±10° is acceptable; to steer within ±5° is good; to steer a precise course of (say) 241° is impossible. That impossibility makes it reasonable to quote a course of 'about 240°' and let the reader make the necessary corrections.

Distances

Readers have asked for a simple table of distances as an indication of the distances between landfalls. Agreeing that this might be useful, we turned for the information to that excellent passage planner *Crossing the Thames Estuary* by Roger Gaspar (Imray). Roger kindly gave his permission to use the data he'd developed and helped us with additional material not directly covered by his book. We highly recommend *Crossing the Thames Estuary* as a planning companion to ECP.

Tides

In the first four editions we based all tides on HW Dover, but now refer to the nearest standard port, be that Dover, Sheerness, Walton or Lowestoft. Differences in time are given before (-) or after (+) in hours and minutes, e.g. HW Sheerness +0120 is 1hr 20mins after HW Sheerness.

Landfall waypoints

To provide a starting point for the pilotage notes, we have selected a point in the offing and called it the Landfall Waypoint. It is a point in clear water, which we feel can be approached safely and from which pilotage can reasonably begin. You are strongly advised to plot the waypoint and decide for yourself whether you wish to use it. You may well decide on another position nearby. Do not just put our chosen waypoint into your GPS and passage plan without checking it and agreeing with it.

Chart lists

We have given the numbers of paper charts covering a specific area published by Imray and the Admiralty (UKHO). We have not attempted to list electronic charts, because there are too many permutations of publisher, plotter and 'packages' and compiling the list would waste valuable sailing time.

DISTANCES (IN MILES) USING INSIDE ROUTES

To and from Ramsgate:

Ramsgate (approach Ch) to River Blackwater (Sales Point)
via Fisherman's Gat and Sunk Beacon	38
via N Edinburgh Channel	37
via Foulger's Gat	41

Ramsgate (approach Ch) to River Colne (Colne Bar)
via Fisherman's Gat and Sunk Beacon	34
via N Edinburgh Channel	33
via Foulger's Gat	37

Ramsgate (approach Ch) to River Crouch (S Buxey)
via Fisherman's Gat and Sunk Beacon	33
via N Edinburgh Channel	31
via Foulger's Gat	36

Ramsgate (approach Ch) to Harwich (adjacent to Cliff Foot PHM)
via Black Deep	39
via Barrow No 2 and E Swin	39

Ramsgate (approach Ch) to River Deben (Woodbridge Haven Buoy)
via Black Deep	41
via Barrow No 2 and E Swin	38

Ramsgate (approach Ch) to The Swale (Columbine SHB)	21

Ramsgate to The Medway (entrance to Medway buoyed ch)	30

To and from the Kent Rivers:

Medway to Crouch (S Buxey)	23
Medway to Blackwater (Sales Pt)	29
Medway to Colne (Colne Bar)	25
Swale to Crouch (S Buxey)	24
Swale to Blackwater (Sales Pt)	30
Swale to Colne (Colne Bar)	26

Medway to Harwich
via Wallet	37
via Barrow and Middle Deep	41

Medway to Deben
via Wallet	40
via Barrow and Middle Deep	42

Swale to Harwich
via Wallet	37
via Barrow and Middle Deep	38

Swale to Deben
via Wallet	40
via Barrow and Middle Deep	39

Data reproduced from *Crossing the Thames Estuary* by kind permission of Roger Gaspar.

Coastguard

At the time of writing, HM Coastguard coverage of the East Coast Pilot area is shared between Humber and Dover Coastguard Operations Centres (CGOCs), with London specifically responsible for the River Thames.

There is no firm dividing line between the coverage of the two CGOCs, but in general Dover is responsible southwards from the River Deben entrance, and Humber is responsible northwards from there.

When calling the Coastguard it is best to use the appropriate MMSI from a DSC VHF set; with non-DSC sets, a CGOC can be contacted via Ch 16 using 'UK Coastguard' as the call sign. Whichever CGOC is available, according to workloads, will reply using its own call sign which should be used for the rest of the conversation.

Humber and Dover both pre-announce MSI (Maritime Safety Information) broadcasts on VHF Ch 16, specifying the channels on which they will be made. London CGOC does not make MSI broadcasts.

London Coastguard

DSC MMSI 002320063 ☎0208 312 7380. Covers area from Shell Haven Point (N bank) and Egypt Point (S bank) to Teddington.

Dover Coastguard

DSC MMSI 002320010 ☎01304 210008. Covers Dover Strait and southern Thames Estuary south of Deben entrance. MSI announcements on Ch 16 at 0110, 0410, 0710, 1010, 1310, 1610, 1910, 2210 UTC. MSI aerials Bawdsey Ch 62, Walton Ch 63, Shoeburyness Ch 63, Bradwell Ch 64.

Humber Coastguard

DSC MMSI 002320007 ☎ 01262 672317. Covers area from Deben entrance northwards. MSI announcements on Ch 16 at 0150, 0450, 0750, 1050, 1350, 1650, 1950, 2250 UTC. MSI aerials Lowestoft Ch 62, Caister Ch 64.

National Coastwatch Institution (NCI)

www.nci.org.uk

NCI stations are now equipped to use VHF Ch 65, a channel for their dedicated use in communication with seafarers on a variety of non-emergency routine tasks. Skippers of leisure craft can use it for radio checks if they need to (rather than calling the Coastguard) or to request local information, such as actual weather and sea state conditions. Note that not all NCI stations are open every day, and those that are open generally operate for daylight hours only.

Any other communications, most especially those of an emergency nature, must still be made with the CG via DSC and/or Ch 16.

NCI stations on the coast covered by ECP are as follows, from north to south:

Caister	☎ 07527 977613
Gorleston	☎ 01493 440384
Felixstowe	☎ 01394 670808
Southend	☎ 07815 945210
Holehaven	☎ 01268 696971
Whitstable	☎ 07864 646209
Herne Bay	☎ 01227 744454

Humber Coastguard
MSI 0150 and ev 3 hrs UTC
VHF 62 (South), 64 (North)

Great Yarmouth •
Lowestoft •
Southwold •
R Ore and Alde • Aldeburgh
R Deben
R Orwell • Woodbridge
Ipswich
R Stour
• Harwich
Brightlingsea
R Colne • • Walton on the Naze
R Blackwater
Maldon •
Burnham •
R Crouch
London   R Thames   Southend
Gravesend • • Sheerness
R Medway   Swale   North Foreland
Whitstable • Ramsgate

Dover Coastguard
MSI 0110 and ev 3hrs UTC
VHF 62 Bawdsey
VHF 63 Walton, Shoeburyness
VHF 64 Bradwell

This pot marker is better than most, but still can't be spotted at night

Danger – pot markers

Poorly marked crab and lobster pots are an annoying feature of the Thames Estuary. It requires a very sharp lookout to spot small floats or empty drinks containers, which may be half submerged in a strong tide. At night it is all but impossible to see them until it's too late.

All of this makes motoring or motor sailing a time for extreme caution, especially at night. Indeed, such is the problem that it may sometimes be wise to take a longer route or remain further offshore to be sure of going around infested areas.

Areas to beware of are off the North Foreland, around the Naze and towards Harwich, off Felixstowe S of the Deben entrance, East Lane (S of Ore entrance), Aldeburgh and Sizewell – there are even scattered pots in Harwich Harbour and the approaches to Lowestoft.

ECP strongly supports the campaign to get pots more clearly marked.

Medical help

For emergency medical help make a VHF call to the Coastguard when at sea or ☎ 999 by phone when in harbour.

For non-emergency help and advice, when in harbour, call the NHS ☎ 111, available 24hr.

Riding lights

The International Regulations for Preventing Collisions at Sea, 1972 (ColRegs), require vessels of more than 7m length to display a black ball during the day and an all-round white light at night when riding to an anchor.

In these days of crowded anchorages and heavy traffic, our advice would be for ALL vessels including those on moorings, to display these signals, particularly at night, when crew are on board.

Wind farms and commerce

Large wind farms are now a fact of life in the outer extremities of our waters. The nearest to shore are Scroby Sands off Great Yarmouth and the Gunfleet Sands off Clacton. The London Array is in the very middle of the Thames Estuary, while the Gabbards affect those of us who aim to venture across the North Sea. The Kentish Flats wind farm has been expanded and needs care to pass in the shallows off the North Kent coast. The Thanet wind farm, also being expanded, stands off the North Foreland.

The Thames Estuary is the most crowded sailing area in the UK after the Solent. It has a charm and character that makes it unique, but the commercial traffic using the Thames is so continuously heavy that the Port of London Authority (PLA) is the largest port authority in the country. Felixstowe is the largest container port in the UK, one of the busiest in Europe, and accommodates the very largest cargo ships in the world. The Thames Estuary is the funnel through which much of this shipping travels to reach either Harwich in the N section or the Thames in the S.

The Estuary is becoming even more crowded with expansion of the container port at Felixstowe and the London Gateway in the Thames itself. There is also a rising demand for yachting facilities and, moreover, the explosion in wind farm developments with increasing traffic in the form of large barges used to install and maintain them and fast craft that service them.

As if all that wasn't enough, craft wishing to leave to the N of our area, say beyond Lowestoft or across to the North Dutch or Friesland coasts, will eventually run the gauntlet of a new massive multi-thousand tower wind farm stretching from just S of Lowestoft to as far N as the Dogger Bank with a width greater than half that of the southern North Sea.

To aid ship safety, the towers in all wind farms are painted yellow up to 12m above sea level and the corner towers, plus those at some key points down the sides of the farm, have yellow flashing lights, also at 12m. Red lights on the tops of the towers flash Morse 'W'. There is,

Even dogs get a mooring at Titchmarsh Marina

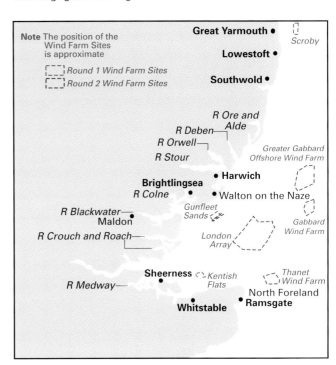

however, doubt that at this height any of these lights will be visible to crews of recreational craft navigating in fog or dirty weather. The farms emit sound signals in fog.

It has been generally agreed that the rotor tip clearance will be 22m above MHWS and at this height 96 per cent of yachts will, if forced into the arrays, pass underneath without being struck by a rotor. Unfortunately, on the Gunfleet, just off Clacton, the clearance is only 20m, bringing the percentage of yachts able to go through without danger of being struck by the rotor tips down to 88 per cent.

General advice to yachtsmen is to avoid the farms as much as possible, but to be aware of their positions, marks and lights, which are shown on current charts.

In this edition; new aerial views of ports and estuaries

THE BEAUFORT SCALE

The Beaufort scale, which is used in Met Office marine forecasts, is an empirical measure for describing wind intensity based on observed sea conditions.

Specifications and equivalent speeds

Beaufort wind scale	Mean Wind Speed		Limits of wind speed		Wind descriptive terms	Probable wave height (m)	Probable maximum wave height (m)	Seastate	Sea descriptive terms
	Knots	ms-1	Knots	ms-1					
0	0	0	<1	<1	Calm	-	-	0	Calm (glassy)
1	2	1	1-3	1-2	Light air	0.1	0.1	1	Calm (rippled)
2	5	3	4-6	2-3	Light breeze	0.2	0.3	2	Smooth (wavelets)
3	9	5	7-10	4-5	Gentle breeze	0.6	1.0	3	Slight
4	13	7	11-16	6-8	Moderate breeze	1.0	1.5	3-4	Slight - Moderate
5	19	10	17-21	9-11	Fresh breeze	2.0	2.5	4	Moderate
6	24	12	22-27	11-14	Strong breeze	3.0	4.0	5	Rough
7	30	15	28-33	14-17	Near gale	4.0	5.5	5-6	Rough-V.rough
8	37	19	34-40	17-21	Gale	5.5	7.5	6-7	V.rough - High
9	44	23	41-47	21-24	Strong gale	7.0	10.0	7	High
7.0	10.0	7	High	25-28	Storm	9.0	12.5	8	V. high
10	52	27	48-55	25-28	Storm	9.0	12.5	8	V. high
11	60	31	56-63	29-32	Violent storm	11.5	16.0	8	V. high
12	-		64+	33+	Hurricane	14+	-	9	Phenomenal

TIDAL STREAMS

The figures against the arrows denote mean rates in tenths of a knot at neaps and springs.
Thus 06,11 indicates a mean neap rate of 0·6 knots and a mean spring rate of 1·1 knots.

TIDAL DIFFERENCES ON DOVER AND SHEERNESS

Location	Dover	Sheerness
Allington Lock	+0210	+0054
Broadstairs	+0037	-0053
Burnham-on-Crouch	+0115	-0015
Canvey	+0125	-0005
Chatham	+0140	+0010
Colne	+0050	-0040
Gravesend	+0200	+0030
Great Yarmouth	-0200	-0330
Harty Ferry	+0120	-0010
Harwich Haven	+0040	-0050
Herne Bay	+0110	-0020
Ipswich	+0115	-0015
London Bridge	+0252	+0122
Lowestoft	-0133	-0303
Maldon	+0130	+0000
Margate	+0045	-0045
Mistley Quay	+0105	-0025
Orford Haven	+0010	-0120
Orford Quay	+0100	-0030
Paglesham	+0110	-0020
Pin Mill	+0100	-0030
Queenborough	+0130	+0000
Ramsgate	+0030	-0100
Sheerness	+0130	+0000
Slaughden	+0155	+0025
Snape	+0225	+0055
Southwold	-0105	-0235
Stone Point	+0040	-0050
Waldringfield	+0100	-0030
Whitstable	+0135	+0005
Woodbridge	+0105	-0025
Woodbridge Haven	+0025	-0105
Woolwich Ferry	+0225	+0055

Cruising down the Ore

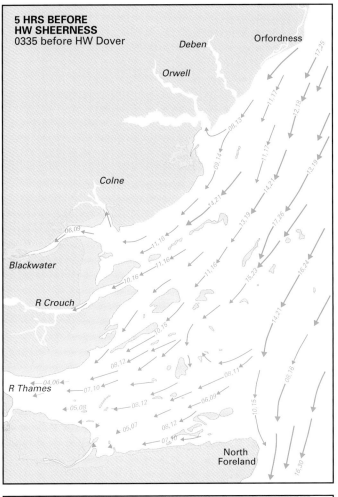

**5 HRS BEFORE
HW SHEERNESS**
0335 before HW Dover

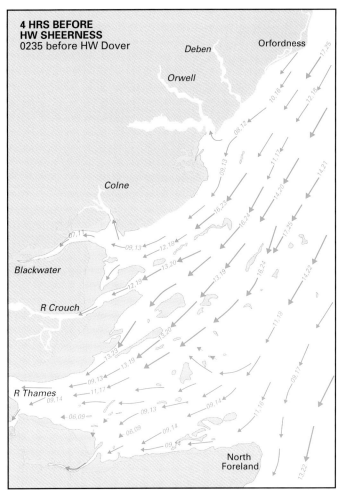

**4 HRS BEFORE
HW SHEERNESS**
0235 before HW Dover

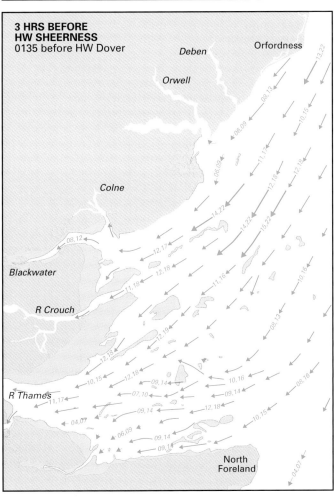

**3 HRS BEFORE
HW SHEERNESS**
0135 before HW Dover

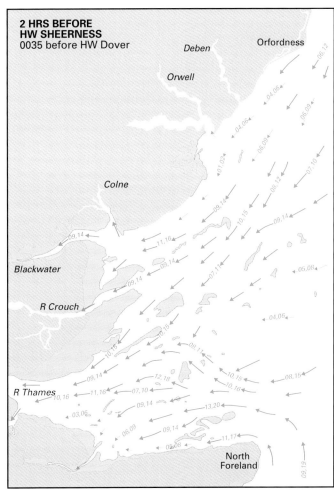

**2 HRS BEFORE
HW SHEERNESS**
0035 before HW Dover

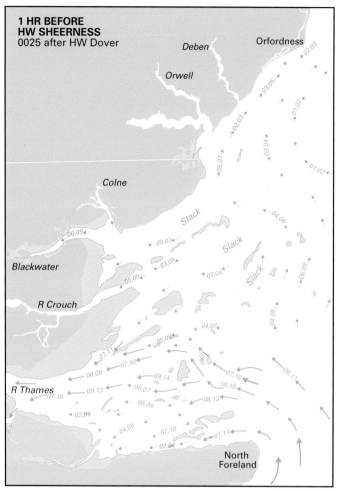

**1 HR BEFORE
HW SHEERNESS**
0025 after HW Dover

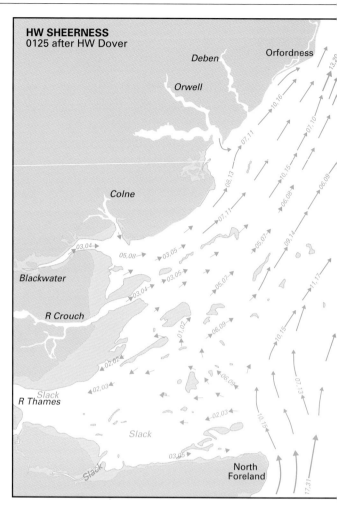

HW SHEERNESS
0125 after HW Dover

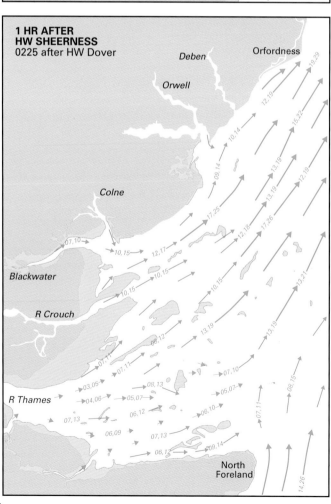

**1 HR AFTER
HW SHEERNESS**
0225 after HW Dover

**2 HRS AFTER
HW SHEERNESS**
0325 after HW Dover

**3 HRS AFTER
HW SHEERNESS**
0425 after HW Dover

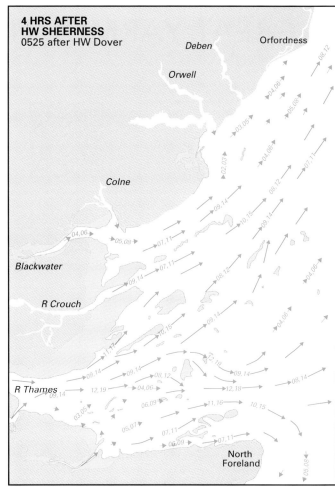

**4 HRS AFTER
HW SHEERNESS**
0525 after HW Dover

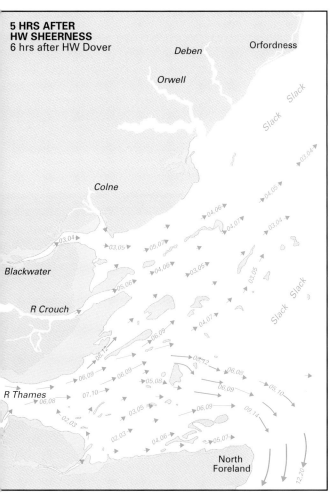

**5 HRS AFTER
HW SHEERNESS**
6 hrs after HW Dover

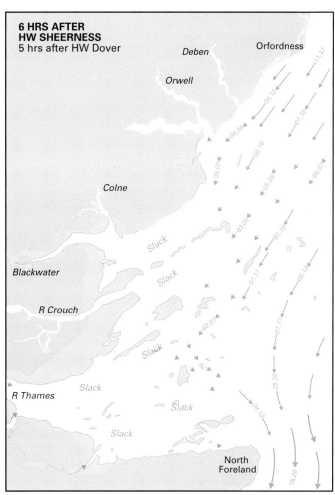

**6 HRS AFTER
HW SHEERNESS**
5 hrs after HW Dover

1. GREAT YARMOUTH

⊕ **Landfall waypoint**
52°34'·34N 001°45'·19E ½M E of entrance
Charts
Imray C28
Admiralty 1543 1534
Tides
HW Lowestoft -0035
Contact
Harbourmaster G Doyle
VHF Ch 12 Callsign *Yarmouth Radio*
☎ 01493 335502
Email GreatYarmouthMarine.Services@peelports.com
www.peelports.com/media/4198/visiting-small-craft-information-
sheet-march2017-1.pdf

Entry to the Outer Harbour is strictly prohibited.

Great Yarmouth harbour is a long, narrow concrete channel running from the entrance at Gorleston to the Haven Bridge, the first of two bridges that give access to the northern Broads via Breydon Water. The harbour was built down either side of the River Yare, which runs through the harbour in a NNW to SSE direction with the man-made entrance flanked by Gorleston Pier to the S and the S retaining wall of the commercial Outer Harbour on the N side. The entrance opens due E and is narrow.

Within a short distance from the pier heads the river turns through 90° to starboard, so visitors are faced by a high blank reinforced concrete wall almost immediately after entering. The bend is blind to traffic in both directions, so it is vital to obey the port control lights mounted on a lattice tower on the N side of the entrance. Beware strong cross currents that can set you against the N pier.

Watch out too for wind farm and oil rig support and supply vessels, which use the space in the entrance to turn around and go astern into their berths further upstream.

Vessels approaching Great Yarmouth from the N should not enter the first entrance they come to as this is the Outer Harbour also known as East Port, which is not open to leisure craft, now being a centre for installation barges and support vessels for the Gabbard and new Anglia One wind farms. Instead, they must pass this entrance and follow the S wall of the Outer Harbour until the entrance to Yarmouth harbour itself opens up.

There is little to commend Yarmouth as a leisure port and we don't recommend it as a port of last resort, because a strong N-S tidal flow, coupled with anything up

The outer harbour is forbidden to yachts

Great Yarmouth harbour *Patrick Roach*

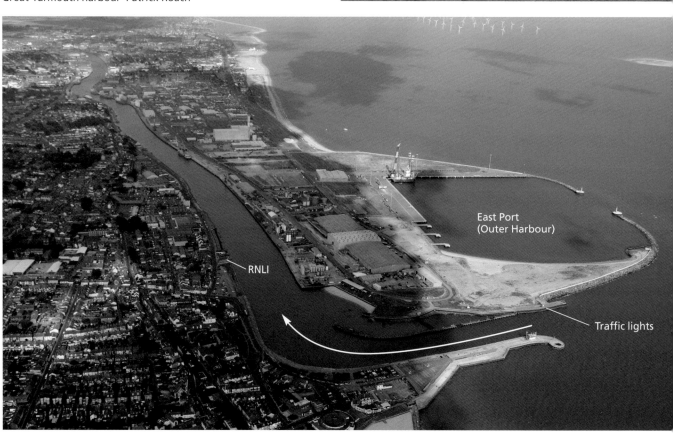

to 6kn of river ebb, gets piled up by strong winds with any E in them. Indeed, it is not advisable to enter with a small yacht in anything over F5. Fortunately, there are no inshore sand banks to worry the careful sailor, although

Gt Yarmouth From East

Landfall waypoint ⊕ 52°34'·34N 001°45'·19E

W Corton FI(3)G.10s

N Holm Q

3·6M 284 T

MID Corton FI.G.2·5s

3·2M 295 T

S Corton Q(6)+LFI.15s

1·98M 319 T

NE Holm FI.R.2·5s

⊕ to enter track 52°32'·56N 001°49'·37E

Gt Yarmouth From South

Landfall waypoint ⊕52°34'·34N 001°45'·19E

White Swan

Holm Sand Q(9)15s

NW Holm FI(4)G.15s

7·25M 350 T

W Holm FI(3)G.10s

N Newcome FI(4)R.15s

SW Holm FI(2)G.5s

Stanford FI.R.2·5s

S Holm VQ(6)+LFI.10s

Newcome Sand Q.R

E Barnard Q(3)10s

1·3M 015 T

⊕ to enter track 52°25'·00N 001°46'·56E

Gt Yarmouth From North

Landfall waypoint ⊕52°34'·34N 001°45'·19E

SW Scroby FI.G.2·5s

Scroby Elbow FI(2)G.5s

Q.R

MID Scroby FI(4)G.15s

MID Caister FI(2)R.5s

NW Scroby FI(3)G.10s

6·62M 180 T

N Caister FI(3)R.5s

N Scroby VQ

1M 197 T

Hemsby FI(2)R.2·5s

⊕ to enter track 52°41'·89N 001°46'·55E

Approach from north

Breydon Bridge (lifting)

River Bure

Fixed Br

Haven Bridge Lt (Opens) Closed 2.90m

Town Hall Quay

GREAT YARMOUTH

R Yare

52°36'N

0₇

6₄

5

6₇

0₇

Britannia Pier 2F.R(vert)11m4M

0₇

6₆

The Jetty 2F.R(vert)7m2M

Wellington Pier 2F.R(vert)8m3M

3₃

6₅

5

3₈

8₆

4₅

5₁

(44) Nelson's Monument

Power Stn Oc.R.10s 42m1M Chy

FI.R.6s5m2M

6₅

3₈

35'

GREAT YARMOUTH

N

Depths in Metres

Great Yarmouth Haven

South Denes

Tanks

4₅

Cranes

Q.G.17m3M

East Port (Outer Harbour)

Q.R.17m3M

Brush Quay

Brush Lt Ho (Disused)

SS

6₁

7₆

Horn(3)60s

SS

Q.G.8m6M

N Pier

FI.R.3s11m6M

0₈

10

Gorleston-on-Sea

34'

8₃

3₅

43'

44'

6₁

1°45'E

Yacht entering Yarmouth harbour

some shoaling can occur in the entrance during strong easterlies with depths reduced by as much as a metre.

The close approach to the harbour entrance is in clear, deep water with depths ranging from 7m to 17m. The entrance is somewhat sheltered by the southern extremity of the Scroby Sands with the deepwater Holm Channel forming a NW–SE gap between the S tip of the Scroby and the N tip of the Holm Sand.

From E Aim for the S Corton (Q (6)+L.Fl.15s (bell)) SCB and turn NW up the Holm Channel until the entrance is abeam, then turn due W to enter.

From N Enter Caister Roads by passing (in close order) the Hemsby (Fl.R.2·5s) PHB and the N Scroby NCB (VQ). The Scroby Sands wind farm opens to port. Continue past East Port while opposite the Great Yarmouth entrance, turn to starboard and head due W to enter.

From S Pick up the E Barnard ECB (Q(3)10s) S of Lowestoft, follow the Stanford Channel and continue N past the entrance to Lowestoft Harbour. Ensure you keep to port of two cardinal buoys about ½M off the end of Lowestoft Ness (an SCB (Q(6)+L.Fl.15s (bell)) and an ECB (VQ(3)5s (bell)) marking a charted obstruction. Follow the coastline N until opposite the Yarmouth entrance.

At night the entrance is marked on the S side by a red light (Fl.R.3s11m6M) erected on the red brick building on the seaward end of Gorleston Pier, at a height of 11 metres and with an arc of visibility of 105° from 235° through to 350° from seaward. The N side of the entrance is marked with a green light (Q.G.8m6M) 150 metres NE of the Gorleston Pier entrance light, at a height of 8m with an arc of visibility 098° from 176° to 078° from seaward.

Gorleston Pier and Brush Bend Lights: At the eastern extremity of Gorleston Pier are two all-round vertical fixed red lights two metres apart, with an additional six sets of lights, of the same characteristic, along the northern edge of the Pier, up to and around Brush Bend.

North Training Wall and Skeleton Works lights and marks: The extreme end of the training wall (at the start of the Outer Harbour south breakwater) is highlighted with illuminated white painted panels. Along the Training Wall and Skeleton Works there are five poles each displaying two all-round vertically mounted fixed green lights (2 F.G. (vert)), the outermost light is opposite the end of Gorleston Pier and the innermost light marks the end of the Skeleton Works. The Training Wall and Skeleton Works are downlit throughout their length.

Marine Services controls the port operations on VHF Ch 12 with the call sign *Yarmouth Radio*. Contact should be made prior to entry or departure and, if outward bound from the Broads, when passing through Haven Bridge. You can also contact them by phone or email.
Marine Services ✆ 01493 335511
Email marineservices@eastportuk.co.uk

Small craft must comply with the Port Traffic Signals displayed at the harbour entrance on a lattice tower on the N side. These are IALA signals showing 3 Fl.R for harbour closed and also do not proceed until instructed, 3Fl.G proceed, G/W/G proceed only when told to. For leaving harbour, 3R(vert) means no vessel should proceed down river of the RNLI station sited just above the entrance bend on the Gorleston or W side. These outbound signals are sited on a tower at Brush Bend at the root of Gorleston Pier.

Vessels required to wait outside for an outbound vessel must stay clear of the port entrance, to give departing ships adequate room to manoeuvre.

A good time to enter the river is at slack low water which occurs approximately 90 minutes after high or low water.

Charges

Vessels are liable for tolls, but waivers are in place for vessels visiting the Norfolk Broads.

Berths

Small craft moorings are available on Hall Quay, just south of Haven Bridge on the E side of the river (opposite the red brick Town Hall building). There are mooring tails to help mooring. Vessels should moor adjacent to the access ladders.

There's a minimum depth of at least 3m alongside the berths on Hall Quay at MLWS. You should also allow for the strong tide when turning into the moorings and take care not to be swept into the Haven Bridge on the flood. The Hall Quay berths are close to the town centre. A five-minute walk along Regent Road will take you to the Market Place.

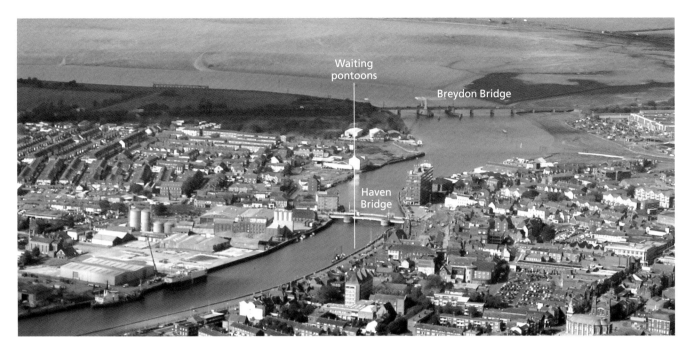

Top end of the harbour *Patrick Roach*

Small craft berthing is also available about halfway up the channel on the starboard side on East Quay just before the river takes a slight turn to port (going up).

Haven and Breydon bridges

The Haven Bridge is only manned when a lift is due to take place. Breydon Bridge is manned from 0800 to 1700 during winter months and from 0600 to 2200 or sunrise to sunset (whichever is the shorter) during the summer months, i.e. from Easter until the end of October.

Requests to lift the Haven Bridge between sunset and sunrise incur a charge of £200.

Bridge booking

To request a lift for the Haven or Breydon Bridges, contact the Port Operations Office prior to 1645 on the previous working day (Monday to Friday) on ✆ 01493 335522. Breydon Bridge will be lifted in conjunction with the Haven Bridge, but a Breydon Bridge lift can be booked in isolation using the same contact details. A vessel at sea may relay a message via Port Marine Services (*Yarmouth Radio*) on VHF Ch 12.

Passing through the port

Both the Haven and Breydon Bridges have river traffic control lights on the bridge buttresses. These traffic signals are not exhibited constantly but are switched on approximately 10 minutes before a planned lift and are initially switched to red (stop) in both directions.

Small craft that can pass under Breydon Bridge without needing a lift should use the side spans, which have a greater air draught clearance. Vessels requiring a Breydon Bridge lift pass through the centre span. The bridge operators will advise if there is two-way traffic.

Mariners should be careful when approaching either of the bridges not to be set onto them, as tides can be strong and, at the Haven Bridge, the rates can exceed 3kn.

Outbound vessels should initially contact Breydon Bridge (or Haven Bridge, if Breydon Bridge is not to be used) on Ch 12. When through the Haven Bridge vessels should contact *Yarmouth Radio* on Ch 12 to advise their intentions. They should obey the IALA traffic signals exhibited at Brush Bend, where the channel turns sharply E towards the entrance and, if a stop signal is shown, hold their vessel north of the stop sign that is displayed on the W bank to N of the RNLI lifeboat station.

Vessels navigating through the port should be aware of large vessels manoeuvring or swinging in the narrow channel. There is a maximum speed limit of 7kn, although a slower speed may be appropriate.

Wind and tide

The tidal range within the harbour is approximately 2m and tidal flows can be swift, particularly during spring tides when rates can rise to 4kn, however, during certain wind and weather conditions, tidal flows can reach 5-6kn. Slack water at the harbour entrance is approximately 90 minutes after HW/LW, but this may vary with weather conditions.

At the entrance to the harbour sea conditions can become confused with wind over tide, particularly on the ebb or with wave reflection from the pier structures.

Inside the harbour, there is generally good shelter, however wind over tide with N or S winds can cause uncomfortable conditions on the berths at Hall Quay and fenders should be carefully adjusted.

Nelson's Monument stands N of the harbour

2. LOWESTOFT

⊕ **Landfall waypoint**
52°28'·18N 001°46'·06E ½M E of entrance
Charts
Imray C28, 2000
Admiralty 1535, 1543
Tides
HW Lowestoft
Contact
Harbourmaster Gary Horton
☎ 01502 572286
Lowestoft Port Control VHF Ch 14
Callsign *Lowestoft Port Control*
www.abports.co.uk/locations/lowestoft
Port Control Lights
Three vertical reds – Do not enter
Green, white, green vertical – Clear to enter (or depart) on specific orders from Port Control.

Before entering or leaving, request permission on Ch 14. Small craft and yachts without VHF may take the green, white, green signal as clearance to go ahead, but with extreme caution and navigational courtesy; those vessels in the Yacht Basin must contact the Port Control before departure.

Mariners should note that both Port Control, which is located at the harbour bridge, as well as departing vessels within the Outer Harbour basin, have extremely limited vision to the N of the entrance piers and should navigate accordingly.

Main hazards

Shifting sand banks make it imperative for the first time or occasional visitor to stay in the marked channels. With wind against tide, heavy seas can build off the entrance, which is quite narrow and marked by two lighthouses on the pier ends.

The entrance tends to get choppy in anything over F5, and downright rough in F7 or more, especially with wind against the tide, which sets strongly across the entrance. With care it can be entered in almost any weather and along with Harwich can be considered a port of last resort.

The whole Lowestoft approaches area is under almost continuous survey, because of the formation of sand waves, which can give rise to rough waters in certain conditions, and continually moving sand banks.

Once inside the harbour watch out for low flying helicopters. There's a helipad on the buttress between the outer harbour and Waveney Dock. You may be asked to stand off if one is landing or taking off.

Landmarks

Half a mile N of the entrance stands Gulliver, the tallest and most E'ly wind generator on the English mainland, which makes a good landmark, being visible from well out to sea. From N or NE the white-painted Lowestoft Lighthouse on top of the cliffs N of the harbour is also

Lowestoft Outer Harbour entrance

Looking west across the harbour and town of Lowestoft *Patrick Roach*

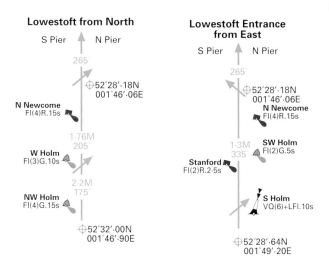

Lowestoft from North

S Pier ↑ N Pier

265°

⊕52°28'·18N
001°46'·06E

N Newcome
Fl(4)R.15s

1·76M
205°

W Holm
Fl(3)G.10s

2·2M
175°

NW Holm
Fl(4)G.15s

⊕52°32'·00N
001°46'·90E

Lowestoft Entrance from East

S Pier ↑ N Pier

265°

⊕52°28'·18N
001°46'·06E

N Newcome
Fl(4)R.15s

SW Holm
Fl(2)G.5s

1·3M
335°

Stanford
Fl(2)R.2·5s

S Holm
VQ(6)+LFl.10s

⊕52°28'·64N
001°49'·20E

Lowestoft from South

S Pier 265° N Pier

N Newcome
Fl(4)R.15s

⊕52°28'·18N
001°46'·06E

SW Holm
Fl(2)9.5s

Stanford
Fl.R.2·5s

2·1M
350°

S Holm
VQ(6)+LFl.10

Newcome
Sand
Q.R

1·3M
015°

E Barnard
Q(3)10s

⊕52°25'·00N
001°46'·56E

conspicuous and a good mark to aim for. Inland from Gulliver stands a complex of pale coloured factories.

Two white pagoda-shaped lighthouses on the pier heads distinguish the harbour entrance itself. The S pier is canted to face NE so that the prevailing swell from SW doesn't drive into the harbour. Immediately N of the entrance can sometimes be seen a gas rig accommodation platform under construction or repair or at other times it is possible to see huge blades from wind turbines in for repair, jutting up against the skyline.

Most of the town is low lying, but a good reference point is the top of the grain silo N of, and behind, the harbour. Because of the offset of the entrance, this silo will appear at first to be S of the harbour.

Approaches

From E Make for the East Newcome PHB (Fl(2)R.5s). Although this buoy lies E of the entrance to Lowestoft, a direct course in is blocked by the shallows over the tail of the Holm Sand. With light enough draught and some local knowledge you can head straight in, however for the first timer we recommend the following slightly longer route.

From the E Newcome steer roughly SSW to round South Holm SCB (VQ(6)+LFl.10s) before turning NW. Follow the Stanford Channel towards the harbour, passing between Stanford PHB (Fl.R.2·5s) and SW Holm SHB (Fl(2)G.5s). On reaching the N Newcome PHB (Fl(4)R.15s) turn due W towards the entrance piers with their twin white pagoda lighthouses.

Britain's first lighthouse makes a good landmark coming from N

Lowestoft from S

In fair weather and calm conditions and with a sufficient rise of tide, many skippers will take the direct route W from E Newcome to N Newcome, crossing the Holm Sand tail in about 3·5-4m of water, and then on into the harbour, keeping clear of two wreck or foul ground buoys just N of the entrance.

From S Pick up the East Barnard ECB (Q(3)10s) on the 10m contour marking the edge of the Newcome Sand. To the N lies the Newcome Sand PHB (Q.R), which marks the N extremity of the sands and is the S gate to the Stanford Channel.

Follow the Stanford Channel, passing between Stanford PHB (Fl.R.2·5s) and SW Holm SHB (Fl(2)G.5s). On reaching the N Newcome PHB (Fl(4)R.15s) turn due W towards the entrance piers with their twin lighthouses. Do not be tempted to cut the corner from the S Holm direct to the S pier, because it shoals to 1·9m at LAT and any onshore wind cuts up a nasty, short, steep sea.

From N Keep within sight of the shore in the buoyed channel through Corton Roads and inside the Holm Sand until abreast the entrance piers.

Watch out for a pair of cardinal buoys about ½M off the end of Lowestoft Ness – ECB (VQ(3)5s Bell) and SCB (Q(6)+L.Fl.15s Bell). They mark a charted obstruction, so do not try to pass between them.

The South Pier shows a set of international port control lights: G over W over G meaning clear to enter; 3 vert R meaning do not enter. Seek permission on Ch 14 from Lowestoft Port Control to enter. Both pier heads are lit; the North Pier (Oc.G.5s 8M), the South Pier (Oc.R.5s 6M). Beware an eddy in the entrance between the two piers.

At night a good guide to finding the entrance is the white sector of the Kirkley Light (Oc. WRG. 10s 17m10M) to the south the entrance itself.

Entry

The entrance is narrow (maximum commercial ship beam is 22m) and canted at an angle so that vessels leaving or entering cannot see each other. This makes it essential to call Lowestoft Port Control for permission to enter. The narrowness and angle of the entrance prevents very heavy S swells driving in, but it's open to NE winds and seas.

Strictly observe the Narrow Channels Rule 9(b) of the ColRegs - '*a vessel of less than 20 metres in length or a sailing vessel shall not impede the passage of a vessel which can safely navigate only within a narrow channel or fairway*'. There is a minimum of 4·3m of water, although 6m is more generally found.

Once inside, the harbour opens out into a series of basins.

Just inside Lowestoft Outer Harbour

LOWESTOFT HARBOUR

The harbour entrance widens into the main or outer harbour, from which a number of lesser basins branch off.

There is a shallow area in the SW corner of the outer harbour. Off to starboard is the entrance to the Waveney and Hamilton Docks, both having charted drying areas on the E or NE sides and are dredged to a minimum of 4m elsewhere. Up river to starboard is the entrance to the Trawl Dock where there's a waiting pontoon for the Lowestoft Harbour bridge. Smack in the middle of the harbour on the W buttress to the Waveney (Fish) Dock is a busy heliport, with priority given to low-flying helicopters

Opposite the Trawl dock, to port, is the yacht basin at the head of which stands the Royal Norfolk and Suffolk YC (RN&SYC). The RN&SYC marina has visitors' berths on the N side of the first linear pontoon and on the W of the cross pontoon in front of the clubhouse. It is essential to call the club's harbourmaster on Ch 80 (call sign *Royal Norfolk Harbourmaster*) for directions before entering. Yachts over 12m LOA should lie against the large bumper tubes against the outer wall (to starboard inside the entrance) and guard against warps chafing on the rough stone quay. Enter with care, because boats may be manoeuvring inside. Be aware too that there's a shallow sand bar on the corner of the starboard (W) entrance buttress, especially at lower

The Royal Norfolk and Suffolk YC

ROYAL NORFOLK & SUFFOLK YC   NR33 0AQ

Contact
VHF Ch 80
☎ 01502 566726 (0730–1930)
Callsign *Royal Norfolk Harbourmaster*
Email admin@rnsyc.net
www.rnsyc.net
Facilities WC, showers, launderette, WiFi
Fuel Diesel from berth below marina office at head of marina alongside the slip
Electricity On pontoons
Water On pontoons
Launching slip (trailers)
Launching crane (2½T)
Pump-out Berth near slipway
Pressure wash Coin-operated at head of slipway
Provisions Shops nearby
Pubs/restaurants Bar/restaurant on site and in town
Local services Include chandler, electronics, engineer, rigger and sailmaker
Transport Rail station 10 mins, buses
Taxi ☎ 01502 515151, 511771 and 500000.

stages of the tide. On leaving, obey the light signals on the E side of the marina entrance (green, white, green – go with caution; three reds – do not go). Port Control must approve departure (Ch 14).

The Lowestoft lifeboat is also moored in this basin alongside the pontoon serving the Lowestoft Historic Ships museum.

Just up river from the RN&SYC marina is the Lowestoft Harbour Bridge. Passage through is free, but opening times are strictly observed (see next page). Yachts waiting to go up river may get permission to wait in the Trawl Dock if they can't get into the marina. Do not approach the bridge unless the green light on the N wall is showing.

Lowestoft Harbour Bridge

The Lowestoft Harbour Bridge, between the outer and inner harbours, is only opened on demand to commercial shipping and then not between 0815 and 0900, 1230 and 1300, 1700 and 1730 to allow commuter traffic unimpeded access.

Small craft may pass through at the time of opening for commercial shipping, so long as Port Control has

The Lowestoft Harbour Bridge - commercial ships have right of way. Traffic signals control flow agreed beforehand. If yachts give at least 20 minutes notice of passage, the bridge can be opened for them at 0300, 0500, 0700, 0945, 1115, 1430, 1600, 1900, 2100 and midnight on weekdays and 0300, 0500, 0700, 0945, 1115, 1430, 1600, 1800, 1900, 2100 and midnight at weekends and Bank Holidays.

Call Port Control on Ch 14 or ☎ 01502 572286.

Approaching the bridge from the E there are traffic lights on the N quay.

Small craft and yachts in a flotilla should make every effort to keep together and pass through the bridge as quickly as possible, bridge operators are instructed not to wait for stragglers. Once the bridge has been lifted the red lights on the east and west side may both be switched to green, allowing inwards and outwards movements at the same time. Boats must not proceed if the lights remain red, or until instructed by the bridge operator, keeping clear of vessels using the main channel.

With the bridge down there is 2·2m clearance at MHW springs (approximately 2·4m on the tide gauge) with a reduction of 0·5 metres for the arch sides. Vessels able to drop masts and aerials and which can pass under the bridge, may do so, once they have received permission from Port Control

There is a pontoon in the SE corner of the Trawl Dock (opposite RN&SYC) to use while waiting for the bridge.

The inner harbour and Lake Lothing

Above the road bridge is the Inner Harbour, which swells out into Lake Lothing. The channel is buoyed and dredged to 4·7m up to a point abreast the Lowestoft Cruising Club pontoons on the starboard hand. It shelves to 1·8m from there to the Carlton Road railway swing bridge.

Lake Lothing (looking W)

Opposite Lowestoft CC is the Lowestoft Haven Marina. Although the general environment is that of an industrial area, visitors are welcome at all Lowestoft's yacht basins, which are in the forefront of the redevelopment of Lowestoft into a major yachting centre.

LOWESTOFT CRUISING CLUB NR32 3LY

Contact
☎ 07810 522515
www.lowestoftcruisingclub.co.uk
Facilities WC, showers
Water On pontoons
Electricity At each berth
Slipway
Mast crane On quayside
Berths To book, phone Peter Hytch, LCC moorings officer,
☎ 01502 732970 or 07810 522515
There are 70+ berths in finger boxes. Visitors should use the E end hammerhead or empty berths on the S side of the main pontoon with a green triangle indicating they are vacant then call the berthing officer.
Provisions, banks, pubs
Transport Trains 10 minutes walk
Taxi ☎ 01502 515151 and 500000.

The bridge waiting pontoon in the Trawl Dock

Lowestoft Haven Marina | Lowestoft Marina | Carlton Rail Bridge | Oulton Broad
Lowestoft Cruising Club | Mutford Rd Bridge

LOWESTOFT HAVEN MARINA   NR33 9NB

Contact
VHF Ch 80
Callsign *Lowestoft Haven Marina*
☎ 01502 580300 (0730–1930)
www.lowestofthavenmarina.co.uk
(also www.transeuropemarinas.com)

Facilities WC, showers, launderette, WiFi (PAYG)
Water On pontoons (use own hose)
Electricity On pontoons
Fuel Diesel (on hammerhead of pontoon A)
Gas Calor
Pub/restaurant The Third Crossing ☎ 01502 583596
Boat hoist 70-T (out of hours by arrangement)
Workshop
Engineers, riggers, electronics and chandlers/support services
Contact marina office
Boat sales ☎ 01502 580300
Transport Trains to Norwich and Ipswich, buses
Taxi ☎ 01502 515151 and 500000.
Note The Hamilton Dock Marina is no longer available to yachts.

Close by the Carlton Road rail bridge on the S bank is Lowestoft Marina a small friendly 40 berth marina right at the gateway to the Suffolk Broads.

Mutford Lock

Lowestoft is the main gateway to the S Broads. To make the final transition from Lake Lothing into Oulton Broad itself, boats have to go through (in order from the E) Carlton Railway Bridge, Mutford Road Bridge and Mutford Lock.

It is advisable to book transits in advance with the lockmaster. VHF Ch 73 or 14, ☎ 01502 531778 (Lock) or 01502 574946 (Yacht Station). The lock is operated by the Broads Authority and is 22m long and 6·5m wide with a minimum 2m depth (plus state of tide). There is a fee for each lock transit or day return.

The bridges and lock open on request during the following hours daily: April to October 0800–1800. November to March 0800–1100. The lock is crowded at weekends and bank holidays.

LOWESTOFT MARINA   NR33 9NQ

Contact
☎ 01502 588811 (call at least two days before arrival)
Mobile 07972779371
Email enquiries@lowestoftmarina.net
www.lowestoftmarina.net

Facilities WC, showers, laundry, disabled facilities, free WiFi, CCTV
Water On pontoons
Electricity On pontoons
Transport Trains to Norwich and Ipswich, buses
Taxi ☎ 01502 515151 and 500000

Mutford Lock gateway to Oulton Broad

Carlton Rail Bridge (foreground) with Mutford Rd Bridge and Lock behind. The red flag indicates the rail bridge will open on request

3. SOUTHWOLD

Landfall waypoint
52°18'·78N 001°40'·54E About ½M SE
of entrance

Charts
Imray C28
Admiralty 2695

Contact
Harbourmasters Peter Simmons and Gerry Hilder
℡ 01502 724712
(0800-1800 in July-Aug and 0800-1600 Oct-Mar)
VHF Ch 12
Callsign *Southwold Port Radio*
www.eastsuffolk.gov.uk/visitors/harbours-and-waterways/
southwold-harbour

Tides
HW Lowestoft +0105

Main hazards

There are shifting sand banks close to and within the entrance. There is a sand bar across the entrance that extends NE of the N pier. With wind against tide heavy seas can build up off the entrance and the depth over the bar can alter drastically after E gales.

Do not attempt an entrance during strong E or NE winds, especially if they are blowing against the tide.

Strong tides run athwart the entrance and in some conditions a 'bore' or standing wave runs in between the piers. There's between 0·9m and 1·3m of water on the yacht track at chart datum.

Visiting vessels must contact the Harbourmaster (Ch 12) for entry and berthing instructions before approaching the entrance and again before leaving their berth for departure.

The town's lighthouse and church are prominent landmarks approaching from N

Landmarks

The town of Southwold lies 1M N of the harbour entrance, which is the mouth of the River Blyth. A white lighthouse (Fl.10s.37m24M, MMSI 992351019) stands in a prominent position on top of the low cliff on which the town stands. Also prominent is a Norman-style church built by wealthy local wool merchants. The seafront is marked by rows of colourful beach huts and, further inland, at the back of the marshes, is a large conspicuous concrete water tower.

Approach

From any seaward direction there is clear and deep water to within a short distance of the entrance. Along the coast in both directions the depth runs from 5m close in to 10m or more ½M out. There are no off-lying marks or buoys, so aim for the landfall waypoint. From there the entrance bears about 310°.

Entry

Entry signals

Three vertical F.R. lights or, during daylight, two red flags, mounted on a pole at the end of the N Pier, indicate 'harbour closed'. If displayed, contact Southwold harbourmaster or, if outside the listening hours of 0800–1700, contact Humber Coastguard for advice. Three vertical greens or no flags means it's clear to enter

Southwold harbour entrance

Fuel berth serves red and white diesel

Entrance is best attempted from 30 min before HW or, if there is sufficient depth, near LW when the coastal tide cross stream is at its slackest. HM will advise on depths over the bar. HW at the harbour bridge is about half an hour after HW at the bar.

The North Pier is marked with a light (Fl.G.1·5s) and the South Pier with a Q.R. Do not stray into the bay N of the North Pier where the water is shallow, and the sand bank keeps moving.

Enter along the centreline of the channel parallel to the S pier. The entrance is narrow, 36m, and the stream runs hard both ways, reaching 3-4kn on flood and 5-6kn on ebb. In addition, the coastal tide flows at right angles across the entrance, both rising (southward) and falling (northward) at anywhere between 2·5 and 4kn.

Keep to the middle between the piers as far as the Knuckle (2F.G.(vert)), at the landward end of the N Pier, marked with a 4kn (through the water) speed limit sign mounted on a post, which is in turn mounted on an iron frame jutting out into the entrance.

Just past this, turn hard to starboard and aim to be close alongside and parallel to the concrete retaining wall on the starboard side of the river just before the RNLI station and RIB launching crane.

Follow this wall almost to its end then head back into the middle of the river. Keeping close to the wall avoids sand and shingle that's building up on the S side of the channel but take care to maintain steerage way above the tidal flow, otherwise eddies can swing the boat and push her against the wall. Usually there is at least 2m of water at low tide along the wall. At the far end of the wall, a sand spit juts out into the stream to catch the unwary.

Despite the sign on the Knuckle indicating a 4kn speed limit, the Harbour Authority has imposed a maximum speed limit of 'dead slow'. This is described as the minimum speed at which steerage and progress can be maintained and applies from the Knuckle to the bridge at the top of the harbour. The bridge, which carries a yellow light on the central support, links Southwold with nearby Walberswick on the other side of the river. Vessels exceeding this speed limit will be considered as not complying with ColRegs Rule 6.

All skippers are requested to navigate with caution and to avoid excessive wash, especially near the rowing ferry that operates across the River Blyth about 3 cables from

Visitor moorings have been increased

the entrance to the harbour during summer months, it has right of way. Warning signs are positioned 100m either side of the ferry crossing.

Vessels moving in the harbour are required to keep a listening watch on Ch 12 and to report their intentions and movements to the HM.

Berthing

There are 16 visitor berths alongside stagings opposite the Harbour Inn pub, where boats can form rafts up to four abreast. Shorelines are obligatory to cope with the 6kn ebb tide and, because departure should always be on the flood, the suggestion is to moor with the boat heading down the harbour so that she can be eased out ahead into the stream and motored cleanly away.

There's usually around 2m of water at low tide and the bottom is hard and steeply shelving. There are ladders on the staging and the harbour authority thoughtfully supplies fender boards to straddle the piles. Remember to leave them behind on departure.

A further eight visitor berths are available alongside two floating pontoons adjacent to the Harbour Office. In 2017 the harbour owners, Waveney District Council, installed new pontoons on the Walberswick side of the river opposite the pub. These have no water or electric services and deeper draught boats can ground especially at the upriver end. Should all the visitor berths be fully booked, phone HMS back downstream on the N shore who may be able to find you a space.

Harbour Marine Services ✆ 01502 724721

Take care turning around in the harbour. There are stagings on both sides of the river, but just up river of the new visitors' pontoons the S bank is clear, and it is recommended that bigger boats should turn here, using full power plus propeller kick to turn tightly in the space. A local trick is to put the boat's stem into the muddy bank opposite and let the tide swing her round, but it takes some courage to do it first time.

Above the moorings is a low bridge taking the footpath from Southwold across to the village of

SOUTHWOLD HARBOUR IP18 6TA

Contact
Harbourmasters ✆ 01502 724712 (0800–1800 July-Aug, 0800-1600 Oct-Mar)
VHF Ch 12
Callsign *Southwold Port Radio*
Out of hours call Humber Coastguard on VHF Ch 16
Email southwoldharbour@eastsuffolk.gov.uk
Access 24hr depending on tide, draught and weather
Berthing On stagings and floating pontoons adjacent to Harbour Office and on S bank. Additional berths can be arranged with Harbour Marine Services ✆ 01502 724721
Facilities WC, showers
(Both at Harbour Office during manned hours and caravan site near harbour entrance, accessed with mooring receipt)
Slipways At boatyard and SC
Electricity Connection points on staging. (Pontoon connections at top of staging gangway use long leads)
Water Taps and hoses on the staging
Gas Calor and Gaz at chandler
Boatyard/Repairs HMS (Harbour Marine Services) ✆ 01502 724721 30-T travel-hoists and large slip, full services
www.southwoldboatyard.co.uk
Fuel Arrange with HM. Fuel station close to lifeboat station on N entry wall; red and white diesel
Chandler Next to boatyard at seaward end of foreshore
www.southwoldboatyard.co.uk/chandlery
Club Southwold SC www.southwoldsc.org
Phone At pub. Emergency phone at RNLI station
Provisions Some from café near chandler. Shops 1M in town
Pub/restaurant The Harbour Inn ✆ 01502 722381, Sole Bay Fish Co. Restaurant ✆ 01502 724241 and in town
Taxi ✆ 01502 723400

Walberswick. Boats have been known to end up against the bridge, carried there by the strong tide. The bridge is lit with a yellow light on the centre support and great care needs to be taken at night or in bad weather when manoeuvring in its vicinity.

Be aware of the low bridge at top of harbour

Southwold is a bustling mix of leisure and inshore fishing boats

4. RIVERS ORE AND ALDE

⊕ **Landfall waypoint**
52°01'·56N 001°28'·20E Within sight of
Orford Haven SWB

Charts
Imray 2000, C28
Admiralty Leisure Folio 5607, 2052 and 2695

Tides
Orford Haven Bar Walton -0028
Orford Quay Walton +0040
Slaughden Walton +0105
Iken Cliff Walton +0130

ECP Honorary Port Pilot
(Orford and Ore / Alde entrance)
Philip Attwood ℡ 07528 092635 or VHF Ch 08/16
Email orfordhaven@eastcoastpilot.com
www.aldeandore.org

A transit from the Orford Haven buoy to this bungalow will keep you in the best water (2019)

Main hazards

Rather as with the Deben entrance, there are a lot of gloomy reports about going into the Ore and Alde. True, the entrance to the Ore and Alde is subject to frequent quite massive changes, especially following E gales, but with careful planning, a cautious approach and taking note of the latest information available via www.eastcoastpilot.com and perhaps a call to ECP HPP Philip Attwood (see box details), you should have no real problems getting in. The buoys are taken away for the winter and placed in new positions each spring following a new survey. An entrance chartlet can be downloaded from the ECP website.

Ideal time to enter the Ore is about 2hr before HW.

Streams in the river run strongly, at up to 5kn on spring floods and over 6kn on the ebb.

Entrance to river Ore, summer 2019

RIVER ORE

52°
04′
N

N

Depths in Metres

03′

Barthorp's Creek

North Weir Pt

North Shoal

Bungalow

Weir

South Shoal

Shingle Street

CG

02′

Oxley
R

Orford Haven
RW
LFl.10s
Bell

Martello Tr AA

Obstn

Flybury Pt

Lower Gull

Dovey's
YB

The Narrows

River Ore

Water Skiing

Long Reach

Hollesley Bay

Drying shingle banks and breaking water

1°28′E

27′

29′

30′

Entry should not be attempted in strong SE or E winds when seas can break heavily.

Landmarks

Orfordness Lighthouse is prominently conspicuous, especially from N, while the bluff of Bawdsey Cliff, topped with a lattice radar tower, stands out to the S. Trinity House has discontinued the light at Orfordness, although the lighthouse tower itself remains as a good daylight landmark. We do not recommend entry to the Ore after dusk.

Approaching the Landfall Waypoint, the hamlet of Shingle Street appears behind the steep gravel bank due W. To the S stand three Martello towers: the one furthest S stands on the N end of Bawdsey Cliffs, the middle one has a distinctive glass pagoda-like top and the northernmost stands W from the Orford Haven buoy at the S end of the hamlet of Shingle Street. A row of white painted ex-coastguard cottages with a CG radio mast is prominent to the N of the hamlet and marks the entrance, which is difficult to identify until close in as the shingle banks extending S from Weir Point visually merge with the shingle of the W bank.

Entry

From N Crossing Hollesley Bay pass the Ness in about 8m of water and about a cable (200 yards) off the shingle and set a course of roughly 235° towards the Orford Haven SWB (RW L.Fl.10s), which should keep you well clear of the Whiting Bank that runs on your port side roughly parallel with the coast.

From N and S There's clear and deep water to within a short distance of the entrance. Along the coast in both directions the depth runs from 5m close in to 10m or more only ½M offshore.

Pick up the Orford Haven SWB and aim for the Oxley PHB (unlit); in summer 2019 safest water is on a transit between the Haven Buoy and the bungalow prominent on the shingle bank, and then to port of the Weir SHB (unlit). It is essential that the first-time visitor finds the Orford Haven SWB (L.Fl.10s Bell) and then spots the Oxley PHB to the W and beyond it the Weir SHB.

Keep to the centre of the river until passing the Weir SHB and turn up river staying in the middle and with an eye on the depth. The river narrows opposite Weir Point where two spurs have extended out from either side. Here also are a series of exposed hard London Clay ridges, which rise vertically on the W bank close by

Weir marks the S extremity of the Ness

Orford Haven buoy. The yacht in background has just turned upriver at the Weir buoy hidden by the shingle bank

Large sections of concrete remains make it imperative to stay in the centre of the river

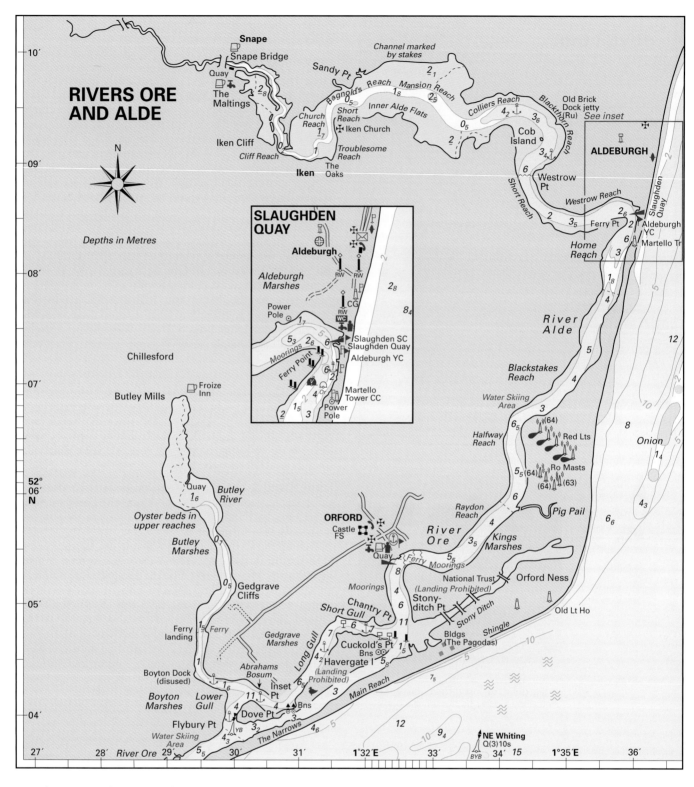

Depths in Metres

Chillesford

Butley Mills

SLAUGHDEN QUAY

Barthorp's Creek. Do not hug the W bank, as opposite Weir Point, you'll likely run into a collapsed concrete gun emplacement that slipped down the shingle and makes a hard hazard to run into. Stay in the middle of the stream. Depths below keel with a 1·8m draught in 2018 were generally in the 2m range. The lowest recorded depth 1½ hours before HW was 1·4m below keel over the bar itself opposite Weir Point.)

With wind against tide, heavy seas build up off the entrance and the depth over the bar can alter drastically after SE gales. If you are unsure of the conditions call up ECP HPP Philip Attwood to obtain the latest available information about the entrance before attempting it and avoid it entirely in strong onshore winds.

An occasional foot ferry runs across the Butley River. Beyond the staging lie local boat moorings

TWO RIVERS

Although one long river, navigable from the entrance right up to Snape Bridge, alongside the famous Snape Maltings concert hall, it's a waterway with two names. From the entrance to about 1M above the village and quay at Orford it's the Ore; from this point in Halfway Reach up to Snape it's the Alde.

The Ore

For much of its length, the Ore divides around Havergate Island, a bird sanctuary that's home to a great variety of wading and marsh birds, including one of the biggest breeding colonies of avocets in Britain. Landing is prohibited.

Having successfully negotiated the entrance to the Ore, the first major landmarks are the incinerator chimney and buildings of HMP Hollesley Bay on the W bank. There is a short drying creek called Barthorp's Creek in the W bank, which was used by barges taking produce from the prison farm to London.

The rather featureless Long Reach is a straight stretch of water running NE inside Orford Ness and is a favourite area for water skiing. At the top end of the reach is an unlit SCB marking the S end of Havergate Island. Leaving the buoy to starboard leads you into the Lower Gull where there is a good anchorage under the port bank.

Butley River

The Butley River branches off NW just beyond the Lower Gull anchorage, but there's a sand spit jutting out from the W bank and the entrance to the creek is well over against the N shore. The channel is marked with withies topped with old paint cans and there are oyster beds in the top half of the creek above the ferry landings, but there's a good anchorage in a little over 2m at LW in the lower reaches of the creek below the disused Boyton Dock.

You can also find good holding ground above the Dock, where the river turns due N for ½M before curving to starboard towards Gedgrave Cliffs, which is about as far as a sea going yacht of any noticeable draught will want to venture. From here on up the riverbed is home to oysters and anchoring is forbidden. Down river of the Cliffs is a number of moorings and it takes a bit of care to wend your way through them. Just before the moorings two long jetties stick out from either side into the river from which an occasional foot ferry operated by volunteers carries walkers and cyclists across. Medium draught boats can anchor in the stream between the top of the moorings and Gedgrave Cliffs, but above here the river virtually dries to a trickle.

Butley River to Orford

Past the Butley River entrance, the river Ore runs briefly SE then NE through Long Gull and turns E into Short Gull before joining once more with the other branch that flows S of Havergate Island through Main Reach. There's a good anchorage in Abraham's Bosum, just upriver of the Butley River, and in both Gulls under the lee of Havergate Island. Main Reach is virtually a straight cut through the marshes and forms a shorter, but less interesting, route to Orford. Deeper water in this reach is to be found on the E side. There are gradually sloping mudflats extending from the Island.

SCM marks the dividing of river around Havergate Island

Can topped withy marks the end of the spit at the entrance to the Butley River

Orford church lies at the centre of the village

ORFORD

Approaching Orford from S, the 90ft high Norman Keep, which is all that remains of the once royal castle, stands out to the left of the village, while in the centre is the church proud on the crown of the hill.

The main channel is clearly marked by two lines of moorings each side of the river. On the outer trot of starboard-hand moorings are five laid for visitors, each with an orange or pink pick-up buoy marked 'single visitor'. To find a vacant mooring is sometimes difficult and if you do pick up one other than a visitor-marked mooring, leave someone aboard, don't leave the boat unattended and don't raft up either. Call the Orford HM as you approach the lower moorings and seek advice.

Don't anchor within the area of the moorings, where the bottom is foul, and don't anchor between the two danger signs either side of the river at the N end of the moorings. These mark pipelines laid in the riverbed

ORFORD   IP12 2NU

Contact
Harbourmaster and Quay Warden ① 01394 459950
① 07528 092635
VHF Ch 08 or 16
Callsign *Chantry* (0930–1700 in season)
Email orfordquayuk@gmail.com
Water From standpipes on the quay
Provisions In village
Pubs/restaurant Several in the village
Post office/stores opposite King's Head
Scrubbing posts Near quay
Telephone Cardphone in car park at back of Orford SC
Slipway At quay, fee pay. Club slipway at Orford SC
Club Orford SC ① 01394 450997 www.orfordsail.org.uk
Transport Buses to Ipswich and surrounding area
Taxi ① 01394 459447

taking services to the National Trust buildings on Orford Ness. It's best to anchor well above the main areas of moorings and go ashore by dinghy but be careful of the swiftly flowing tide. You can stay for a short time alongside the quay, up to an hour or so either side of HW but watch for the ferry that runs from the quay across to the landing stage on the Ness; other riverboats also use the quay.

Continuing up river from Orford, the next prominent feature is the nest of large BBC World Service radio transmitter masts to starboard. The National Trust owns the marshes surrounding them and landing is strictly forbidden.

It is here, at Pigpail Sluice, that the Ore becomes the Alde.

Orford

HM office | Orford SC | Aldeburgh | River Alde
Quay and ferry | Moorings
Moorings | Moorings

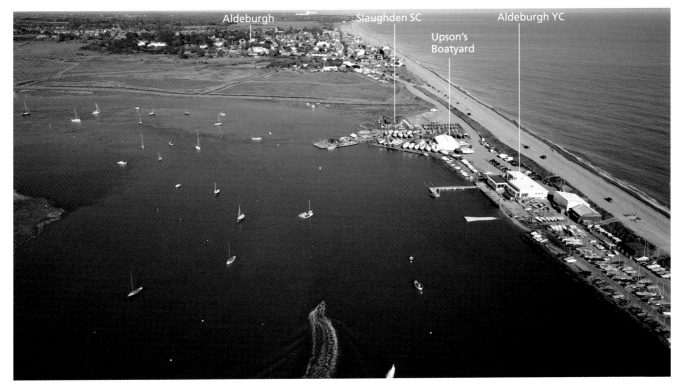

Slaughden is a busy yachting centre

The Alde

Under its new name, the river continues in a winding, but generally N direction through flat marshland up to Slaughden Quay, which is on the outside of a hairpin bend inland. The first prominent landmark is a Martello Tower on the starboard side where the shingle bank between the river and the sea is hardly more than 50 yards wide. The tower is known as 'CC'.

Slaughden Quay

Slaughden is sited on the apex of the bend in the river, which, having run NNE, now swings almost due W as it heads inland.

A good anchorage can be found in the bay 150 yards S of Aldeburgh Club, between the designated visitor moorings and the Martello Tower. Anchoring in the fairway between moorings is strongly discouraged as the ground is foul. There are three visitor moorings just downriver of the club, in line with the Martello Tower. Each is large enough to raft three yachts. Other visitor moorings are provided by Brian Upson (RF Upson & Co ☎ 01728 453047). The club runs a launch between shore and moorings at weekends and all through August, call the launch on ☎ 07531 071303.

Visitors are welcome at the club, Aldeburgh YC, and can land at the floating pontoon. There's water available via hosepipe at the end of the pontoon. There's a crowded beaching area between the clubhouse and Slaughden Quay. There are two boatyards: Upson's on the quay and Aldeburgh Boatyard, which lies further back. Behind Upson's slipway and yard lies the clubhouse of Slaughden SC, which again welcomes visitors when open.

SLAUGHDEN QUAY (ALDEBURGH)   IP15 5NA

Contact
Harbourmaster Brian Upson ☎ 01728 453047
Boatyards Upson's Boatyard ☎ 01728 453047
Aldeburgh Boatyard (Demon Yachts) ☎ 01728 452019
Fuel Diesel from Upson's Boatyard, petrol in Aldeburgh town
Chandler Upson's and Aldeburgh Boatyards
Rigger Aldeburgh Boatyard
Visitors' moorings Contact Upson's Boatyard ☎ 01728 453047 or David Cable ☎ 01728 452569.
Electrical and mechanical engineer Upson's Boatyard
Slipway Upson's Boatyard
Facilities (All at Aldeburgh YC) WC, showers, telephone
Club Aldeburgh YC ☎ 01728 452562
www.aldeburghyc.org.uk Slaughden SC
☎ 01728 454335 when open
www.slaughdensailingclub.co.uk
Bar/food Aldeburgh YC (hours vary)
Pubs/restaurants Several in town
Water Standpipe on quay and Aldeburgh YC pontoon
Provisions Aldeburgh (about 1M)
Transport Buses
Taxi ☎ 01728 833621 and 452142

Slaughden SC

Aldeburgh YC

The steel post on the end of Cob Island has a distinctive swan emblem as a topmark. The best water is well over to starboard and well clear of the long spit that juts out from Cob Island. There is a line of small boat moorings round the outer edge of the bend.

At Cob Island the river swings W and widens out into a shallow lake with the winding channel marked by withies. Here too the character of the river changes with well wooded rolling countryside interspersed with arable fields and church steeples reaching skyward, all so characteristic of the Suffolk countryside.

Deep draught boats can find good holding in Colliers Reach, so crews can mount a dinghy excursion through the winding waterways to Snape. Shoal draught boats can anchor off Iken Church, The Oaks and Iken Cliffs in 1m and 2m of water at low tide, but care is needed as a number of moorings have been laid in these holes. Landing on the Iken shore is restricted and there's only a footpath along the bank to Snape.

Above Iken Cliffs the river winds N and finally NW to the quay and bridge at Snape where the world famous Snape Maltings concert hall stands. It is possible to lie alongside the quay, but it dries at low tide and fender boards are recommended, because the face of the quay is quite rough. Do not moor outside a barge or other flat-bottomed boat, because the ground here slopes and if the inner boat slides, the outer could be pushed over. For a panoramic view of the upper Alde it's well worth a stroll up to the crossroads on the 'hill' in Snape.

General advice about the upper reaches

When planning a trip up river above Cob Island, aim to begin as early on the flood as possible. By doing so, the channel can be picked out more easily and the channel markers understood. Note these markers are withies,

For a longish stay it's worth contacting either Brian Upson or David Cable (see box page 27) for a mooring but expect to have either a longish row or to use an outboard, as the tide is quite strong. Although facilities are limited at Slaughden it's a fairly short walk into the town of Aldeburgh and its well-stocked High Street.

From Slaughden up to Westrow Point the river is lined on either side with moorings and, at the point itself, is crossed by an underwater power cable. Above that, the river turns NE in Island Reach and good places to anchor can be found between Cob Island to port and the Old Brickyard Dock to starboard or round the corner in Collier's Reach.

From Slaughden the river wends W towards Snape

Cob Island marker now has a distinct lean

The remains of the Old Brickyard Dock

with port hand marks topped with red cans and the starboard withies have branched tops and occasional green cans. They tend to come and go from season to season, so once the mud is covered, there may be no marks to guide you or they may be confusing. Starting early may also make a stop at Snape for lunch and a drink at the Plough and Sail possible before hurrying back down to deeper water.

The famous Snape Maltings

5. RIVER DEBEN

Hazards

Don't believe all that the doom-mongers tell you about the entrance to the Deben being treacherous and difficult; true the entrance is subject to frequent changes, especially following E gales, however, by dint of prudent seamanship and carefully following the buoys and entering at the right state of the tide, you should have no real problems getting in. It is essential to obtain the latest information from www.eastcoastpilot.com which carries a chartlet drawn from the latest Trinity House survey, the specialist Deben and Ore website or the Woodbridge Cruising Club's website.

www.debenestuarypilot.co.uk
www.woodbridgecruisingclub.org

The Woodbridge Haven SWB is at 51°57'·99N 001°23'·62E (2019). It is essential for the first-time visitor to check current information before approaching the entrance and we suggest calling the Felixstowe Ferry HM and ECP HPP, John White, for pilotage or advice (see contact details in Felixstowe Ferry or River Deben information panels).

The ideal time to enter is about HW -2hr. Streams in the river mouth are quite strong. Entry should not be attempted in strong SE or E winds or at night. Unless you have considerable spare engine power don't try entering against the ebb either, which can run at up to 5kn on springs.

The entrance to the River Deben at LW, spring 2019

Woodbridge Haven buoy

Landmarks

The tall lattice frame of the last remaining radar tower at Bawdsey is the best landmark when approaching from a distance to the entrance to this most beautiful river. The entrance lies between Bawdsey Manor, visible in the trees on the E bank and two Martello Towers on the W side of the river.

Entry

From the Woodbridge Haven SWB (Mo(A)15s) steer a course that leaves the West Knoll PHB to port followed in close order by the Knoll Spit PHB also to port, which marks the spit on the S shingle bank, and the Mid Knoll SHB to starboard. Beware of very strong cross currents, especially on the S going flood, which can push boats onto the S-side shingle spit.

As you pass the Mid Knoll SHB and turn up river, keep hard over towards the W shore and follow close in under the shingle bank until at least halfway to the large Deben PHB marking a shingle bank off the Felixstowe Ferry SC. At first sight this buoy appears to be almost on the E shingle shore.

Approaching Knoll Spit from the Woodbridge Haven buoy

Keep clear of a line of steel posts topped with PH marks standing out from the shingle beach. These mark the ends of groynes and recent erosion has meant they are now well out from the bank. Just past the last of the posts set a course to angle across the river towards the starboard shingle bank to pass through the relatively narrow deep-water gap between the Deben PHB and the Bawdsey shingle shore. (Don't be tempted to follow the local fishermen and shallow draught boats through the

RIVER DEBEN

gap between the Felixstowe Ferry pier and the Deben PHB – there's not a lot of water and the tide runs very hard just there.)

After passing the Deben buoy, keep over on the starboard side of the channel for the deeper water and slightly less fierce tidal stream. The relatively narrow entrance channel between the shingle banks then opens out into Felixstowe Ferry itself. Close by the Bawdsey shore is a line of five visitor moorings, often with boats on them, but the bulk of moorings lie in the channel to the W of Horse Sand.

FELIXSTOWE FERRY

On the W bank lies Felixstowe Ferry with Felixstowe Ferry SC and the new grey painted HM's office prominent on the bank, just down river from the ferry steps and the slipway to Felixstowe Ferry Boatyard. Close by is an assortment of shacks, mostly used by local fishermen for gear storage, although one is a good fresh fish shop and there's another fresh fish shop at the head of the ferry landing. There's a pair of scrubbing posts on the upstream side of the slipway. There is no public access to the river; launching licences are available from the boatyard office or East Suffolk Water Ski Club (details on a board at the head of the slipway).

The Ferry Café stands behind the boatyard, while the boatyard's owners have opened a new café at the head of the ferry jetty, Winkles Cafe.

FELIXSTOWE FERRY — IP11 9RZ (Ferry Boatyard)

Contact
Harbourmasters John White and Stephen Read
☎ 01394 270106 or 07803 476621
VHF Ch 08
Callsign *Odd Times*
Water taxi VHF Ch 08, Callsign *Deben Ferry* or ☎ 01394 282173
Facilities WC behind FFSC
Water From standpipe by the boatyard
Chandler At boatyard (limited stock)
Provisions Shops in Old Felixstowe 2M
Pubs/restaurant Ferry Boat Inn ☎ 01394 284203
Ferry Café ☎ 01394 276305, fish & chips and all-day breakfasts
Winkles Café ☎ 07947 100242
Repairs Felixstowe Ferry Boatyard ☎ 01394 282173
www.felixstoweboats.co.uk
Crane At head of slip. Contact boatyard
Scrubbing posts Close to slip. Contact Harbourmaster
Slipway Contact Harbourmaster
Club Felixstowe Ferry SC ☎ 01394 283785, www.ffsc.co.uk
Telephone Payphone near Ferry Boat Inn
Visitors' moorings Contact Harbourmaster
Taxi ☎ 01394 284000, 271116

On the opposite bank of the river, at Bawdsey, is Bawdsey Manor, which is now a school but was once the centre of radar research. There's a jetty and dinghy slipway and a clean sandy beach. The one-time servicemen's houses along the front are now holiday homes.

Inside the entrance bar

Tide turning on the Horse Sand

Do not anchor in the main channel where the holding is highly suspect and the tide runs extremely strongly. A visit to either Felixstowe Ferry or Bawdsey involves finding a mooring – call the HM for an allocation – or anchoring a mile up river in good holding mud in Sea Reach with a long trip to and fro in the tender.

The local boatyard now runs the foot ferry between Felixstowe and Bawdsey, which will also act as a water taxi to get crews to and from the shore between runs. It operates between 1000 and 1800 hours throughout the summer months (see the information panel for contact details).

Above the Ferry, just about in mid-stream, lies the Horse Sand. The deep-water channel is on the E side, while the shallower channel on the W side is crammed with moorings. This channel has silted up in recent years restricting the size of boats it can accommodate.

The stretch of water above the last of the moorings and almost as far as the next bend in the river is the only section to which a universal 8kn speed limit does not apply. It is a designated water ski and speedboat area and on the W bank is a pontoon and ski ramp.

The river is clearly defined by the banks here and any buoys are racing marks for either FFSC or the up river Waldringfield SC. This section of the river is also the least exciting visually where it runs between high sea defence banks through Falkenham Marsh to port and low-lying arable land to starboard.

At Green Point, where the river turns N and the view of Ramsholt opens out, the Deben reveals its true character with gently rolling slopes covered in woodland and well tended farmland.

Note that all the buoys above Felixstowe Ferry are unlit.

RAMSHOLT

Ramsholt stands on the E bank and consists of an old stone barge jetty and a pub, the Ramsholt Arms (IP12 3AB ☎ 01394 411209), plus a red telephone box. There are no services there, but it's a pleasant spot to stretch the legs and 'take refreshment'. For information about moorings contact the HM, George Collins, ☎ 01394 384318 (evenings) or 07930 304061 during the day when he's usually to be found on his own boat *Brio* on a mooring opposite the jetty. There are over 200 moorings at Ramsholt and the fairway is sometimes difficult to identify, but there is good holding in the middle, if you wish to anchor, so long as you don't mind the wash from passing craft.

Ramsholt

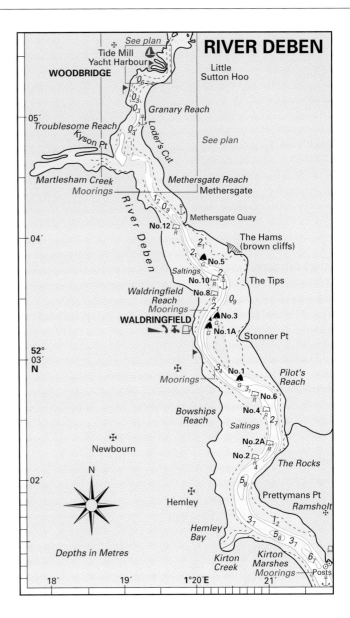

THE ROCKS

Above Ramsholt, the channel swings gently NW round Kirton marshes, where the drying Kirton Creek joins the river, before heading NE round Prettyman's Point into an area below Ramsholt Woods known as The Rocks, because the riverbed is strewn with them. There is a low sandy cliff forming a sheltered anchorage with a beach for swimming and picnicking, but it's often crowded at weekends. There are no roads or facilities and visitors are requested not to cut down trees to make fires.

Opposite the Rocks is the first of the river buoys, which continue right up to Melton.

The first four buoys are PHBs marking the edge of mudflats extending out from the W shore, pushing the channel well over to the E side of the river until it sweeps back to the W side above No.1 SHB below Waldringfield. Give No.4 and 6 a good berth, because the mud and sand spit they mark is growing.

The Rocks is a popular weekend anchorage

WALDRINGFIELD

No.1 SHB marks the downstream extremity of Stonner Island where the main channel bears to port and is marked by triple lines of moorings all the way through Waldringfield itself.

There are no designated visitor moorings, however the owners of Waldringfield Boatyard have introduced a novel scheme, using clients' vacant moorings, to each of which is attached a 12ft orange-painted rowing boat with *Visitor* clearly marked on the sides; oars and rowlocks are attached. Alternatively, ask the HM if he has a spare mooring. (There are no official mooring fees, but a donation is gratefully received for local sailing charities). Anchoring in the main channel is not recommended, because it is quite narrow, there is much traffic, the bottom's foul and the holding's suspect. Generally, moorings will take boats up to 35ft (10·4m).

If no vacant mooring is available, go up as far as No.3 SHB, at the top of the moorings, and anchor roughly in line with it and No.5 the next buoy up on the bend. Again, such is the pressure for all-tide moorings that this area is now being populated with moorings as well, so be careful anchoring and use a trip line for safety.

There is clean landing on the beach at Waldringfield near the HM's hut and there are some pretty walks

WALDRINGFIELD   IP12 4QZ (Boatyard)

Harbourmaster Tony Lyon ☎ 01473 736291 / 07925 081062
Email waldringfieldhm@btinternet.com
Boatyard Waldringfield Boatyard ☎ 01473 736260 VHF Ch 80
www.waldringfieldboatyard.co.uk
WiFi (on the water)
Water From taps at boatyard quay or outside sailing club
Fuel Diesel and petrol in cans from garage 1M up the Woodbridge road
Boat repairs Slipway and 40T crane
Scrubbing posts In front of sailing club (care with bilge keels)
Facilities Public phone box near inn. Toilets in boatyard, code on payment of mooring fee
Pub/restaurant The Maybush ☎ 01473 736215
www.debeninns.co.uk/maybush
Club Waldringfield SC ☎ 01473 736633
Provisions None
Transport Occasional bus or taxi into Woodbridge or Martlesham

around the area, but services are limited. There is a pontoon jetty reaching out from the boatyard to which dinghies can be moored during a stroll ashore or a drink or meal at the Maybush, and a river trip boat moors across the end of the pontoon.

Maybush   Boatyard

Waldringfield

WOODBRIDGE

Above Waldringfield the river becomes increasingly attractive with wooded banks. It also shallows and, below half tide, great care is needed not to ground. From No.3 SHB, at the N end of Stonner Island, the river runs into a bay at the N end of which are The Hams, brown cliffs with a fine sandy beach, while to the S a promontory called The Tips marks downriver extent of the bay. A spit from the opposite, W, bank is marked by Nos.8 and 10 PHBs. Landing at The Tips is possible, but only for a short period either side of HW.

The river swings over to the other shore just above The Hams and then straightens for the run up past Methersgate on the starboard side. There's another stone jetty here, Methersgate Quay, which was originally used for loading local farm produce into barges, but now landing is strongly discouraged. However, you can pick up a vacant mooring in deepish water on this reach.

From the Quay and No.12 PHB, almost all the way to Woodbridge, the river is marked with both buoys and moorings. There are now so many moorings that it takes considerable care to identify the main channel. At No.14 PHB the river turns 90° to port in Troublesome Reach and heads W towards Kyson Point, which also marks the entrance to Martlesham Creek (drying), before swinging 90° back N again. The saltings that caused these violent changes in direction were cut through in the 1890s to accommodate barges. The cut, called Loder's Cut, can be used by shallow draught (max 1·5m) craft at about HW ±1hr.

There is a small boatyard, Martlesham Creek Boatyard, on the S bank of the W-running Martlesham Creek with pontoons, which dry out, and fresh water and power, plus showers and toilets. The yard can launch boats up to 10 tons and offers boat repairs and both inboard and outboard engine servicing.

Martlesham Creek Boatyard IP12 4PQ
☎ 01394 384727
www.martleshamboatyard.co.uk

The creek is buoyed for much of its length and there are moorings at the upper end for boats that can take the ground. The bottom is generally good east coast mud.

Roughly half way up Granary Reach, between No.13 SHB and No.16 PHB, the river almost dries at LW, but deepens again as it passes the Deben YC. From there,

This boathouse snuggled under the woods marks the turn W from Methersgate to Troublesome Reach

YACHT CLUBS AT WOODBRIDGE

Deben YC ☎ 01349 385400
www.debenyachtclub.co.uk
Woodbridge CC ☎ 01394 386737
www.woodbridgecruisingclub.org
Facilities WC, showers, bar (at weekends only).

WOODBRIDGE

through Woodbridge and right up to Wilford Bridge, just above Melton, the river dries to a mere trickle at low water.

Boats unable to take the ground can find a least depth of 2m inside the Tide Mill Harbour, the main marina at Woodbridge although the sill restricts entrance or exit to

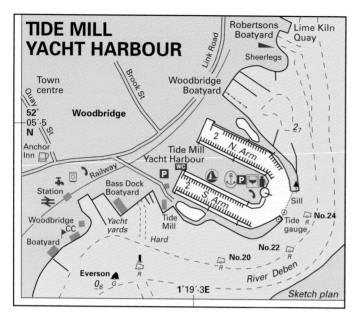

TIDE MILL YACHT HARBOUR

(map labels:)
Robertsons Boatyard
Lime Kiln Quay
Sheerlegs
Link Road
Brook St
Woodbridge Boatyard
Town centre
Quay St
Woodbridge
52° 05'·5 N
Anchor Inn
Railway
Station
Bass Dock Boatyard
Tide Mill Yacht Harbour
N. Arm
S. Arm
Sill
2 7
Woodbridge CC
Yacht yards
Tide Mill
Hard
Tide gauge
No.24
No.22
No.20
Everson
0·6 G
River Deben
1°19'·3E
Sketch plan

TIDE MILL YACHT HARBOUR   IP12 1BP

Contact VHF Ch 80
Callsign *Tide Mill Yacht Harbour*
Harbourmaster Mike Ellis ☎ 01394 385745
Email info@tidemillyachtharbour.co.uk
www.tidemillyachtharbour.co.uk (includes useful daily predictor of heights over the sill)
Access HW±1½hr
Facilities WC, showers, launderette, WiFi (only close to the HM's office)
Water On pontoons
Electricity On pontoons (adaptor required from office)
Gas Calor and Gaz
Telephone At railway station
Boat repairs 16T crane, 35-T boat hoist, full service workshop
Fuel Diesel on berth at entrance
Chandler A few basics on site
Sailmaker Suffolk Sails ☎ 01394 386323 outside marina gate
Rigger Evolution Rigging ☎ 01473 655089
Brokerage Howard Ford Marine Sales ☎ 01394 385577
Provisions In town, 10 minutes
Pubs/restaurants In town
Transport Train station close by, buses
Taxi ☎ 01394 333888

HW ±1½hr. Depth over the sill is indicated by a tide gauge marked in metres on the port side of the sill.

Those happy to take the mud can moor at the quay along the front of the old Tide Mill Granary. Sadly, the opportunity to take a mud berth in Bass' Dock isn't possible any more as the dock is full of live-aboard craft. The old Whisstock's Boatyard has been redeveloped into modern flats and shops. The old Ferry Hard stretching right down to the middle of the river bed has been abandoned and now lies under a foot of mud, the end is still marked by a post (PHB). (At low water springs you could wade across in calf-deep water.)

Woodbridge is an historic town with a good shopping centre and easy access by bus, taxi or train to Ipswich and onward. Much of the surrounding countryside is well worth a visit and the Sutton Hoo Viking burial site is a major attraction.

BOATYARDS AROUND WOODBRIDGE

Woodbridge Boatyard ☎ 01394 385786
www.eversonsboats.co.uk
Crane, slipway

Robertson's ☎ 01394 382305 Alan Fuller
Email info@robertsons-boatyard.co.uk
www.robertsons-boatyard.co.uk
Access HW±1·5hrs
Boat repairs Two slipways, 14-T hoist, crane, rigging, boat repairs (specialists in wooden boats)
Facilities WC
Water On quay
Electricity On quay

Melton Boatyard ☎ 01394 386327 Simon Skeet
Email info@meltonboatyard.co.uk
www.meltonboatyard.co.uk
Berthing By prior arrangement
Access HW ±2hr (at springs), HW ±1 (at neaps)
Boat repairs Specialists in steel and aluminium, 40-T hoist Small chandlery, 30-berth marina
Café Deben Cafe, on HMS Vale ☎ 01394 358643

Larkman's Boatyard Melton ☎ 01394 382943
www.larkmansboatyard.co.uk
Email larkmansboatyard@btconnect.com
Boat repairs and wintering yard (250 spaces) with chandler
Crane 15-T crane for lifting boats over sea wall Limited facilities

Deben YC

Final approach to Woodbridge. Tide Mill Marina behind Tide Mill

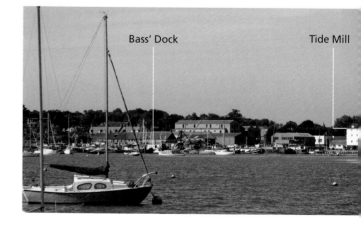

(photo labels:) Bass' Dock   Tide Mill

Bass' dock   Station   HM   Depth gauge   Fuel berth   Sill   WC/showers

Tide Mill Marina, Woodbridge

Opposite the entrance to the Tide Mill the river narrows under a wooded bank. There are a number of moorings that can be temporarily picked up while waiting for the tide to give enough clearance over the Tide Mill sill.

Past the marina the river swings W and opens out into a marshy bay on the W side. This is a good place for over-wintering in mud berths. Here also is Robertson's Boatyard and the remains of an old Lime Kiln and attendant quay.

Further up river lies Melton Boatyard and marina and, next door upriver Richard Larkman's laying up yard. There is a well-buoyed, if rather tortuous, channel right up to the yards, with Wilford Bridge, the point of final navigation on the Deben, a straight run further on. Melton Boatyard's pontoon moorings are dredged to 2m while Larkman lifts boats over the river wall at high tide. Anyone staying in the Tide Mill Marina should consider taking the dinghy and exploring the upper reaches and even ducking under Wilford Bridge into some pretty countryside up to Ufford. Remember though, the river virtually dries at low water, the mere trickle left being almost fresh water.

The Deben above Woodbridge

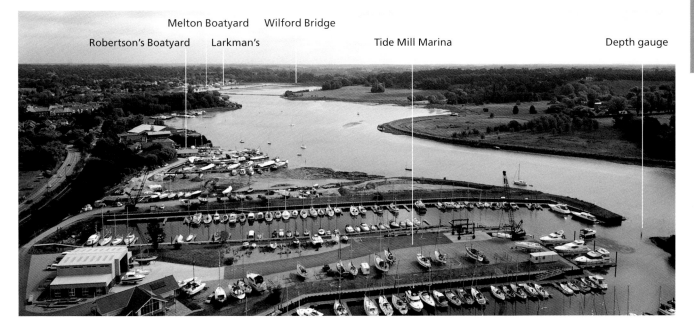

Robertson's Boatyard   Melton Boatyard   Wilford Bridge   Larkman's   Tide Mill Marina   Depth gauge

6. HARWICH HARBOUR

⊕ **Landfall waypoint**
51°55'·23N 001°18'·39E SW of Landguard NCB (Q) on recommended yacht track

Charts
Imray 2000, C1, Y16
Admiralty SC5607, 1491, 2693

Tides
Walton HW +0005

Harbourmaster
Harwich Port Control Ch 71
Callsign *Harwich VTS*
Harbourmaster Mike Dunn ☎ 01255 243030
hha.co.uk/leisure

HARWICH AREA CONTACTS

Harwich Haven Authority ☎ 01255 243030
Harwich Harbour Control (VTS) ☎ 01255 243000

PORT CONTROL

Harwich Harbour is accessible at all times and is one of only two ports of last resort on this stretch of coast. It is imperative that small craft keep clear of the main shipping channels and berthing manoeuvres of container ships. The harbour authority maintains a round the clock radar and radio watch (on Ch 71) and all yachts are requested to listen on this channel from Landguard to Fagbury, on the River Orwell, and to past Erwarton Ness beacon on the Stour. Call on Ch 71 in an emergency only, such as being unable to get out of the way of an announced shipping manoeuvre.
Harwich VTS ☎ 01255 243000.

The authority also produces an excellent yachtsmen's guide detailing the recommended yacht tracks, which is available from local marinas and chandlers or by writing to Harwich Haven Authority. Harbour launches patrol the harbour.
Harwich Haven Authority, Harbour House,
The Quay, Harwich CO12 3HH
☎ 01255 243030
The guide is also available at hha.co.uk

Landmarks

On the E side of Harwich Harbour is Felixstowe Container Port, the largest in the UK and following extensions to the Felixstowe quays is bigger and busier than ever. The most prominent landmarks are the huge blue cranes that stretch the length of the Trinity and Felixstowe South Quays, all along the E side of the harbour.

On a clear day, from the Landfall Waypoint, the disused lighthouse on the Dovercourt Beach is visible, looking rather like a pale coloured, over large dovecote on stilts at the back of the beach. The tall steeple of Harwich Town church, together with the white roof of the Ro-Ro shed on the end of Harwich Quay make good aiming points. On the E side of the entrance is a south cardinal beacon SCM on the tip of Landguard with, just inland, the lower fortifications of Landguard Fort, as well as one of the several radar towers (white) that are dotted about the harbour.

Harwich Church steeple is a good landmark

Main hazards

Big ships and ferries.

The recent extension of Felixstowe South Quay, on the E side of the harbour, has resulted in an almost uninterrupted quay face from Landguard Beach to the N end of Trinity Quay opposite Babergh PHB in the mouth of the Orwell. From several miles out to sea the veritable forest of blue container cranes make the harbour conspicuous. Beware of big ships swinging round to face seawards when berthed.

There are areas of shallow water in the harbour that need care and attention, including the Harwich Shelf on the W side of the entrance and the Shotley Spit, which is marked by Shotley Spit SCB (Q(6)+LFl. 15s) in the centre of the harbour.

At the entrance to the harbour, beware the Cliff Foot Rocks patch E of the end of Blackman's Breakwater on the W side of the approach. The bottom is foul at LW and there are strong eddies. Further in, keep to starboard of the seasonal (March to November) Harwich Shelf ECB (Q(3)10s), which marks the E limit of the Harwich Shelf – at LWS it all but dries in the centre.

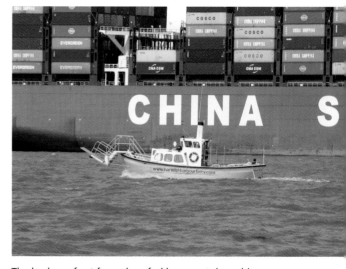

The harbour foot ferry dwarfed by a container ship

Approaches

The approaches to Harwich are well marked. In particular, the deepwater shipping channel is heavily buoyed, but, because of the number, tonnage and size of shipping using the channel, there are recommended yacht entry tracks shown on charts, which must be used. All of them converge on the Landfall Waypoint, roughly halfway between the Landguard NCB (Q) and Pye End SWB (L.Fl.10s).

Once round Landguard and squaring up to enter harbour, a good point to aim for is the white roof of the Ro-Ro shed at the seaward end of the Navy Yard at Harwich. About opposite the Redoubt Fort marked on the chart, turn a few degrees to starboard and aim for the Harwich Shelf ECB. It's quite a small buoy and is often difficult to spot against the background of ships and

The world's largest container ships berth at Felixstowe

HARWICH HARBOUR

Stour Bathside Bay Trinity Pier Trinity House Ha'penny Pier Orwell Shotley Spit SCB

Harwich Harbour

quays. Although lit (Q(3)10s), it's drowned at night by the working lights on the container quays and care is needed to identify it.

The working lights on the quays and ships themselves can be seen many miles out to sea and make a night entrance difficult, especially from the N and E. If in serious doubt, make S to the Medusa SHB (Fl.G.5s), which lies E from Walton on the Naze, and return N towards Harwich using the Medusa Channel past the Stone Banks PHB (Fl.R.5s). It adds distance but can be the easier approach.

In spite of the background light pollution problems, Harwich is an all-weather, all-tide, 24hr, remarkably easy harbour to enter.

From seawards In daylight and after a North Sea crossing, yachts will pick up the Cork Sand Bn (Fl(3)R.10s) or the nearby Cork Sand Yacht Bn NCM (VQ) and, keeping S of the deep water channel, proceed to pass well to port of Landguard NCB (Q) to keep well clear of the bend in the shipping channel.

From N Perhaps having departed the Rivers Ore and Alde or Deben, pass close to Wadgate Ledge SHM (Fl(4)G.15s) and cross the deep-water channel at right angles between the Platters SCB (Q(6)+L.Fl.15s) and the Rolling Ground SHB (QG) to join the recommended yacht track coming in from E.

Harwich Haven Authority recommends crossing the deepwater channel between waypoints 51°55'·83N 001°20'·29E on the N side of the channel and 51°55'·23N 001°20'·39E on the S side, to give the shortest right-angle crossing.

Approaching from S Follow a course of about 345° from the Medusa SHB (Fl.G.5s) through the Medusa Channel to pass close to the Stone Banks PHB (Fl.R.5s) and join the recommended yacht track at the Landfall Waypoint or, at most, three cables S of Landguard NCB (Q).

Yachts approaching Harwich from almost due E and from the direction of the Galloper will have to negotiate the Sunk Gyratory System. Navigate in this area using only the latest charts on which the system's buoyage and traffic separation lanes are marked. It will pay you to give Sunk VTS a call on VHF Ch 71 to let them know

Harwich Shelf ECM

ard PHB   Felixstowe container port   Landguard Point

your position and projected track before entering the system. If you have an AIS transceiver switched on they'll pick you up anyway.

Close approach (pilotage) to Harwich Harbour will be by either the S route through the Medusa Channel or the N route via Cork Sand Yacht Bn.

Inside the Cork Sand to the E and the shipping channel to the N and extending SW into Dovercourt Bay are a number of yellow seasonal racing marks.

Entry

Progress through the harbour must be via the recommended yacht tracks shown on current charts. Keep a sharp lookout for pilots and other working boats crossing between Harwich and Felixstowe. At the Guard PHB (Fl.R.5s Bell) either turn W along the Harwich waterfront to reach the moorings at Halfpenny Pier or cross the mouth of the Stour to Shotley Spit SCB (Q(6)+L.Fl.15s).

At Shotley Spit, turn W either towards Shotley Marina or to proceed on up the River Stour, keeping to the Shotley side until clear of Parkeston Quay, or continue N from Shotley Spit into the River Orwell. Keep close watch on the depth anywhere near Shotley Spit.

HARWICH

Halfpenny Pier

The only facilities for yachts at Harwich are at Ha'penny Pier. From the Guard PHB make W past the Ro-Ro terminal and Ha'penny Pier lies to port. The approach is clear but beware of swells from passing ships while going alongside. The gate at the top of the gangway between the leisure vessel pontoons and Ha'penny Pier itself is locked daily at 1730 for security

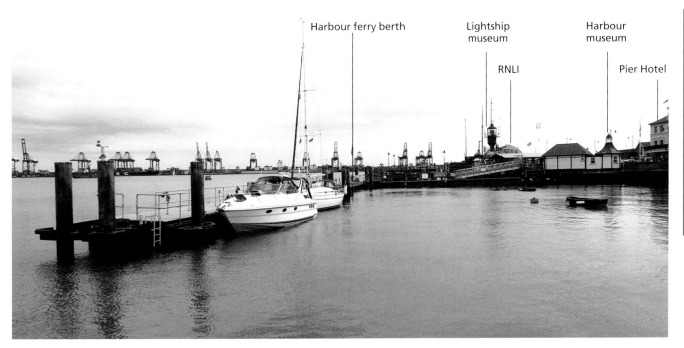

Harbour ferry berth   Lightship museum   Harbour museum

RNLI   Pier Hotel

View across Harwich Harbour from inside Ha'penny Pier

reasons. Access between 1730 and 0900 is only possible using a code obtained from the PM. The office is located at the entrance to Ha'penny Pier (see Halfpenny Pier box for details).

Harwich Yacht Clubs

There are two yacht clubs based at Harwich: Harwich Town SC, which is a dinghy racing club with a clubhouse overlooking the main harbour, and Harwich and Dovercourt SC, which is a cruising club. Its headquarters are at the top of Gashouse Creek, a drying gutway between the Trinity House jetty and Bathside Bay.

There is a foot ferry between Harwich Town, Felixstowe (Landguard beach) and Shotley Marina.

HALFPENNY PIER   CO12 3HH

Contact
Pier Master ☎ 01255 243030 or 07748 154039 (phone manned until 2100)
Pier manned by PM 0800-0900 and 1630-1730 April-Oct (incl. weekends and bank hols). 0800-0900 and 1230-1730 during school summer holidays.
Berth Alongside pontoons. (20m LOA limit) Watch for wash from passing ships. No charge between 0900-1600, but charges apply overnight
Facilities Water and electricity on pier; WC and showers via coded lock, see PM
Provisions In town
Pubs/restaurants café at root of pier; many more nearby in town
Sailmaker Dolphin Sails ☎ 01255 243366
Transport Trains, buses
Taxi ☎ 01255 506070, 01255 551111
Note Harwich Navy Yard has no facilities for yachts. The pilots and harbour launches use it

HARWICH AND DOVERCOURT SC

Contact
www.hdsc.org.uk
Clubhouse on landing barge (LBK6) alongside quay. Bar open Friday evening and Saturday and Sunday lunch times. 5 mins walk from Ha'penny Pier. Gates may be locked outside opening hours
Access HW±3hr
Facilities WC (when club open)
Water On quayside
Telephone In club
Provisions In nearby town centre
Pubs, restaurants In town

SHOTLEY MARINA

On reaching the centre of Harwich Harbour close to Guard PHB (Fl.R.5s Bell), a low building will be seen off the port bow, which carries the word 'Marina' in large letters. It's at Shotley Marina. A prominent landmark behind the marina is a huge once-green water tower at the old HMS *Ganges* naval base behind the marina.

Entry to Shotley is via a dredged channel (2m at MLWS) and a lock providing 24hr access. Approach from Shotley Spit SCB, running parallel to the deep-water channel towards Ganges SHB (Fl.G.5s). When close to this buoy, turn to starboard and pass between a pair of top-marked beacons, which are lit Fl(4)G.15s on the starboard hand and VQ(3)5s on the port hand ECM. From these beacons, the channel into the lock runs on a bearing of about 340°.

SHOTLEY MARINA
IP9 1QJ

Contact ☎ 01473 788982
VHF Ch 80
Callsign *Shotley Marina*
www.shotleymarina.co.uk
Email sales@shotleymarina.co.uk
Max size (lock) 20m x 6·5m x 2·2m,
(berth) 20m on hammerhead only
Facilities WC, showers and baths, launderette, WiFi
Water On pontoons
Electricity On pontoons
Gas Calor and Gaz
Chandler On site ☎ 01473 788982
Fuel From berth immediately to starboard inside lock (24hr)
Provisions From chandler in summer, local shop/PO in village 20 min walk
Bar/restaurant and B&B The Shipwreck ☎ 01473 788865; Bristol Arms (10 min walk) ☎ 01473 787200
Boat repairs Shotley Marine Services ☎ 01473 788982. 40-T boat hoist, 20-T crane
Transport Foot ferry to Harwich and Felixstowe ☎ 01728 666329 *Email* chris@harwichharbourferry.com www.harwichharbourferry.com. Bus service from Shotley Gate (10 min walk) to Ipswich.
Taxi ☎ 01473 222222, 407777, 255555

Locking into the marina is governed by traffic lights (red and green) and there is a waiting pontoon, which is also used by the ferry, to port on the outside of the entrance. There is an INOGON directional leading light mounted on the starboard lock knuckle with lit arrows to keep approaching craft on line up the narrow approach channel. If the arrows point to the left, steer to port, or if they point to the right, steer to starboard, to maintain your track up the channel. Inside the lock are floating bumpers with cleats and grab lines on top.

Entrance to Shotley Marina lock,
green traffic light and Inogon directional light

Shotley Marina

7. RIVER STOUR

⊕ Landfall waypoint
51°55'·20N 001°18'·50E SW of Landguard NCB on
recommended yacht track

Charts
Imray 2000, C28
Admiralty SC5607, 1491, 1594, 2693

Tides
Walton HW
Mistley Quay HW Walton +0025

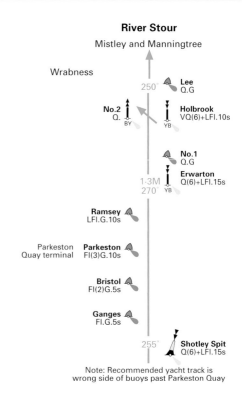

River Stour
Mistley and Manningtree

Wrabness

Lee Q.G
No.2 Q. BY
Holbrook VQ(6)+LFl.10s YB

No.1 Q.G
Erwarton Q(6)+LFl.15s YB

Ramsey LFl.G.10s

Parkeston Quay terminal
Parkeston Fl(3)G.10s

Bristol Fl(2)G.5s

Ganges Fl.G.5s

Shotley Spit Q(6)+LFl.15s

Note: Recommended yacht track is
wrong side of buoys past Parkeston Quay

Introduction
The Stour forms the boundary between Suffolk and
Essex and is one of the most attractive waterways on the
East Coast, arguably running a close second to the River
Deben. Less populated than the latter it is nevertheless an
integral part of the 20-odd square miles of sheltered
water within the Harwich Haven area. When winds
blow hard from E or W you take to the Orwell, but if it's
blowing from N or S, the Stour comes into its own,
offering sheltered anchorages and good holding for most
of its length.

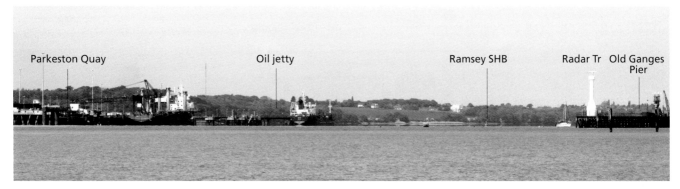

Entering the Stour from Harwich Harbour

Sailing down the Stour past the oil refinery

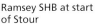
Ramsey SHB at start of Stour

Erwarton SCM

Landmarks and approach

After crossing to the N side of the main shipping channel at the Guard PHB (Fl.R.5s Bell), turn W at Shotley Spit SCB (Q(6)+L.Fl.15s). Pass Shotley Marina control and workshop buildings to starboard (the roof of the workshop is marked MARINA in big black letters), below the Ganges Cliff, on top of which is a conspicuous pale green water tower.

The next landmark to starboard is the old Ganges jetty with a white radar tower on the seaward end. Between Shotley Spit and the jetty are a number of unlit ships' mooring buoys, often with a couple of Trinity House light vessels awaiting refit.

Lunch break in Erwarton Bay

Around the Ganges and Shotley jetties are several yacht moorings that extend up river into Erwarton Bay. Over on the S side of the river is the Harwich International Port (Parkeston Quay), where the ferries berth. At the lower end is a wind farm rig berth and at the up river end is an oiling wharf with a major fuel storage depot behind it. There are two green buoys, Bristol (Fl(2)G.5s) and Parkeston (Fl(3)G10s) opposite the quays and yachts should keep the wrong side of these to leave room for ships turning and berthing or leaving. A third green, Ramsey (LFl.G.10s) marks the change from Harwich Harbour to the River Stour proper. The river here is subject to an 8kn speed limit.

River Stour to Erwarton Ness

The river is at its widest here where it opens out into Erwarton Bay on the N side. At the W end of Erwarton Bay is Erwarton Ness with a SCM (Q(6)+L.Fl.15s). Erwarton is a popular anchorage, although it lacks shelter in either E or W winds. There's good holding up river from the beacon but take care down river where there can be patches of kelp. There's good clean landing on a sand and shingle beach at HW ±1½hr and a slightly muddy landing can be made at other times using an old barge hard that extends out from the shore to the base of the Ness Bn, almost to LW. There are several footpaths along the foreshore, one of which goes N across the fields to the village of Erwarton.

In S winds, if the Erwarton anchorage becomes uncomfortable, it is possible to find shelter across on the S shore in Copperas Bay in 4-6m of water.

From Erwarton the river runs almost straight for a good two miles with the deepest water a little N of the centre line with only one particular hazard to watch out for – a large ships' mooring buoy on the S side of the channel, W of Erwarton Ness. Occasionally you may find the most oddest of things moored here, such as 1,000m long pipes for feeding wind farm cables under the river Deben!

Erwarton to Wrabness

About ¾M W of Erwarton Ness SCM is the first SHB, No.1 (Q.G). Around 1M further W there's a pair of beacons. One is the Holbrook Beacon SCM (VQ(6)+L.Fl.10s) to starboard and the other is No.2 Beacon NCM (Q) to port. The pair act as a gateway to Wrabness.

The Holbrook Beacon also marks the entrance to the drying Holbrook Creek. This little waterway meanders N across Holbrook Bay towards the palatial buildings

Quiet night in Copperas Bay under S bank

Royal Hospital School, Holbrook, dominates the N shore

Looking NW across the saltings at the head of Holbrook Creek

No 2 NCM E of Wrabness

Wrabness can be uncomfortable in E or W winds against tide

and prominent clock tower of the Royal Hospital School standing on the N shore. The NE corner of the bay is a popular wind- and kite-surfing area and has moorings for local boats.

There are two or three moorings laid in the lower reaches of the Creek. Anchoring positions are best found below half tide and by careful depth sounding.

WRABNESS

There are many moorings at Wrabness, which is marked by a plethora of beach huts under a low cliff on the wooded S bank; landing, except in emergency, is strongly discouraged as the beach is private. It is usually possible to pick up an empty mooring for a short stay but anchoring in the main channel is not recommended, because the holding is poor and it's used by small coasters bound to or from the Baltic Wharf at Mistley.

On the N side of the channel, opposite the cliffs, lies No.3 SHB (Q.G.), designated Lee. Do not stray N of this mark, because it shallows very quickly and even at high tide there's little depth of water.

Most other parts of the river offer good holding in some wonderfully glutinous East Coast mud and some of this can be found above the Wrabness moorings towards No.4 PHB (Q.R).

Wrabness to Mistley and Manningtree

The river is well marked all the way to Mistley, largely to assist the coasters that use the waterway, and it is essential to avoid sailing too far away from the buoyed channel, because the whole area dries extensively. This is another East Coast area where visitors are advised to set off up river before the mud banks are covered and to be aware that buoys can be blown across the banks they are marking.

Leaving Wrabness and carrying the tide with you, pass No.5 SHB (Fl.G.5s) to starboard and aim for the No.6 beacon (Fl(2)R.5s) about ¾M above the Wrabness moorings. It marks the N edge of the Smith Shoal, which moves the channel and best water well over towards the N side of the river at Stutton Ness. There's a good anchorage opposite No.6 under Stutton Ness, which has a sandy beach that can be reached by dinghy and is popular for picnics.

Leaving No.6, the channel is well buoyed and fairly straight with the buoys all well within sight of each other. Deeper draught boats should keep pretty well to the channel, although it's often tempting to follow a small bilge keel or centreplate cruiser gaily tramping across wide expanses of open water between Smith Shoal and Ballast Hill. Unless you have good local knowledge or are sure of your depth sounder and have an adventurous spirit, don't try it. You could find yourself stuck on some really sticky mud or some very hard gravely ground from which the aptly named Ballast Hill gets its name. In days of yore barges would settle on the hill and load shingle ballast.

Landing at Mistley Quay is no longer allowed. Will this fence come down?

No.6 PHM   No.12 NCB

After passing the unlit No. 12 NCB at Ballast Hill, the channel dives SW towards Mistley Quay. Head for Nos.13 (Fl.G.5s) and 15 (Fl(2)G.5s) SHBs and the Quay lies straight ahead. Keep close to the quay, because the whole area to starboard dries at low water.

Yachts used to lie alongside Mistley Quay at HW ±1½hr, depending on draught, the bottom being fairly level soft mud, but landing is now strictly forbidden and made impossible by a 6ft high steel mesh fence installed along the outer edge of quay. Unfortunately, the bollards are within this fence, so finding a ring or projection to secure to and rest before heading back down river is now not possible. As ECP went to press the Supreme Court had ruled the fence should come down and that the quay was public space open to all.

Mistley Marine runs a small drying marina on the S bank just down river from the Baltic Wharf (where small coasters unload building materials and general cargoes). Mistley Marine also runs a small boatyard and marine engineering works and operates a dredging barge. River moorings and quayside moorings dry out. There are no toilet or shower facilities.

Mistley Marine
VHF Ch 71 ☎01206 392127, 07850 208918

With care and a shallow draught, it's possible to reach ½M beyond Mistley to Manningtree at HW. Approach Manningtree by following the channel buoys carefully and remember that the whole area dries soon after HW. Boats with a draught greater than 1·5m need to avoid a nasty sand bank some 50m in front of the Stour SC clubhouse and quay. The advice is to skirt along the line of moorings.

Those who sail into Mistley but then go the extra half mile to Manningtree will find there are three visitor's moorings or a short-term quayside berth, and a warm welcome at the Stour SC with its waterfront clubhouse, small hard jetty and slipway. Best to call the Club's mooring master to ensure you get one, though. You must also be able to take the ground comfortably if you plan a stay. Visitors are few, but increasing, as people get to know about this attractive little town that has all a crew needs close to hand, including pubs, restaurants, shops, banks and a train service to London.
Stour SC CO11 1AU ☎ 01206 393924
Mooring master ☎ 01206 399006
www.stoursailingclub.co.uk

Manningtree is the head of the navigable Stour and is also on the doorstep of the Dedham Vale and 'Constable country'.

Manningtree has a substantial quayside and acres of soft east coast mud

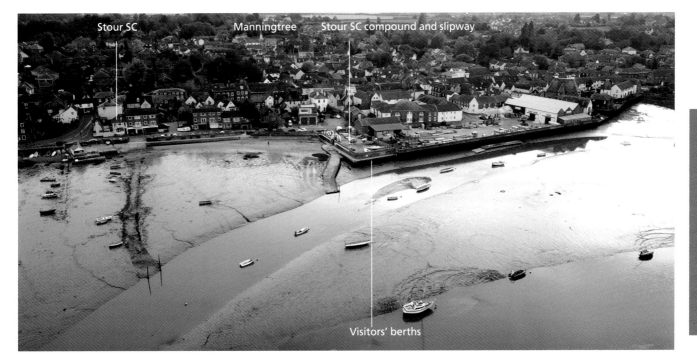

Stour SC   Manningtree   Stour SC compound and slipway

Visitors' berths

8. RIVER ORWELL

⊕ **Landfall waypoint**
51°55'·20N 001°18'·50E
SW of Landguard NCB on recommended
yacht track

Charts
Imray 2000, C28, Y16
Admiralty SC5607, 1491, 2693

Port Authority
ABP (From Fagbury to Ipswich Wet Dock)
Ipswich harbourmaster ☎ 01473 231010
Ipswich lockmaster ☎ 01473 213526 (VHF Ch 68
Callsign *Prince Phillip Lock*)

VHF Channels
Monitor port operations Ch 71 from Pye End to Fagbury
Monitor port operations Ch 68 from Fagbury to Ipswich

Tides
Harwich HW Walton +0005
Ipswich HW Walton +0025

Hazards

The Orwell carries a busy mix of commercial and leisure traffic, everything from general cargo boats to Thames Barges, East Coast smacks and several hundred small craft, all bustling about day and night. The danger for visiting yachtsmen is the commercial traffic, which is very quiet and a sharp lookout must be kept astern. Ships are constrained by draught and yachts must keep well clear. If a ship is manoeuvring near the docks it is frequently best for yachts to heave to and wait until passage is clear again.

The port authority (ABP) has warned of the danger of wash and the subsequent draw down effect from passing ships in the river at LW, especially at LWS. They are particularly concerned about possible swamping of tenders or the temporary grounding of yachts and urge great caution together with the wearing of lifejackets when going to and from moorings and the shore.

If anchoring anywhere in the Orwell, keep clear of the main channel. Remember to display a black ball during the day and a riding light at night, but it is also advisable to do the same if lying to a mooring, because it tells the skippers and pilots of passing ships that there are people on board.

Keep a good look out for commercial ships

This advice is the result of some 'incidents' between ships and moored and anchored yachts in the past.

The river is subject to an 8kn speed limit decreasing to 6kn above Woolverstone.

The Orwell – lower reaches

The River Orwell, or the Ipswich River as it's often known locally, is attractive and remarkably unspoilt, yet increasingly commercial. It is 9M from the end of the Trinity Quay at Harwich to the lock gates into Ipswich Wet Dock and getting on for ½M wide in places at HW.

Because of the commercial shipping, the main channel has been dredged to a depth of 5·6m at LW and is about 400m (2 cables) wide. Gently rising mudflats merge into either narrow sandy beaches or heavily wooded banks on either side.

Entering the Orwell from Harwich Harbour, stay W outside the dredged channel, leaving the Guard PHB (Fl.R.5s Bell) to starboard and, after crossing the narrowest part of the deep water channel, leave the Shotley Spit SCB (Q(6)+L.Fl.15s) also to starboard, then leave the Shotley Horse buoy (Fl(4)Y.10s) close to port. This buoy is a yellow turning mark that allows yachts to turn in deep water without having to go round Shotley Spit SCB and stray into the main harbour channel. From Shotley Horse make about NW towards the College PHB (Fl(2)R.10s).

Leave College close to starboard. It marks the W edge of the deep-water channel opposite the Trinity container berths and is there for big ships. There's plenty of depth between the buoy and the Shotley Spit, which runs out from Shotley Point (roughly half way along the marina retaining wall) to Shotley Spit SCB. If a big ship is manoeuvring on the up-river Trinity Berth, keep to port of the Pepys and Babergh PHBs to remain clear of the main channel.

Heading down Long Reach in a brisk breeze

Entering the Orwell past Fagbury Point

The changeover from Harwich Harbour Authority to Associated British Ports is at the Fagbury SHB (Fl.G.2·5s) off Fagbury Point, close N of the container berths. Nearby is a clearly marked underwater cable, which must be avoided if anchoring to await the tide.

The river is well buoyed and generally there is plenty of room and water outside the channel to avoid large vessels (which have total right of way and often use their horn to assert it). Remember most of them have to do 8-10kn just to maintain steerage way in what is quite a winding and confined channel.

Shotley Spit to Butterman's Bay

Bay
Q.G

No.4
Q.R

No.3
Fl.G.2·5s
Suffolk
Yacht
Harbour

290°

Collimer
Q.R

Stratton
Q.G

335°

No.2
Fl.R.2·5s

Trimley
Fl.G.2·5s

000°

Orwell
Q.R

No.1
Q.G

Fagbury
Fl.G.2·5s

340°

Babergh
Fl.R.2·5s

Pepys
Fl(4)R.15s

Shotley Pt

305°

College
Fl(2)R.10s

Trinity
Container
Berths

Shotley Horse

325°

Shotley Spit
Q(6)+LFl.15s

Note: Recommended yacht track is wrong side of PHBs opposite container berths

RIVER ORWELL
TO IPSWICH

N

Depths in Metres

The deep water channel has been pushed further over to the Shotley bank by developments and extensions of the Trinity Quay and a PHB, Babergh (Fl.R.2·5s), has been installed between the Pepys and Orwell PHBs, almost opposite the first SHB, Fagbury (Fl.G.2·5s). Once past the end of Trinity Quay you are in the Orwell proper.

To port, a little N of Shotley Marina, the river opens out into a gentle bay, called Stone Heaps, the name being a legacy from the old barging days, which offers a good anchorage, if a little rough when ships pass. The holding is good, water is plentiful at all states of tide and a shingle beach offers clean landing for a walk round the back of the marina to Shotley.

Trimley Marshes

Trimley Marshes lie on the E side behind a raised flood protection bank. Once a marshy bird sanctuary, they have been excavated and flooded by breaching the sea wall to make a proper wetland for wading birds. A walk along the wall with binoculars is always rewarding for birdwatchers.

Landing is possible at HW on a sandy beach backed by cliffs. It's a popular place to picnic and swim, but the bay is also a designated speedboat and water-ski area.

The down river end of Trimley Bay is marked by the Trimley SHB (Fl.G.2·5s) and on the opposite (W) side of the channel is No.2 PHB (Fl.R.2·5s), which marks the start of the NW bend in the river round Collimer Point.

Off Collimer Point is a PHB marked Collimer (Q.R) and a SHB marked Stratton (Q.G). On the W bank also is the remnants of a tide gauge giving the depth of water over the natural riverbed, do not try passing inshore of it or you will pile into the remains of one of the many old barge hards once in regular use on the river. The river turns NW at this point.

SUFFOLK YACHT HARBOUR (SYH)

The first major landing point on the river is at Suffolk Yacht Harbour, a few hundred yards down river from the entrance to Levington Creek (drying) on the starboard bank. The entrance to the marina is a well dredged, 30m wide by 2m deep (at LWS) channel, marked with a SWB at the start of the approach then port and starboard hand posts with fluorescent topmarks along the channel. Tides set across the channel and care is required not to be pushed onto the posts, especially at springs. They are substantial steel tubes and will do serious damage to topsides.

At night there are leading lights (outer Iso.Y and inner Oc.Y.4s); the lower light is on a post behind and slightly to port of the visitor's berths and the upper on a taller post near the head of the West Dock, their transit gives an approach up the starboard side of the entrance

Suffolk Yacht Harbour

SUFFOLK YACHT HARBOUR · IP10 0LN

Contact
VHF Ch 80
Callsign *Suffolk Yacht Harbour*
Harbourmaster ☎ 01473 659465/240
Email enquiries@syharbour.co.uk
www.syharbour.co.uk
Access 24hr
Facilities WC, showers, launderette, WiFi
Water On pontoons
Electricity At each berth
Fuel Diesel and petrol from berth at entrance
Chandlery and Classic Marine On site
Provisions Some from chandler
Gas Calor and Gaz
Boat repairs Slipways (two), 75-T, 30-T and 10-T boat hoists, 20-T crane
Scrubbing posts At head of West Dock, turn to port at entrance
Shipwrights On site
Sailmaker On site
Electrical engineers On site
Rigger On site
Mechanical engineer On site
Electronics On site
Club Haven Ports YC (in old light vessel in marina)
☎ 01473 659658 www.hpyc.com
Pub/restaurant Ship Inn, Levington (1 mile) ☎ 01473 659573

channel (see chartlet) from the SWB. Changes to the security lighting in the marina have made them easier to distinguish at night.

Visitors' berths and the after-hours harbourmaster's office lie directly opposite the entrance with the fuel berth just to starboard. To port is the main slipway and the entrance to the West Harbour used by large yachts.

SYH is in an isolated location 1M from the nearest bus stop to Ipswich and Felixstowe, but food and drink are available to visitors in the marina aboard LV87, the lightship home of the Haven Ports YC. There is also the Ship Inn at the village of Levington 1M away.

SYH has an imposing harbour office combining chandler, small general store and commercial offices.

SUFFOLK YACHT HARBOUR

Depths in Metres

Yard
Service Companies
West Dock
Workshop
Oc.Y.4s
Harbour Function Room
Public
Haven Ports YC
Iso.Y
Sea Wall
River Orwell Dredged to 5·6M
Water Skiing Area
Stratton Q.G
1°16'·5E
51° 59'·7 N
59'·5
16'

Levington Creek

Leaving SYH and travelling up river, the next buoy, No.3 SHB (Fl.G.2·5s), lies off the entrance to Levington Creek. Visitors can pick up a vacant mooring and, approaching HW, take a dinghy up to the old barge quay at the top. From there it's a short walk to the Ship Inn at Levington. The channel in the creek is marked with withies but watch out for old iron posts and strapping near the quay.

Above Levington Creek, almost as far as the high-level Orwell Road Bridge, both shores of the river are lined with moorings between the deep-water channel and the drying banks.

Nacton

The Nacton Foreshore runs between Levington Creek and Nacton Quay, the next major landmark on the N side. The flat mud runs up into a narrow sandy beach, popular for picnics and teaching youngsters to swim, because the water gets very warm as it comes in over the mud in mid-summer. It's a good place to see cormorants standing on mud humps at LW with their wings held spread out to dry.

Long Reach and Butterman's Bay

Long reach is the wide section of the river running from Collimer to No 4 PHB (Q.R.) and Bay SHB (Q.G.) the entrance to Butterman's Bay, the reach up to Pin Mill. Off Long Reach to W is Colton Creek opposite Levington Creek, where there are a number of yacht moorings on both sides of the channel and a recognised anchorage for sailing barges. During the summer there's often one or more of these stately craft anchored there.

At the top end of Long Reach, nestling under the end of a wooded cliff, sits a prominent, solitary white cottage, called Clamp House, which is reputed to have been a smuggler's den. No.4 PHB (Q.R) is directly opposite the cottage on the W side of the deep-water channel and, opposite that, the Bay SHB (Q.G). Upriver from both these buoys are double and triple rows of moorings, with a wide-open space in the lines of moorings under the trees on the S side, which is a good anchorage, sheltered from S and SW winds. On the S bank, lies one of the jewels of East Coast sailing, Pin Mill.

PIN MILL

Much has been written about Pin Mill and the famous boatbuilding yards of Harry King and Fred Webb, though even more column inches have probably been given over to the riverside pub the Butt and Oyster, which has one of the finest views of the river in both directions from the bar window.

Visitors to Pin Mill should look for a number of moorings with small orange pickup buoys with "visitor" painted on them. There are signs on the buoys giving you further information on using them. Getting ashore at Pin Mill requires a dinghy and a pair of boots, because there's a lot of mud, especially at LWS. A long hard is laid out from the shore almost to LW mark, so landing is possible at most states of the tide, but, if you go ashore at LW or early on the flood, pull the dinghy all the way up. There's a small rill – the Grindle – that runs down the upstream (W) side of the hard, enabling dinghies to float a long way up.

Pin Mill waterfront

PIN MILL
IP9 1JW

Moorings Contact King's Boatyard, operators of Tony Ward Moorings Ltd, ② 01473 780258; 07867 640650; or 07714 260568 (for visitor mooring enquiries) www.kingsboatyard.co.uk
Pub/restaurant Butt and Oyster ② 01473 780764
Provisions From shop in Chelmondiston. Early closing Wednesdays
Water Tap at Pin Mill SC
Boat repairs Two boatyards:
FA Webb ② 01473 780291
Harry King & Sons ② 01473 780258
Scrubbing post Contact King's Boatyard
Telephone In car park 100 yards up road
Club Pin Mill SC ② 01473 780271
www.pmsc.org.uk

Similarly, if landing at HW or on the ebb, be prepared for a long drag back down. A vacant mooring may usually be used for an hour or two, if one can be found, but for longer stays, call King's Boatyard. A drying pontoon runs out in front of the yard.

Pin Mill is a small, unspoilt hamlet that lies in a steep valley running back from the shoreline up to the nearby village of Chelmondiston, from which buses run regularly to and from Ipswich. There's a grocer, butcher and Post Office at 'Chelmo', as it's known locally. Pin Mill Sailing Club welcomes visiting yachtsmen. Next to the Butt and Oyster is the start of the Arthur Ransome's Walking Trail.

The barge hard and posts are still used by Thames barges and almost invariably there is one being worked on at weekends.

From Pin Mill, the river turns more N up Potter Reach and then back NW at Hall Point between the Park Bight

SHB (Q.G) and the No.6 PHB (Q.R) into Cathouse Reach with the channel tucking under the wooded slope that shelters Woolverstone Marina and the Royal Harwich YC from SW winds.

Opposite Woolverstone Marina is the Cathouse SHB (Fl.G.2·5s).

WOOLVERSTONE

The clubhouse of the Royal Harwich YC, which has its own jetty and 55 deep water pontoon berths on the S bank, is the next port of call. During the summer the club welcomes visitors, who can use the showers, bar and restaurant in the clubhouse.

Arriving from Harwich, the first pontoon is 'A', while pontoons B and C are within the marina pond, with D the row nearest the Orwell Bridge. Berth 1 is the first berth inside the hammerhead for each row.

ROYAL HARWICH YC
IP9 1AT

Contact
RHYC office ② 01473 780319
Berth Master VHF Ch 80 ② 07742 145994
(voicemail checked daily if unattended).
Alternatively, call the RHYC office
www.royalharwichyachtclub.co.uk

Visitors' berths By arrangement
Access 24hr
Facilities WC, showers, laundry (in clubhouse)
Water On pontoons
Electricity On pontoons
Bar/Restaurant In clubhouse
Slipway (dinghies only)

Royal Harwich YC and Woolverstone Marina

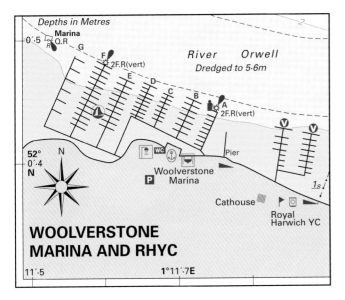

Depths in Metres
Marina
0·5 Q.R
R G
F 2F.R(vert)
E D C B A 2F.R(vert)
River Orwell
Dredged to 5·6m
52° N
0'·4 N
WC Pier
Woolverstone Marina
P
Cathouse
Royal Harwich YC
1·8

WOOLVERSTONE MARINA AND RHYC

11'·5   1°11'·7E

WOOLVERSTONE MARINA

IP9 1AS

Contact
VHF Ch 80
Callsign *Woolverstone Marina*
Harbourmaster ☎ 01473 780206, ☎ 07803 968209
Email woolverstone@mdlmarinas.co.uk
www.mdlmarinas.co.uk
Access 24hr
Visitors' berths As available. Swinging moorings
with taxi service
Facilities WC, showers, laundry, WiFi
Water On pontoons
Electricity On pontoons
Fuel Diesel from fuel station on pontoon A hammerhead
Gas Calor and Gaz
Chandler On site
Boat repairs Crane, boat hoist, slip
Engineer On site
Pub/Restaurant On site
Provisions Basics on site. Shops in Chelmondiston

If arriving out of hours, please tie up to one of the hammerheads and enquire at the bar.

Snuggled into the trees between the club and the marina lies the fabled Cathouse, another smugglers' den. It is said that, when the coast was clear, a lamp was shown, but when the Revenue men were prowling, a white cat sat in the window as a warning.

Next door, up river, is Woolverstone Marina, an open-river 235-berth marina with pontoons held by massive piles driven into the riverbed in a deep pool S of the main channel. Its situation under the wooded shore is attractive, but it suffers from strong tidal streams through the berths and almost constant swell from passing traffic. Recent developments have included the installation of a new fuel berth on the hammerhead of the first pontoon. Alongside it is a wide slip called the Cathouse Hard, also belonging to the marina.

The marina also has 110 swinging moorings in the river and runs a water taxi service on demand.

From Woolverstone up river, leave the No.7 SHB (Q.G) to starboard and the Marina PHB (Q.R) to port into Downham Reach. Here the channel begins to narrow markedly with unspoilt Suffolk parkland to be seen on either shore. Up ahead and spanning the river is the high level Orwell Road Bridge.

On the W shore of Downham Reach stands Deer Park Lodge, nestling in the woods with its own landing stage, and then the Stoke SC clubhouse and moorings providing a foreground to a Victorian folly. Called Freston Tower, the folly was reputedly built by one of the Paul family (famous for their barge fleet) as a garden

The Orwell high-level road bridge

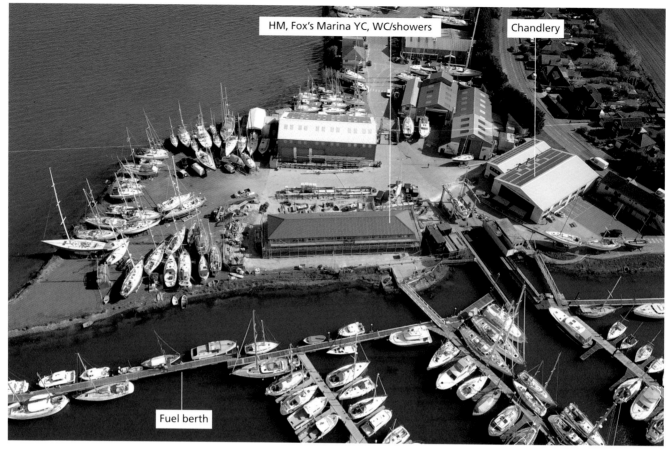

HM, Fox's Marina YC, WC/showers

Chandlery

Fuel berth

Fox's Marina and Orwell YC moorings

dining room for entertaining guests to fine food and wine and views of the company's vessels plying up and down the river. Others say it was built for the education of their daughter with one floor for each day of the week.

The channel here is quite narrow but extremely well buoyed. When a ship is sighted, keep just outside the line of buoys on either hand until she passes. At the bridge itself, the channel narrows down to 92m (300ft) between the artificial islands that protect the bases of the eight piers carrying the bridge. The air draught is 43·07m (141ft) at LWS (128ft – 38M at HWS). Do not attempt to pass under the bridge at the same time as a ship, whatever her size.

Ostrich Creek

Once through the Orwell bridge – and do look up when passing under it, the deck is made in two sections with a considerable gap between them – there is a SHB E Fen (Fl.G.5s) marking the E side of the channel between the bridge and the down river end of the Cliff Quay complex. Opposite is the West Power PHB (Fl.R.5s) and this should be left very close to starboard to stay just W of the deep water channel and clear of the shipping activities at Cliff Quay. About ¼M further N is the No.12 PHB (Q.R) that also marks the entrance to Ostrich Creek where both Fox's Marina and the Orwell YC are to be found.

Ostrich Creek home of both Fox's Marina and Orwell YC

Fox's

Wherstead Road Bridge

Orwell YC

Enter Ostrich Creek from the No.12 PHB, passing between the posts topped with R and G markers. The Orwell YC, on the N shore, has some drying moorings and water can be obtained from the clubhouse or from a floating pontoon. Fuel and oil are available at a garage adjacent to the clubhouse. There's a regular bus service into the centre of Ipswich.

Orwell YC https://orwellyachtclub.org.uk

Fox's Marina

Opposite Orwell YC, on the downriver side of Ostrich Creek, lies the 100-berth Fox's Marina and Boatyard, which has one of the largest chandlers on the East Coast, plus a club and a restaurant. Fuel and water are available from the clearly marked fuel berth.

FOX'S MARINA & THE RIVER ORWELL TO IPSWICH

FOX'S MARINA   IP2 8SA

Contact
VHF Ch 80 Callsign *Fox's Marina*
Harbourmaster ☎ 01473 694680 ☎ 07703 472222
Email john.jonas@foxsmarina.com
www.foxsmarina.com
Access 24hr, dredged to 3m MLWS
Boat sizes Max 25m LOA, draught 3m
Facilities WC, showers, WiFi (free)
Water On pontoons
Electricity On pontoons
Telephone On corner of YC at head of pontoon gantry
Chandler On site ☎ 01473 688431
Gas Calor and Gaz
Fuel Diesel from fuel berth on S side of entrance
Club Fox's Marina YC www.fmyc.org.uk
Pub/Restaurant On site
Provisions Shops nearby
Boatyard Boat repairs and all services on site up to 70T, masts to 110ft

Ipswich Wet Dock

Although there are a number of buoys on the approach to the lock gates into the Ipswich Wet Dock, there is deep water from quayside to quayside and sufficient lighting to see when going in at night. The port's working channel is VHF Ch 68 and the call sign is *Prince Philip Lock*. Call from about buoy No.9 (below the Orwell Bridge) if wishing to enter.

Although originally designed for commercial shipping, the lock has been refurbished and fitted with rope travellers on the high wall on the port side and a floating pontoon to starboard (when going in) for yachts to moor against as they progress through (you will need to set fenders low for this pontoon). On the very rare occasion that a ship or large vessel (a sail training ship for example) passes through they have priority and the pontoon is slipped and towed out while the vessel locks through.

Ipswich Lock open on high tide free-flow

IPSWICH HAVEN MARINA

IP3 0EA

Contact
VHF Ch 80
Callsign *Ipswich Marina*
Harbourmaster ☎ 01473 236644
Email ipswichhaven@abports.co.uk
www.ipswichhavenmarina.co.uk
Facilities WC, showers, laundry, WiFi
Water On pontoons
Electricity On pontoons
Boat size Max 20m
Boat repairs Crane, 75-T boat hoist
Fuel Diesel from fuel berth pontoon C
Gas Calor and Gaz
Telephone In office lobby
Electronics On site
Engineers Volspec On site
Chandler On site
Bar/restaurant Last Anchor ☎ 01473 214763 on site, and nearby
Provisions Shops 10 minute walk
Transport Trains (15 mins walk)
Taxi ☎ 01473 289289, 222222, 257777

There is a waiting pontoon to starboard, just upstream of Cliff Quay on the approach to the lock, if you have to wait long, but most boats prefer to jill about – a lot of ducks and gulls use the pontoon with clear consequences. The lock holds up to 20 x 9·75m yachts at a time, but usually it takes between six and 12.

Visual signals for entering or leaving the lock, which opens virtually on request, are a set of red and green traffic lights located above the Orwell Navigation Service's building on the E (or starboard) side of the lock.

NEPTUNE MARINA

IP4 1AX

Contact
VHF Ch 80
Callsign *Neptune Marina*
Harbourmaster ☎ 01473 215204
Email enquiries@neptune-marina.com
www.neptune-marina.com
Facilities WC, showers, WiFi
Boat repairs all services available, crane, 30-T boat hoist
Water On pontoons
Electricity On pontoons
Diesel From fuel berth by hoist and workshop to starboard of final approach
Gas Calor and Gaz
Provisions Shops 10 minute walk
Taxi ☎ 01473 289289, 222222, 257777

Once inside the wet dock, aim for the far end (it's actually a dogleg), where the Neptune Marina lies ahead on the starboard side with the Haven Marina to port, visitor moorings for the latter usually being allocated near the office, which is round the bend to port and several hundred yards further on at K pontoon. Both marinas offer the usual facilities and are equidistant from the town centre shops, a 10 minutes walk away in the town itself. Haven Marina has its own bar and restaurant, while the N dockside is steadily being redeveloped with bars and restaurants; it is a pleasant walk right round to the lock. Ipswich itself boasts restaurants, pubs, cinemas, a large park and a highly regarded theatre.

Visitor berths in Ipswich Haven Marina

Neptune Marina

Looking up the New Cut towards Debbage Marina with the buttresses of the new flood relief barrier in the foreground

The New Cut

To port of the entrance to the Wet Dock is a stretch of water called The New Cut. It is the point at which the river Gipping (from which Ipswich got its original name of Gyppeswick) joins the Orwell. Here Debbage Yachting has a yard and small marina situated about halfway between the entrance and the Wherstead Road Bridge, above which navigation is by dinghy only. Boats lie alongside pontoons and dry out. You can obtain fuel and water.

Debbage Yachting ☎ 01437 601169 / 07774 694226
Email office@debyacht.co.uk

A flood relief gate crosses the entrance to the New Cut; it normally lies on the riverbed, but when required it is raised to close the Cut. There are large warning signs and three vertical red traffic lights indicate when it is raised and that access to boats is denied.

9. WALTON BACKWATERS

⊕ **Landfall waypoint**
51°55'·1N 001°17'·9E Close N of Pye End buoy
Charts
Imray 2000, Y16
Admiralty SC 5607, 2695
Tides
HW Walton
ECP Honorary Port Pilot
Alec Moss ☎ 01255 850266 *Email* walton@eastcoastpilot.com

Main hazards

The Walton Backwaters lie S of Harwich, well protected by the Pye Sand and Sunken Pye on the seaward side of the narrow Pye Channel approach. This sand is unyieldingly hard and grounding should be avoided, particularly in onshore winds or when a swell is running. In fact, it would be unwise to attempt entry to the Backwaters at all in strong NE winds when big seas are running.

Approaches

Ideally you should locate the Pye End SWB (L.Fl.10s) before approaching the Backwaters. The buoy is of good size and, with the help of GPS, is fairly easy to find, even in choppy seas, although a good pair of binoculars will be useful. This is especially true at night when the light

may be hard to identify against the background of Felixstowe dock lights if an approach is made from SE. It can also be hard to spot from the NE against the late afternoon sun.

The two main landmarks when approaching the Harwich area are the cranes of Felixstowe container terminal and the Naze Tower standing on the cliffs just N of Walton-on-the-Naze. Either or both can be seen from several miles away in clear conditions.

From N Approaching the Backwaters from Harwich, follow the charted yacht track to stay W of the deep water channel until near Cliff Foot (Fl.R.5s) before turning SW towards the Pye End Buoy. This course avoids the Cliff Foot Rocks and the shallow waters over the Halliday Flats off Dovercourt.

From NE Following the coast S from the Deben or Ore, cross the Harwich deep water channel by way of the charted yacht track to arrive at Inner Ridge PHB (Q.R) on the S side, then alter course W for the Pye End buoy.

Pye End SWB must be located for entry into Pye Channel

Walton Backwaters from N. Stone Point in centre with Walton Channel all the way to Walton; Twizzle branches off to right for Titchmarsh Marina and Horsey Mere. Line of sunken barges on N shore of Horsey Island; Hamford Water running off to right past them *Patrick Roach*

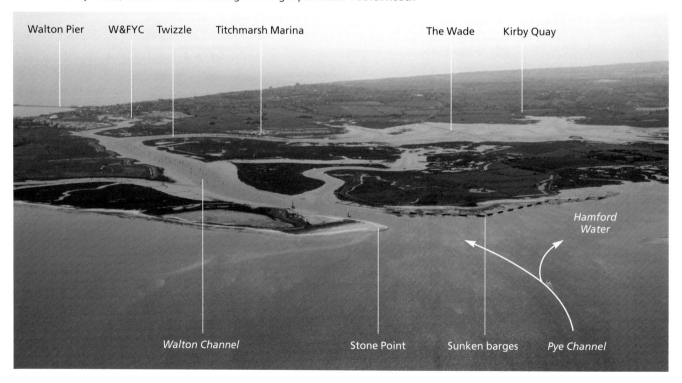

Walton Pier   W&FYC   Twizzle   Titchmarsh Marina   The Wade   Kirby Quay

Hamford Water

Walton Channel   Stone Point   Sunken barges   Pye Channel

Walton Backwaters

Island Point (Q.)

No.10
Baines
Q.R
No.8

195°

Harry-
Moulton
No.6
No.4a

Julia G
No.7
Fl.G.10s

220°

No.4
High Hill
Fl.R.10s

225°

Heather J
No.5

Crab Knoll
No.3
Fl.G.5s

228°

No.2
Fl(2)R.5s

240°

Pye End
LFl.10s

⊕ 51°55'·1N
001°17'·9E

Pye End
LFl.10s
RW
1₉

0₈

0₂

1₂

Sunken
Pye

No.2
Fl(2)R.5s
1₄

Crab Knoll
No.3
Fl.G.5s

0₅

Heather
No.5
G

1₂

High Hill
No.4
Fl.R.10s

0₉

No.7
Fl.G.10s

No.4A

Pye
Sand

Pennyhole
Bay

No.6

3₄

1₃

1₆

No.8

0₃

Irlam's Beach

Bramble
Island

Dugmore Creek

Oakley
Creek

Pewit
Island

Island Point

No.10
Q.R

No.12

1₈

Water Tr

Water

Hamford

No.14
No.9
Fl.G.5s

Stone Point

Stone
Creek

New
Island

Exchem

3₂

No.16
No.11
Fl.G.10s

G

Garnham's
Island

Exchem
BYB

5₄

3₆

6₃

0₈

1₂

Maze Creek

4₄

1₃

No.13

2₆

2₅
2

51°
53'
N

Landermere
Creek

Wind pump

Dardanelles
Creek

0₃

Cormorant Creek

Quay

Horsey Island

Nature Reserve

THE
NAZE

1₅

Oyster Beds

Kirby Creek

Skippers I.

Ambrose Pt

Honey I.

0₂

Salt Fleet

3

Walton Channel

Moorings

CG

Naze
Cliff

Power
lines

1₆

3₈

Oyster Beds

Landing

3₄

Hedge End
Island

The Naze Tr
(conspic 49m)

Beaumont
Cut

Beaumont
Quay

Landermere
Quay

2₄

Horsey
Mere

Causeway/The Wade

Twizzle Creek

3

2₁

0₈

Oysters beds

1₈

Titchmarsh
Marina

See
plan
p.61

BY

Bonoud

3₁

Foundry
Reach

N

Peters Pt

See
plan
p.63

Walton and
Frinton YC

1

Depths in Metres

White House

Kirby
Quay

See
plan
p.63

Bedwells Boatyard
and Halls Boatyard

WALTON

CG

0₈

WALTON BACKWATERS

Kirby-le-Soken

1°15'E

11'   12'   13'   14'   1°15'E   16'   17'   18'

Horsey Island   Honey Island   Skippers Island   Oakley Creek

Horsey Mere

Hamford
Water

Island Point

Walton Channel

Stone Point

Pye Channel

Pye Sand

Looking W up Hamford Water with Walton Channel and sunken barges on Horsey Island at left. Kirby Creek branches off left and Oakley Creek to right. Pye Channel runs in from right *Patrick Roach*

Passing Pye End on a rising tide

From E Arriving from the continent see *North Sea Passage Pilot* (Imray) for passages to the Harwich area and follow local routes.

From S When arriving from the Blackwater, Colne or Crouch via the Wallet and the Medusa Channel in clear weather, the Naze Tower and the cranes of Felixstowe docks will be sighted while still S of Walton Pier.

Pass the Medusa SHB (Fl.G.5s), which is positioned 2¼M seaward of Walton Pier, and Stone Banks PHB (Fl.R.5s), while aiming for the Felixstowe cranes. This course should keep you E of the Pye End buoy but bring you close enough to spot it and identify it.

Once N of Walton Pier, all the way to Pye End, keep a sharp lookout for pot markers and fishing floats. You will also encounter a number of yellow racing marks in the area.

Entry

It is usual, when entering the channel, to pass close to starboard of the Pye End SWB. From the buoy, shape a course of about 240° for just under 1M to reach the PHB No.2 (Fl(2)R.5s). Take care especially in murky conditions or with the late afternoon sun in your eyes as the buoys are quite small.

At this stage a look ahead will show no sign of a break in the coast; the Backwaters do not reveal themselves until much closer in. Not for nothing did Arthur Ransome name his famous book *Secret Water*.

The next buoy to make for is Crab Knoll No.3 SHB (Fl.G.5s), distant ⅓M, followed closely by an unlit SHB No.5.

The lit PHB High Hill No.4 (Fl.R.10s) marks the N end of a deeper section of the channel towards the unlit No.4A and then the lit SHB No.7 (Fl.G.10s) and unlit PHB No.6. From there pass No.8 PHB and head directly for PHB No.10 Baines (Q.R) and look for the small Island Point NCB (Q), which is not always easy to find and often appears to be out of position to the W.

First time visitors should keep a close eye on the depth and not stray outside the marks; the sand is as hard as concrete! Small boats in particular should be wary of a swirl or mini whirlpool that forms on the upriver side of Stone Point on the flood and again on the down-river side on the ebb. Both are strong enough to cause a sudden change of direction if not expected.

The channel is narrowest opposite No.16 PHB and care must be taken when passing a vessel going the other way, especially on the ebb, which runs strongly. Take your time and follow the buoys carefully.

It is common to enter the Backwaters in the afternoon and the sun's glare on the water at that time can mean a very hard time spotting and identifying buoys until almost upon them. Polarising sunglasses may help and binoculars always do.

Because the Pye Channel is so narrow, running between banks of hard sand, the tide funnels through it and can easily reach speeds of more than 2kn, particularly on the early ebb.

Departing the Backwaters at night can also be an interesting experience, because the buoys that are lit tend to be hidden among the background lights of the docks at Felixstowe, while the unlit ones simply disappear in the darkness. It's essential to work out rough courses to steer. This is one occasion when an up-to-date chart plotter can be of real benefit.

The winding narrow channel into the Walton Channel

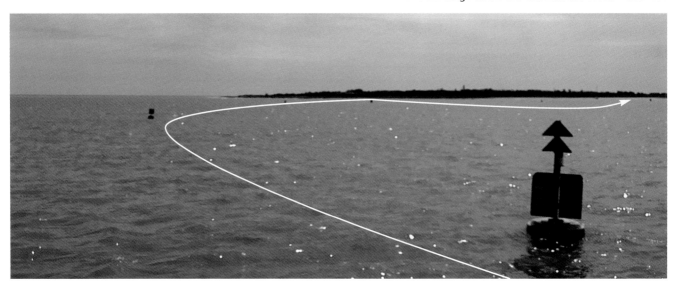

Speed limits

There is an 8kn speed limit in the approaches and within Hamford Water and this reduces to 6kn in creeks and channels leading off Hamford Water and to 4kn in congested areas.

The Walton Channel

Major changes have taken place at the junction of the Pye Channel with Hamford Water and the Walton Channel. Massive sand shifts meant the twisting channel around Stone Point had to be dredged and re-buoyed. The new channel is narrow and steep sided and ebb tides at springs can run to a fierce 6kn at peak flow (in the second hour). At LWS there is around 0·6m over chart datum, but the bottom is uneven with ridges left from plough dredging operations. A useful up-to-date chartlet of the area can usually be found on the downloads page at www.eastcoastpilot.com, and also on the WFYC website.

When bound up the Walton Channel towards Titchmarsh Marina or Walton town, leave the Island Point NCB (Q) to starboard and bear round SE to follow the line of unlit red PHBs. These and the No.9 SHB (Fl.G.5s) mark the way past Mussel Scarfe where the channel is narrow and, at LW, the buoys are often blown well out of position and lie over the banks or in the channel. Careful consideration has to be given to tide and wind direction before deciding how close to pass these buoys and a sharp eye should be kept on the depth, which varies considerably.

The channel runs very close in to the beach around Stone Point where that side is steep to and forms a popular anchorage off the sandy beach. The water is relatively deep and tides run fast (3–6kn on a spring ebb), so care must be taken when setting an anchor. On occasion this may be tricky and more than one attempt may be needed to ensure a good grip. Nonetheless, it's a popular anchorage.

Landing is possible at all states of the tide and the beach away from the point is good for swimming or having a picnic, but there is a nature reserve nearby and care must be taken not to disturb birds or damage plant life. Indeed, since the whole of the Backwaters is a Site of Special Scientific Interest (SSSI), such care must be taken throughout the area.

W of the anchorage is a SHB No.13 where a shallow creek branches off to starboard around the E end of Horsey Island. The Walton Channel starts here with lines of moorings showing where the best water is and extending S for almost 1M to the Spit NCB. This NCB marks the end of a spit between the Walton Channel, which runs on S past the buoy as Foundry Reach, and

Give the Spit NCB a wide berth entering Foundry Reach

The Twizzle, which turns W towards Titchmarsh Marina and Horsey Mere. The spit is extending so if turning from The Twizzle into Foundry Reach stand well out round the mark.

Walton & Frinton YC

The W&FYC has buoyed and marked the drying channel right up to its clubhouse, but the channel is tortuous, occasionally shallow and some of the buoys can be hidden by nearby moored boats, revealing themselves only at the last moment.

It is wise to wait until above half flood before heading up Foundry Reach, but then enter it by leaving the Spit NCB to starboard and heading straight through the

W&FYC   Bedwells

Walton

'gate' formed by No.2 PHB and No.3 SHB. Ahead you'll see a landing place on the E bank at No.5 SHB, but this is not for public use and does not offer access to the town.

Follow the port and starboard hand buoys in careful sequence. You will see the W&FYC clubhouse ahead from around No.7 SHB, but continue to follow the channel buoys as far as No.8 PHB. At that buoy, if you intend to lie alongside the W&FYC quay on the W side of the clubhouse or to visit Bedwell's boatyard, turn to starboard between a green topped SHM post and a small flat topped buoy painted black over yellow with 'N cardinal' written on it. Be sure to leave this NCB to port (i.e. stay N of it). Then leave a red-topped post PHM to port and make for the quay ahead to port or turn to starboard, keeping close around boats in mud berths, and head on for Bedwell's quay.

The W&FYC quay is accessible at or near HW and there is a two-hour time limit on boats lying alongside it. There is a good hard and concrete ramp for dinghies right under the front of the clubhouse (its N side) where the end of the concrete landing is marked by a red topped PHM post, which must be left to port if going alongside the club quay.

The Walton Yacht Basin is entered through a 15ft wide break in the sea wall from the creek on the E side of the W&FYC. A retaining gate (opened by arrangement) is lowered to the creek bed to allow entry or exit for a short time at HW when there is 2–2·5m over it. A tide gauge is positioned beside the gate. Contact Bedwell & Co. or W&FYC, as you approach (details in box). It may not be possible to open the basin's gate on low neap tides.

If you have made arrangements with the club or Bedwell's to enter the yacht basin or are planning to approach the Frank Halls boatyard, turn to port round No.8 PHB, leaving the NCB to starboard, and follow the PHBs to No.12 (keep close to the end of the W&FYC pontoon at No.10 PHB for the best water). From No.12 locate some thin white poles leading into the narrow entrance to the gated basin. As you approach, your view of the entrance between sheet piling will open up and so too will the channel between the white poles. If you see a triangle on top of a pole in the centre of the entrance to the basin, do not attempt entry – this mark stands on top of the raised gate. Only enter when the gate and its mark have been lowered beneath the water and sufficient depth is shown on the tide gauge beside the gate.

WALTON ON THE NAZE   CO14 8PF

Contact
Walton & Frinton YC ☎ 01255 678161
www.wfyc.co.uk
Access HW ±2hr
Facilities WC, showers
Slipway (contact club)
Water At W&FYC and in basin
Electricity On pontoons in basin
Provisions In town
Telephone At W&FYC
Post Office In town
Boat repairs Frank Halls ☎ 01255 675596
Bedwell & Co ☎ 01255 675873
Both located by W&FYC with cranes/slips
Pub/Restaurant W&FYC and many in town
Taxi ☎ 01255 675910, 676887, 674444

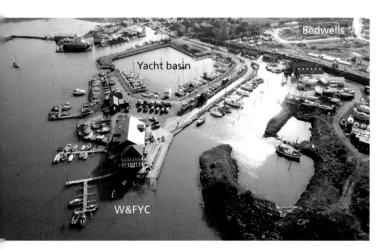

Walton's busy waterfront with Walton Yacht Basin at the centre

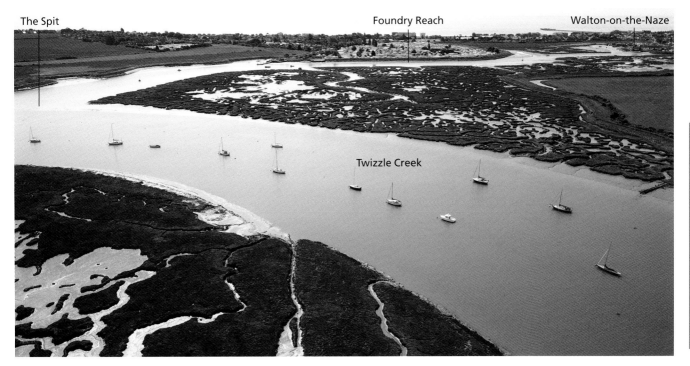

The Spit   Foundry Reach   Walton-on-the-Naze

Twizzle Creek

Looking SE across Twizzle Creek towards Walton

At the time of writing the Trust, which owns the basin had embarked on a £130,000 redevelopment to increase the number of berths to 60 and improve facilities. The entrance has been widened to enable larger boats to use the basin.

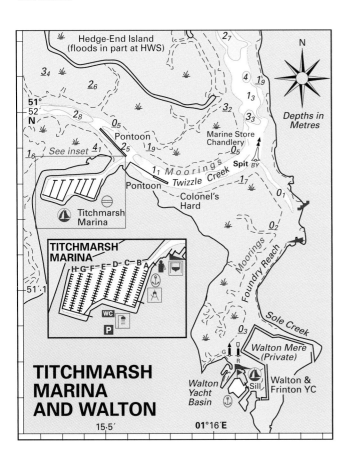

The Twizzle

The Twizzle (or Twizzle Creek) runs W and NW from the Spit NCB, in the Walton Channel, along the S shore of Hedge End Island and W into Horsey Mere. Titchmarsh Marina is cut into land on the SW side of the channel.

From the Spit NCB, moorings continue on both sides of the creek and, just over a cable in, there are pontoons on the SW side (just as the creek turns NW) where boats berth alongside. Watch your depth passing the start of these pontoons, as boats lying alongside take the ground at low water and there are shoal patches in the channel.

Titchmarsh Marina

The entrance to Titchmarsh Marina is between the NW end of the pontoons and the SE end of a second line further up the creek, also on the SW side. A tide gauge on the SE end of the further pontoons shows the depth in the marina's entrance channel.

Turn in as soon as the entrance opens up. There's a slipway to port with the fuelling pontoon beside it (at the head of 'A' pontoon) and the marina offices are in the building above. Once past the fuelling berth the channel turns hard to starboard past the ends of each pontoon. 'A' is nearest to the marina office, 'H' the furthest away.

The majority of pontoons have hoops rather than cleats.

Note that it's about 1½M into Walton itself, so you may wish to get those bikes out to get there or to Frinton. Walton town centre is busy and there are grand views south across the Thames Estuary.

TITCHMARSH MARINA   CO14 8SL

Contact
VHF Ch 80 (0800–1900 in season)
Callsign *Titchmarsh Marina*
Harbourmaster ✆ 01255 851899
Marina Office ✆ 01255 672185
Email info@titchmarshmarina.co.uk
www.titchmarshmarina.co.uk

Access HW±5hr (1·3m in entrance at LWS)
Fuel Diesel and LPG at berth in entrance
Facilities WC, showers, WiFi
Water Taps on pontoons (no hoses, but can be borrowed from office). Also on fuelling berth where hoses are provided
Electricity On pontoons, by card purchased from office
Gas Calor and Gaz
Phone Overlooking marina by office block
Chandler Westwater Chandlery ✆ 01255 676411, on site
Slipway Contact marina office
Provisions In town plus some basics at chandler on site
Post Office In town
Boat repairs 2 x 35-T travel-lifts, 25-T mobile crane, engineers and electronics on site
Scrubbing berth Against wall near fuel berth
Pub/Restaurant Harbour Lights on site ✆ 01255 851887
Taxi ✆ 01255 675910, 850888

Horsey Mere

Above Titchmarsh the Twizzle continues to wind its way NW and then W out into the open area of Horsey Mere. It is navigable to the W end of Hedge End Island by shoal draught boats at most states of the tide, but care must be taken to avoid grounding on oyster layings marked by withies.

At HW the Mere is a large expanse of shallow sailing water, but at LW it is just a sea of mud. A causeway, The Wade, crosses the middle of the Mere from the mainland to Horsey Island. Boats with a draught of not much more than 1m can cross it, but it must be close to HW, preferably on spring tides. There is no obvious point at which to cross the Wade or where you can expect the greatest depth of water; it's a case of watching the depth sounder and taking it gently while being prepared to retreat.

View W from Titchmarsh Marina across Horsey Mere

At HW springs, if heading westward across the Mere, take care on the approach to Kirby Creek where it's hard to spot the submerged, marshy extremity of Horsey Island. Stand well off the island until you're sure you're into the deeper waters of Kirby Creek.

On the W side of the Wade, Kirby Creek (see page 65) leads away NW and runs round the W end of Horsey Island to join Hamford Water. An even less well-defined arm of the creek heads off S towards Kirby Quay. Readers of Arthur Ransome's book set in the Backwaters, *Secret Water*, will recognise Kirby Quay as Witch's Quay and Horsey Mere as the Red Sea with Hamford Water as the Secret Water of the title. Unfortunately, Kirby Creek, where it winds S to Kirby Quay, is not so well marked as in the book, but it still provides a wonderful area to explore by dinghy.

Hamford Water

Hamford Water – sometimes known locally as the West Water – runs SW from the Island Point NCB (Q) at the S end of the Pye Channel (the entry channel to the Backwaters). Leave the Island Point buoy to port and Hamford Water opens up ahead.

Depths are good up past the SHB marked Exchem, where the channel bends more to the W, and on as far as the ECB, also named Exchem, at the entrance to Oakley

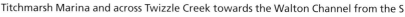

Titchmarsh Marina and across Twizzle Creek towards the Walton Channel from the S

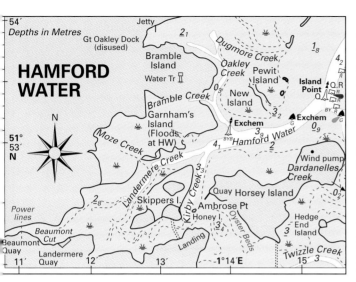

Creek. This is a popular reach in which to anchor, but can be uncomfortable if the wind picks up from NE or E. An anchor ball or riding light is strongly advised.

Oakley Creek

The Exchem ECB, which carries a radar reflector, marks the end of a spit out from Garnham's Island on the W side of the entrance to Oakley Creek. Leave the buoy close to port to avoid the mud on the E side when entering Oakley. Silting has created a bar across the entrance, but it's not enough to prevent entry after half flood (earlier with shallow draught). Seals often bask on the exposed mud inside the entrance.

Oakley creek runs N between Bramble Island and Pewit Island with a branch, Bramble Creek, turning off W along the S side of Bramble Island. Posts topped with red squares or green triangles mark the winding channel in from the entrance and must be followed carefully.

At the top of Oakley Creek is the Great Oakley Dock, which serves an explosives factory at the head of the creek. Small coasters call in, usually at weekends and this, combined with the narrowness and lack of water above Bramble Creek makes Oakley a place where you shouldn't anchor. However, if you enjoy exploring creeks and gutways on the tide with a good chance of seeing plenty of seals, it's worth visiting as the tide rises, even if only by dinghy.

Landermere Quay

Back in Hamford Water, the short stretch between Oakley Creek and the entrance to Kirby Creek is a popular anchorage with good depths.

Kirby Creek

Running S from Hamford Water, between Horsey Island and Skipper's Island, Kirby Creek turns SE around the corner of Horsey out into the Mere.

When approaching the entrance to Kirby Creek, keep a close eye on the depth, but it is best to enter from E along the Horsey Island shore to avoid the long spit out from the NE corner of Skipper's Island, which is unmarked and seems magnetic to yacht keels.

The oyster beds and no anchoring signs in Kirby Creek have been abandoned and it is possible to anchor right up to where Kirby Creek divides around Honey Island (both branches are shallow), before heading E into Horsey Mere. It is possible to land by dinghy on the mainland shore opposite the SE corner of Skipper's Island. From there it's a sea wall walk of about 1½M to Kirby-le-Soken for shops and a pub.

Landermere Creek

Immediately W of the entrance to Kirby Creek there is a mud bar where the spit from Skipper's Island has broadened across the main channel. Depending on draught, it may be necessary to wait until above half tide to cross this bar into Landermere Creek itself. Once over it, there is a ½M reach in which to find depth enough to anchor before the creek turns sharply SW around the corner of Skipper's Island towards Landermere Quay.

In the reach along the W side of Skipper's Island there are a couple of moorings, but still plenty of room to anchor N of them. Immediately S of the moorings the creek divides with one arm rounding the SW corner of Skipper's Island and returning E to join Kirby Creek, and the other continuing W towards Landermere Quay.

For going ashore at Landermere Quay it is best to anchor or borrow one of the moorings then go in by dinghy, because the approach is not clear and is unmarked.

Towards HW it is also possible to explore by dinghy above Landermere Quay, even reaching Beaumont Quay, the most W'ly point of the Backwaters by way of Beaumont Cut, a straight, dug channel that is crossed by low power cables, preventing anything much larger than a dinghy with a mast from reaching the quay. Guy's Hospital, London, built the quay in 1832 using stone from the old London Bridge, which was demolished in that year. There's a preserved lime kiln at the eastern end.

The sad bones of the old sailing barge *Rose* lie in a pool just above the quay, providing a reminder of the days when remote docks such as Beaumont formed a vital trade link to the sea.

10. RIVER COLNE

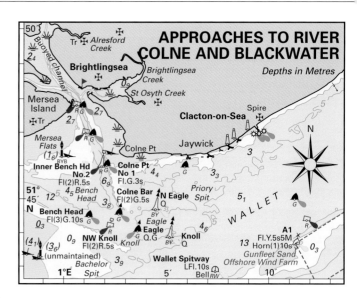

Landfall waypoint
51°44'·0N 001°05'·4E Immediately NE of Knoll NCB

Charts
Imray 2000, Y17
Admiralty SC5607 and 3741 for Colne N of Brightlingsea

Tides
HW Walton +0025

Contact
Harbourmaster
VHF Ch 68
Callsign *Brightlingsea Harbour*
☏ 01206 302200 ☏ 07952 734814

Main hazards

The main hazards to be avoided when approaching the Colne are the long NE–SW stretch of the Gunfleet Sands and Buxey Sand, followed by the shoals of the Knoll, Eagle, Priory Spit, Colne Bar, Bench Head and Mersea Flats.

Channels through or around these hazards are well buoyed, but navigators must identify each buoy carefully and ensure that progress is made from one to the next in the correct sequence. It may be tempting to cut corners, but it's rarely worthwhile. It may appear that you are in clear water with good depth but wander off course and that can change with little warning.

Buoyage does move and is changed to take account of shifts in banks and shoals. It is wise to keep your charts up to date.

Approaches

You can approach the Colne from the NE (Harwich and rivers to the N), the SE or S (across the Thames Estuary or from the Crouch and Thames), and from the W (River Blackwater). For routes from the Continent see *North Sea Passage Pilot* (published by Imray).

From the NE, SE or S All routes from seaward converge on the Knoll NCB (Q), which should be left to port. From there, shape a course to leave first the Eagle (Q.G) and then the Colne Bar buoy (Fl(2)G.5s) to starboard with the NW Knoll (Fl(2)R.5s) to port.

When sailing round from Harwich, a course close to the coast enables vessels to pass N (inshore) of the N Eagle NCB (Q) and from there to make for the Colne Bar buoy.

Above half flood a course direct from the N Eagle to the Inner Bench Head buoy may be considered, but this means crossing the Colne Bar, which can be rough in stronger winds and should be avoided on the ebb. Be aware too that the tide sets strongly to the W here on the flood (and E on the ebb).

From the Bar buoy a course of about 345° will take you to Colne Pt No.1 SHB (Fl.G.3s) and the Inner Bench Head No.2 PHB (Fl(2)R.5s).

Looking N up Colne channel with Brightlingsea harbour on right and Pyefleet on left *Patrick Roach*

RIVER COLNE

N

Depths in Metres

River continues to Colchester

Rowhedge

Wivenhoe
Fl.G.4s
Wivenhoe SC

Tidal Barrier (marked by lights)

Buoyed Channel

Ballast Quay
Oc.WRG.5s

Roman River

Fingringhoe

No.30 Fl(2)R10s
No.28 Fl.R.5s
No.26 Fl.R.3s
No.23 Fl.G.5s

Moorings

No.21 Q.G
No.24 Fl.R.3s

Fingringhoe Wick
2F.R(vert)

No.22 Fl.R.3s

Alresford Creek

No.19 Fl.G Aldboro' Pt

No.20 Fl.R

North Geedon Creek

Geedon Saltings

Fingringhoe Firing Ranges

Fingringhoe Firing Range. No Entry into creeks west of Rat Island when red flags (day) and red lights (night) show

F.R (occas)
F.R (occas)
F.R (occas)

No.18 Fl.R

No.16 Fl.R.3s

River Colne

South Geedon Creek

Rat I

No.17 Fl.G.3s

F.R(occas)
F.R(occas)

Pyefleet Channel
Pewit I

No.15 Fl.G.3s

No.12 Q.R
Fl(3)20s12m

Fl.R

BRIGHTLINGSEA

Bateman's Tr
Westmarsh Pt

Brightlingsea Creek

Flag Creek

Cindery I
Cindery Creek

St Osyth Creek

MERSEA ISLAND

Mersea Stone

East Mersea

East Mersea

Caravans

Caravans

Spit
Q(6)+LFl.15s
Fl(2)G.5s

Martello Tr
No.1 (12)

Mud

Sandy Pt

(11)

Note
Oyster beds lie in the River Colne between No.9 buoy and Aldboro' Pt and in Pyefleet Channel

No.10 Fl.R.3s
No.13 Fl.G.3s

No.9 Fl.G.3s
No.8 Fl.R.3s

Bns

Ray Creek

Mersea Flat

Saint Osyth Marsh

Bns

Lee-over-Sands

Jetty

Molliette (dr 1·6m)

Cocum Hills

Colne Pt

Colne Pt No.1 Fl.G.3s
Inner Bench Hd Fl(2)R.5s

Continuation to Colchester

Colchester
Hythe Quay
Tr
Pylon
King Edward Quay
Sluice
Haven Quay
Sewage works
Hythe Marshes
Rowhedge
Roman River
F.Y

River Colne

0°56'N

River Colne (inset)

Brightlingsea Creek

Brightlingsea Spit
Q(6)+LFl.15s
040°
Fl(2)G.5s

360°

No.10 Fl.R.3s
345°
No.13 Fl.G.3s

No.8 Fl.R.3s
333°
No.9 Fl.G.3s

No.2 Inner Bench Hd Fl(2)R.5s
345°
Colne Pt-No.1 Fl.G.3s

NW Knoll Fl(2)R.5s
300°
Colne Bar Fl(2)G.5s

270°
Eagle Q.G

Knoll Q.

⊕51°44'·0N

The Inner Bench Head is a very tall pillar buoy that marks the beginning of the deepwater Colne channel. Few buoys are now used to mark the channel and the next buoys are a mile distant. These are the No.8 (Fl.R.3s) PHB and the No.9 (Fl.G.3s) SHB.

From W When approaching from the W (the River Blackwater), sea state, tide and draught will dictate how far off the Mersea Flats you need to stand. With a deep draught and rough seas at low water (last of the ebb out of the Blackwater, first of the flood up the Colne) you may need to sail out round the Bench Head SHB (Fl(3)G.10s), towards the Colne Bar buoy and then N

Inner Bench PHB

towards the Inner Bench Head to avoid the very extensive Bench Head Shoal.

With less draught or more water and better sea conditions a course across the shoal directly to the Inner Bench Head may be possible. If taking this approach, beware the large unlit 'Fishery' yellow spherical buoy positioned about a cable W of the Inner Bench Head buoy.

Finally, with shallow draught or towards HW with calm water, an inshore course can be set to skirt the Mersea Flats, keeping S of the Molliette ECM wreck beacon on the Cocum Hills. From there a course of about NE will lead to the No.8 PHB (Fl.R.3s) and the deep water Colne channel.

The Mersea Flats, inside the Molliette ECM, are indeed fairly flat, but only cross them above half tide and with shallow draught in calm conditions. It does shorten the passage to the Colne, but by surprisingly little.

When approaching the Colne from the Blackwater at night, it's best to do so via the Bench Head and Colne Bar buoys. It might be a longer route than you would take in daylight, but it follows the deep water and you have the benefit of lit buoys. Similarly, from other directions, finding the Knoll then approaching from there means a lit approach in deep water all the way. It's certainly a good plan in rough weather at the bottom of the tide.

Entry

Once into the Colne deep water channel, it is marked with pairs of port and starboard lit buoys. The sides are steep to (more so on the W side), so if tacking, keep an eye on the depth and it will be quite apparent when you leave the channel across the line of buoys.

Once past No.8 PHB and No.9 SHB, the shingle bank of East Mersea Stone will be seen ahead to port, probably with a few craft at anchor, and the town of Brightlingsea ahead to starboard with its prominent block of waterfront flats making a clear landmark.

From No.10 PHB (Fl.R.3s) and No.13 SHB (Fl.G.3s) onwards, the river can be quite busy, particularly if there are dinghies out racing, so a sharp lookout is needed to avoid other craft as well as to pick out the necessary navigation marks. Note also that coasters carrying gravel frequently run up or down the Colne on the tide and there is plenty of commercial traffic in and out of Brightlingsea.

The main place for mooring and re-supplying on the Colne is Brightlingsea, while a popular anchorage is across on the W side in the Pyefleet. It's just after No.13 SHB that the courses of inbound vessels diverge according to destination with most going to Brightlingsea.

BRIGHTLINGSEA

From No.13 SHB, in reasonable daylight, a pale coloured tower with a dark conical roof can be seen on the shore beyond the Brightlingsea Spit SCB on Westmarsh Point – Bateman's Tower (Fl(3)20s). Once past No.13 SHB, keep out in the deep water channel with Bateman's Tower clear to the left of the Brightlingsea Spit SCB (Q(6)+L.Fl.15s) until that buoy is almost abeam and you have gone a short way past a green SHM beacon (Fl(2)G.5s) off the Point Clear shore. Only then is it time to turn into Brightlingsea Creek.

A starboard beacon with tide gauge marks the start of the Brightlingsea Channel

Leading marks

Leave the Brightlingsea Spit ECB to port

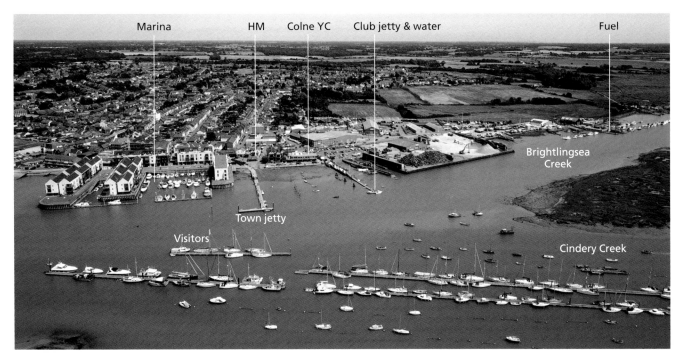

Brightlingsea from the SW

Leave the Brightlingsea Spit SCB to port and the SHM beacon, which has a gauge on it showing depth in metres over the bar, to starboard. The channel has been dredged to 1m below CD right up to Oliver's Wharf. Refer to the depth on the gauge as you enter.

Make good a course of about 040° to keep the two leading marks on the shore in transit. These are vertically striped white/red/white panels on white posts W of Brightlingsea SC's white clubhouse, and are lit at night with 2 F.R. lights. (They can look like white/black/white if the light is poor or the sun behind them.) They can be hard to see from a distance but look for a tall spire that stands up behind them, but not quite in line.

Keeping the leading marks in transit, leave a green SHB (Fl(3)G.5s) to starboard and continue towards a red PHB (Fl.R.5s). As you approach this PHB the creek and harbour will open up to starboard. When about 25m from the buoy, turn to starboard, leaving it on your port side, and head towards Brightlingsea Hard with the NCM on the end of the first mooring pontoon to starboard. A second pontoon is moored parallel to the first and N of it. Head between this second pontoon and the Waterside PHB Fl.R.6s on the N side of the creek.

At night you may have trouble sorting out all the lights. There's the block of flats to port, the Waterside PHB Fl.R.6s, and lights beyond on the end of the long town jetty (2 F.R) and pairs of fixed red vertical lights on the Colne

Inside the entrance channel pass between this pair of buoys

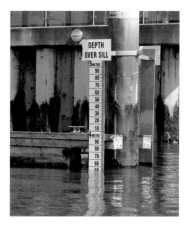

Depth over sill is marked on PH entrance post

YC hammerhead, as well as the wharf just upstream, while ahead to starboard you will see the pontoon NCM (Q), and the second pontoon Fl.G(2+1) 15s.

A variety of cargo ships visit the Oliver's Wharf in Brightlingsea Creek, north of Cindery Island, especially near HW. Keep a sharp lookout for them when entering or leaving the creek, because some of the ships are constrained by their draught, so you must give them adequate room to manoeuvre. You'll also need to watch for the high-speed wind farm personnel and service vessels that use the harbour. They moor on the two seaward pontoons on the starboard side of the river.

Brightlingsea is a crowded and popular harbour where anchoring is prohibited, so it's essential to try, during daylight hours, to make contact with the HM (Ch 68 *Brightlingsea Harbour*) and request a berth on the floating pontoons or, alternatively, in the Waterside Marina, the berthing complex in front of the flats. The HM (or an assistant) will often be out and about on the water to help, advise and guide visitors to a harbour pontoon berth and will probably come out to meet you just to seaward of the pontoon NCM, in a harbour launch with 'Harbourmaster' written on the topsides during working hours.

You may also need to avoid the Brightlingsea/Point Clear/East Mersea Stone ferry, which plies to and fro across the harbour. The speed limit within the harbour is 4kn.

To the SE of the first two pontoons, there are a further two in parallel, which are very long indeed. If you arrive out of harbour office hours, leave the first pontoons to starboard and berth in a visitor's berth at the seaward end of the northern of the two longer pontoons about 150m beyond the NCM.

At LW there is limited depth on the inshore side of the pontoons, so be careful when turning. Tides run swiftly in the creek (up to 2kn) and must be taken into account when berthing alongside or departing.

A water taxi service (also on Ch 68) makes trips ashore from the pontoons easy and it's much safer than crossing from the shore in a laden dinghy when the water is choppy. If the water taxi is not running, call the Harbourmaster on Ch 68 who may be able to help.

The Waterside Marina has a drying sill at 1m over CD and has recently been dredged to a minimum of 2m, a new system of mechanical flushing has also been installed to maintain depths inside the wall and in the narrow approach channel. There is a clear sill depth gauge on the port arm of the entrance, displayed inwards and outwards. Access is around HW±3hr. Enter by leaving the Waterside PHB to port – there may also be a port hand withy between the buoy and the entrance; it gets broken off by boats trying to enter being swept sideways by the ebbing tide. The marina has the obvious advantage of ready access to shore, unlike the harbour pontoons, where visitors must use a dinghy or the water taxi.

Brightlingsea has an attractive waterfront with the Colne YC and a lovely timbered building, now converted to flats, with a cupola on the roof prominent at the top of the busy hard. The older part of the town, between the hard and the shopping centre, has retained its nautical air with various marine companies dotted about and boats appearing over garden walls. It is the home of James Lawrence Sailmakers (largely for traditional craft), the Colne Smack Preservation Society (next to the CYC pontoon) where several smacks are berthed, and the Pioneer Sailing Trust. Sadly the old shipyards have gone now, but boatyards remain busy.

The Hard is a popular launching place for all sorts of craft but is also the location of some of the busiest scrubbing posts on the East Coast. To use them, talk to

Good sized coasters dominate the harbour as they load at Oliver's Wharf

BRIGHTLINGSEA CO7 0AX

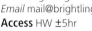

Harbour pontoon moorings
Contact
VHF Ch 68 Callsign *Brightlingsea Harbour*
Harbour office ☎ 01206 302200
www.brightlingseaharbour.org
Email mail@brightlingseaharbour.org
Access HW ±5hr
Water taxi VHF Ch 38, ☎ 07535 508537
Waterside Marina
For berthing contact HM. Water and electricity on pontoons. Public WC in apartment complex closes 2000. New facility opposite requires code from HM's office
Weather Recorded daily inshore waters message ☎ 0844 499 2681 and on harbour website
Scrubbing posts and slipway (Town Hard) call harbour office
Fuel Diesel by arrangement with harbour office, sited by pioneer Sailing Trust shed
Facilities (at Colne YC) WC, showers, laundry (ask in office for access code). New facilities in flats complex.
Pump-out By diesel berth, as above, by arrangement with harbour office
Water CYC hammerhead. Activated by a coin in slot on box on E end wall of CYC
Foot ferry and Colchester ferry details from HM's office
Gas Calor and Gaz from chandlers
Chandler Two nearby
Provisions In town
Post Office In town
Boat repairs At nearby yards
Engineer French Marine Motors ☎ 01206 302133 www.frenchmarine.com
D B Marine ☎ 01206 304391 www.dbmarineeng.co.uk
Sailmakers In town, Lawrence ☎ 01206 302863 jameslawrencesailmakers.com
Clubs
Colne YC CO7 0AX ☎ 01206 302594
Email waterside@colneyachtclub.org.uk
www.colneyachtclub.org.uk
Brightlingsea SC CO7 0DY ☎ 01206 303275
(commodore ☎ 07711 718470)
www.sailbrightlingsea.com

Pub/Restaurant Several nearby, in town and at Colne YC
(weekends and some weekdays)
Taxi ☎ 01206 305006, 307355

the Harbour Office (☎ 01206 302200) or make enquiries at the white hut at the top of the Hard. The same applies for launching on the hard if you wish to launch a trailer-sailer.

The town jetty, just upstream from the block of flats and marina, has a 24m-long hammerhead. A Thames barge often picks up and discharges passengers from the berth, but yachts may lie there for up to 15mins to load or unload, although it's best to check first with the HM. Tenders and small craft can be secured inside the hammerhead or on the access walkway for up to 2hr, but beware the inside may be dry at LW. The jetty is the terminus for the water taxi and the Point Clear foot ferry, and is very popular with children for crabbing.

The small 12-passenger foot ferry operates from the jetty to Point Clear (St Osyth) and East Mersea Stone from Easter to the end of October. For details of service times see www.brightlingseaharbour.org/boat-trips-foot-ferry or ☎ 07981 450169.

A second route operates between the jetty and Colchester, stopping at Wivenhoe and Rowhedge, but must be booked with the Harbour Office by 1300 on the day of travel.

St Osyth

St Osyth Creek runs SE from where the two arms of Brightlingsea Creek and Cindery Creek reconnect at the E end of Cindery Island (see plan on page 67). It's a narrow, twisting and attractive creek with best water at the entrance between the little Pincushion Island and the S bank of the creek.

The creek is unmarked but is well worth a visit in the dinghy on the rising tide, when it's possible you might see seals lolling in the shallows along with a wide variety of

ST OSYTH

Access HW±1½hr
Facilities WC
Water At boatyard
Provisions In village – ¼M
Post Office In village
Boat repairs St Osyth Boatyard, CO16 8EW ☎ 01255 820005
Slipway At boatyard
Pub/Restaurant Several in village

St Osyth Boatyard at the head of Osyth Creek

A summer dawn over slumbering yachts in the Pyefleet

bird life on the way up to the St Osyth Boatyard beside the road bridge at St Osyth. The village is known to have been a port as far back as 1215 and the bay beside the road bridge is full of houseboats and some barges in for repair. There is a line of mud berths at stagings along the waterfront below the boatyard.

Boats of up to 1·5m draught can reach the quay at HW but must either seek a berth alongside and dry out or return down the creek in good time, because it more or less dries at LW. For a berth contact St Osyth Boatyard.

East Mersea Stone

Sometimes known as East Mersea Head, the point has a steep shingle beach with clean landing and the attraction of the Dog and Pheasant pub about a mile inland (☎ 01206 383206). The foot ferry from and to Brightlingsea also lands and picks passengers up from here. It is a convenient way to go shopping for stores in Brightlingsea while lying at anchor off the Stone.

The shore is steep to and if the anchorage is busy it may be necessary to anchor in relatively deep water or just around the point, but the holding is good and an evening stroll ashore pleasant. It is occasionally useful too as a waiting anchorage if catching a tide early in the morning but do keep as close to the Point as possible and show a riding light, because plenty of yachts come and go at night and coasters run up and down the Colne.

A tide rip forms off Mersea Stone on the ebb. Beyond is the entrance to Pyefleet Creek curving away W

The Pyefleet

Pyefleet Creek or The Pyefleet, which runs along the N side of Mersea Island, eventually reaching the Strood (the causeway to the island), is the main anchorage on the River Colne and is a favourite amongst East Coast yachtsmen, which means it can become very crowded during summer weekends.

The entrance lies about 2 cables N of the PHB (Fl.R.5s) and the unlit ECB (a post) marking the wreck of the SS *Lowlands* on the W side of the River above Mersea Stone. Sailing barges often anchor in the mouth of the Pyefleet and several smacks and bawleys have moorings there. Indeed, there are now a lot of moorings in the Pyefleet off the Colchester Oyster Fishery's landing, including a number of large white-buoyed visitor moorings belonging to the Fishery. There is a fee payable for using these – details are marked on a tag on each buoy. There is room, however, to anchor above these moorings between the Mersea shore and Pewit Island, but much beyond that and you come into an area of oyster layings, which you must not anchor or ground on. The creek also shallows rapidly, W of Pewit Island, making it hard to find a hole to lie afloat in clear of the layings.

Holding in the Pyefleet is generally good, though in places the mud is very soft, and boats do drag their anchors unexpectedly. In fact, Pyefleet mud seems to have a character of its own and delights in sticking firmly and in great quantities to both anchor and chain, making recovery a messy business. It is common to see boats motoring seaward as their crews expend much energy dipping buckets and scrubbing the mud off ground tackle, decks, topsides and selves.

The Pyefleet has great charm and a place in the heart of most East Coast sailors, but it can also prove a particularly uncomfortable berth in the wrong conditions. Should the wind draw into either the E or W and blow hard against the tide, the whole creek cuts up rough with boats pitching and tossing all over the place. It occasionally becomes so bad that a boat will dip her head under at times.

Sailing into Alresford Creek

Wivenhoe SC pontoons

A further attraction for a lot of visitors to the Pyefleet is the presence of the Colchester Oyster Fishery's sheds on the S shore from where it is possible to buy oysters and cooked crabs and lobsters.

Colchester Oyster Fishery ☎ 01206 384141
Email info@colchesteroysterfishery.com
www.colchesteroysterfishery.com

Pyefleet to Alresford

Leave the No.12 PHB (Q.R) to port when leaving the Pyefleet to head seawards or to cross to Brightlingsea or to continue up the Colne.

Half a mile up the Colne, the N and S Geedon Channels open up on the W side to surround Rat Island. These channels lead in towards the Fingringhoe firing ranges, where activity is indicated by numerous red flags on the seawall, and cannot be used much, but there is a small hole that local craft sometimes anchor in, just inside the mouth of the S channel.

After passing No.17 SHB (Fl.G.3s) follow the line of red PHBs from No.16 at North Geedon up to No.24 (Fl.R). Pass fairly close to each (as river traffic allows), because they lie along the W edge of the channel while the E side, which shelves gradually, is unmarked until No.19, N of Aldboro Point. Keep a close watch on depths when tacking in this area and beware the dogleg in the channel around No.18.

SHB No.19 (Fl.G) off Aldboro Point is at the apex of a long right hand bend extending from N of No.18 PHB round to No.21 SHB. In the middle of the bend on the W bank, at Fingringhoe Nature Reserve, there's a disused jetty inshore from No.22 PHB, marked 'no landing'.

The next landmark is the gravel works and jetty in Alresford Creek on the E side of the river.

Alresford Creek

Alresford Creek is entered from immediately upstream of No.21 SHB (Q.G) with a line of small port hand pillar buoys and starboard hand conical ones showing the line of the narrow channel.

Laid and maintained by a group of local yachtsmen who have moorings in the creek, these marks are clear and easy to use, but the creek dries out almost completely and there is little space for visiting craft to lie.

Within the creek there is a disused jetty on the N side from which ballast was loaded for many years (the ballast is now taken out by road) and a hard landing at a ford. From the landing it is about a mile to Alresford where there's a pub, the Pointer (☎ 01206 824378), a Post Office and a train station.

Alresford to Wivenhoe

Above Alresford, the Colne continues between wooded banks with Alresford Grange nestling among the trees on the E bank just where the channel runs closest to that shore before sweeping W towards the very active Fingringhoe ballast quay. Small coasters load and depart from the quay on the tide and when they are manoeuvring in the area they use the whole channel and yachts must keep well clear.

There is a line of fore and aft small craft moorings along the E edge of the channel opposite the quay, making this a busy bottleneck area. It is within sight of the Wivenhoe tidal barrier and Wivenhoe itself.

Immediately below the barrier, on the E bank, is the Wivenhoe SC which has a slipway and floating pontoons where vessels of under 2m draught can lie alongside at about HW ±1hr before drying out in soft mud. Visitors are welcomed but stays are limited to 48 hours.

Wivenhoe SC CO7 9WS ☎ 01206 822132
Email clubsecretarywsc@gmail.com
www.wivenhoesailing.org.uk

WIVENHOE

Just above the ballast quay to port and the club to starboard, the river is spanned by the massive structure of the Wivenhoe tidal barrier. It's an unattractive edifice, but the central section is normally open for vessels to pass through unimpeded.

Approach from No.29 SHB with the open section directly ahead. There's a pair of port and starboard hand buoys (Nos 38 and 31), followed by a substantial pair of port and starboard hand beacons (Q.R/Q.G) to guide boats into the passageway through. The barrier is marked on each side by 2F.R/F.G (vert) lights. (These signals are also shown on the upstream side for passage down through the barrier.)

The approach through the tidal barrier to Wivenhoe

Traffic warning signals on the N pier are arranged to show 3F.R.(vert) lights, directed both downstream and up, which are lit to indicate that the barrier is closed or that a large vessel is in transit. In either case, do not try to pass through.

The opening in the barrier is 30m wide, so two-way traffic is practical, but be careful to pass port to port and at less than 5kn.

Once through the barrier, Wivenhoe waterfront opens to starboard with boats berthed bows on in mud berths with all activity watched by visitors to the popular Rose and Crown pub. Unfortunately, there is limited scope for getting ashore. Immediately beyond the barrier, to starboard, there is a modern pontoon jetty but it is private. Another more substantial modern jetty projects from the starboard bank a few yards further on but, like the long quay higher up, it has railings along its edge making it unwelcoming to any visiting boats. Just beyond it is the newer town slipway where you can at least land from a dinghy There is a line of small craft fore and aft moorings to port with some more a little higher up, off the quayside where new houses and blocks of flats overlook the river. Boats can berth briefly on the tide at this quay, but again the railings are right on the edge of the quay, making landing difficult.

There are shops and a Post Office in Wivenhoe, plus pubs and restaurants, doctors, dentists and a chemist.

Sadly, in such an attractive spot, finding a mud berth along the quay is a matter of chance and even then an empty berth may not prove comfortable, once the tide has gone, if your boat's hull does not match the hole made by the resident vessel. It is better to moor at the Wivenhoe SC below the tide barrier.

FINGRINGHOE

There is no buoyage beyond the Wivenhoe barrier, so for best water use charts and/or generally follow the outside of bends. As the river bends away from Wivenhoe, another creek opens on the S shore, just before an extensive new housing development. This is Fingringhoe Creek, commonly known as the Roman River. It mainly dries and should only be explored by shallow draught vessels near HW, when it is an attractive waterway leading up to Fingringhoe, a once thriving port.

Landing pontoon at Rowhedge

ROWHEDGE

Above the mouth of the Roman River, the Colne takes a turn to the N past a development of modern apartments on the old quay and Rowhedge appears on the W bank. Once a busy centre for boat building, plus having a large fishing fleet, the Rowhedge waterfront is now quieter with few obvious signs of its commercial maritime past.

It's still possible to moor along the pretty quayside at Rowhedge, close outside the waterfront pubs, but timing is dependent upon draught and it's likely that you will only have from perhaps HW -2 to HW +1½hr unless planning to dry out there.

The village, which is right by the river, offers several pubs, including Ye Olde Albion and The Anchor on the quay, as well as a Post Office and shops.

There is a floating pontoon upriver of the pubs at which yachts can berth for a visit to the village, but they share it with the ferry from Wivenhoe, although that usually berths on the inside. Boats with a draught of up to 5ft can get alongside at HW ±2½hr, but the pontoon dries completely at LW.

The attractive waterfrontage of Rowhedge

ROWHEDGE TO COLCHESTER

The Colne runs a further two miles from Rowhedge to Colchester and is perhaps of interest only to the curious or the adventurous, although there is a visitor pontoon near the head of navigation. There are attractive tree-lined reaches at first, but soon you are passing rundown industrial wharves and warehouses until you reach King Edward Quay on your port side, at the end of which is a low-level road bridge.

Near to HW there is enough water for a boat of over 2m draught to creep right up to the road bridge, but this would be within an hour of HW and time must be allowed to return down river to deeper water. It is possible to dry out at the King Edward Quay, in gaps you may find between a variety of permanently moored craft, but it should be undertaken with caution – as you might expect, there is debris around, and you should test the depth each side before committing yourself.

There is also a 42-metre visitor pontoon by the quay, not far below the conspicuous lightship (home to various activities including local Sea Cadets), and shoal draught boats up to 9m in length should dry out reasonably level in mud beside this pontoon. Stays are limited to 48 hours. There is electricity and water but no other facilities. Rafting out may be uncomfortable for the outside boats where the mud slopes more steeply.

The skyline of the upper reaches of the Colne is dominated by the tower blocks of Essex University

The section of quay close to the bridge has been renovated and provided with bench seats and lighting, making it tidier than it once was. The town centre is about a mile away while supermarkets and restaurants are closer. A lot of student accommodation is being built nearby. Colchester Borough Council, responsible for the area, can be contacted on ☎ 01206 282222.

There is a winding hole to starboard below the pontoon. It was originally intended for turning coasters, but beware – the main area has silted up very badly.

It's worth noting that the plans for the regeneration of the area include the possible provision of more facilities for visitors, but there is no clear timescale for the work.

Colchester

Visitor pontoon

11. RIVER BLACKWATER

⊕ **Landfall waypoint**
51°44'·0N 001°05'·4E Immediately NE of Knoll NCB

Charts
Imray 2000, Y17
Admiralty SC5607, 3741

Tides
Bradwell HW Walton +0030
Osea HW Walton +0050
Maldon HW Walton +0100

Blackwater River Bailiff
Nigel Harmer ☎ 01621 875837 ☎ 07818 013723
Email nigel.harmer@maldon.gov.uk

ECP Honorary Port Pilot
Nigel Harmer as above
Email blackwater@eastcoastpilot.com

Main hazards

The entrance to both the River Blackwater and the River Colne lies W and NW from the Knoll NCB (Q), which in turn stands at the SW end of the Wallet channel, N of the Buxey Sand and W of the Gunfleet Sand. Approaching the buoy is straightforward if arriving from the NE through the Wallet, but from S, either from the Crouch or Thames, it means crossing the sandbanks. As with everywhere in the Thames Estuary, these banks are hazards to navigation and must be treated cautiously.

From the S, the best approach to the Knoll is via the Spitway between the Swin and Wallet channels, which saves a long haul NE to round the NE Gunfleet and return SW through the Wallet.

From the Crouch, shallow draught craft can cut through the Rays'n, but even they must cross Swire Hole to avoid drying patches on the Batchelor Spit.

The twin sarcophagi of the decommissioned Bradwell nuclear power station are excellent landmarks

Once the Knoll is reached, from any direction, navigation becomes less hazardous although compass courses will be needed in poor visibility.

Approaches

From the Knoll NCB (Q) shape a course to leave the Eagle SHB (Q.G.) close to starboard. Alter course then to pass between the NW Knoll PHB (Fl(2)R.5s) and the Colne Bar SHB (Fl(2)G.5s). From there, steer to leave the Bench Head SHB (Fl(3)G.10s) to starboard. The Bench Head buoy is generally thought of as the beginning of the Blackwater.

Craft approaching the estuary from the NE by way of the Wallet may, if tide and weather conditions permit, shorten their passage slightly after passing Clacton by ignoring the Knoll NCB and leaving the North Eagle NCB (Q) on their port side before making for the Colne Bar SHB.

If crossing from the River Colne to the Blackwater, sea conditions, draught and state of tide will dictate your course. It may be necessary to go right out to the Bench Head buoy near to low tide on a rough day, but a more likely route is out round the Inner Bench Head, then on a

West Mersea with (L to R) Salcott Channel, Thorn, Mersea and Besom Fleets. Hammerhead landing pontoon at right *Patrick Roach*

course made good of about 250° into the deep water channel with the Bench Head buoy bearing about 110°. Shallow draught boats can leave the Colne S of No.8 PHB and make good a course of about 220° to stay S of the ECM (1M distant) marking the wreck of the *Molliette* on the Cocum Hills. From there they can turn onto about 250° with Bradwell Power Station fine on the port bow until again finding the deep water of the Blackwater itself.

Entry

Once past the Bench Head it is often difficult to identify any marks other than the two massive lumps of Bradwell Power Station on the S shore and a general view of 'that's W Mersea' on the starboard bow. Although the power station has been decommissioned, the landmark buildings will remain for many years.

Approaching West Mersea up the Thorn Fleet

From the Bench Head, make good a course of about 290° to clear Sales Point and lead you towards the Nass Beacon ECM (VQ(3)5s6m2M) marking the entrance to Mersea Quarters and Tollesbury, with the option of leaving it to the N and going on up the Blackwater. (Keep checking your position, because you will have tide running athwart your course for the full 4M from the Bench Head to the Nass Bn.)

WEST MERSEA

First port of call on the Blackwater is West Mersea. Enter the Quarters from close E of the Nass Bn ECM (VQ(3)5s 6m2M), following the line of mainly unlit port and starboard buoys towards the mass of moorings. Do not venture into the area close SW of the beacon where there

The Old Packing Shed sits on its island in the middle of the Mersea channels

Approaching the landing pontoon on the West Mersea front

is a dangerous obstruction. A course of about 280° for half a mile will take you from the Nass Bn to the Quarters Spit buoy ECB (Q(3)10s), which must be left to port. Further in, to starboard, you will see No.7 SHB (Fl(2)G.5s). From No.7 inwards you have to rely on the lines of moorings to show where the best water is.

There are boats moored well out in Mersea Quarters, but there is still room to anchor, although it can be rather exposed at HW with a heavy swell if the wind is from E or SE.

Once you're amongst the moorings there is no room to anchor safely and you must seek a mooring. For this it's best to call the West Mersea YC launch, call sign *YC1* on VHF Ch 37, from close to the Nass Bn. The launchman will do his best to find you a mooring and can take you to and from the shore, for which journeys there is a charge, as there is for short term and overnight mooring. (The launch charge may be refunded if you eat or drink in the WMYC.) As an alternative to a swinging mooring, YC1 may ask you to moor fore and aft on either the row of piles or on a number pontoons that hang between some of them in the Ray Channel.

Beyond the Quarters, the channel divides into several separate arms. Each of these generally has a clear lane of best water to follow between the lines of moorings, but at slack water boats may lie athwart the channel, making it hard to pick out.

Steering about NW from a position between the Quarters Spit ECB and No.7 SHB will take you up the Salcott Channel to the W of Sunken Island. Heading a little to starboard, the middle line of moorings leads into Thorn Fleet on the W side of Packing Marsh Island with its distinctive oyster shed. (Following Thorn Fleet will take you to the pile moorings in the Ray Channel.) On the E side of Packing Marsh Island is the shallower Mersea Fleet and the third line of moorings, while way over to the E of Cobmarsh Island is Besom Fleet, which runs right along the West Mersea foreshore.

A narrow channel, The Gut, cuts through from the Thorn Fleet and Ray Channel to Mersea Fleet and the Strood Channel opposite the hard and landing pontoon. The Strood Channel runs on N from the RNLI lifeboat station and Dabchicks SC to turn NE round the back of Mersea Island towards the Strood itself, which is the causeway between Mersea and the mainland. (Beyond this causeway is the head of the Pyefleet, which runs E into the Colne.)

All of the Mersea channels are thick with moorings and their headwaters are really only suitable for exploration by dinghy. Best water is generally found between paired lines of moorings in each fleet or channel. Whatever you do, don't cut across from one fleet to another, the water is shallow and the mud hugs keels. Withies generally mark oyster layings, not good water.

WEST MERSEA   CO5 8PB

Contact
Moorings: WMYC launch
VHF Ch 37 Callsign *YC1*
℡ 07752 309435 (seasonal, daily but hours vary, check club website for details)
Additional Water taxi VHF Ch 72
Callsign *Lady Grace* ℡ 07791 859624
0800-1800 (and evenings by prior arrangement).
Access 24hr
Clubs West Mersea YC CO5 8PB
℡ 01206 382947
Email info@wmyc.org.uk
www.wmyc.org.uk
Dabchicks SC ℡ 01206 383786
www.dabchicks.org
Fuel Garage in town
Water On pontoon hammerhead
Gas Calor and Gaz from chandlers
Chandlers Marinestore Wyatts Chandlery CM ℡ 01206 384745
Scrubbing posts Contact WMYC
Boatyards and repairs Peter Clarke's Boatyard (incl. slipway)
℡ 01206 385905
West Mersea Marine ℡ 01206 382244
Sailmakers Gowen Ocean ℡ 01206 384412
Shipwright David Mills ℡ 01206 382161
Engineers A B Clarke ℡ 01206 382706;
OHM Engineering ℡ 07905 243414
Provisions In town
Post Office In town
Pub/Restaurant Many along front and in town, including WMYC
(℡ 01206 384463 to book)
Transport Buses to Colchester
Taxi ℡ 01206 384666, 731257

Woodrolfe Creek   West Mersea   The Leavings

The approaches to Tollesbury Creek

TOLLESBURY

Tollesbury shares a common entrance with Mersea from the Nass Bn ECM (VQ(3)5s 6m2M), its creeks running W from Mersea Quarters. To enter, follow the line of PHBs in from the Nass Beacon and head W at No.6, leaving the Quarters Spit ECB (Q(3)10s) to starboard, before following the charted channel W and WSW for several hundred yards to find a small PHB No.2, lit Fl.R.5s.

A word of warning is needed here. In common with many East Coast ports, when entering Tollesbury in the late afternoon, the sun will be low and directly ahead. This makes spotting buoys and/or identifying them extremely difficult, so proceed with caution. New visitors are also advised to follow the buoyed channel and not be distracted by local boats whose draught and local knowledge enable them to cross the Nass at the right state of the tide.

The No.2 PHB is the first of three PHBs placed along the N edge of the Nass sand bank. Depending upon wind and tide conditions, at anything less than HW, these buoys can drift over the bank, so watch the depth and be prepared to stand off them a little. The second PHB,

No.4 (Fl.R.5s), is paired with an ECB 'Indigo' (Q(3)10s) at the seaward end of a long spit out from Great Cob Island, forming a 'gate' into the buoyed South Channel. The South Channel, which is the main Tollesbury channel, carries on SW leaving the Indigo ECB on your starboard side. (You might also see local boats make their way to Tollesbury by leaving the ECB to port, entering the North Channel and then on to Tollesbury via the W end of Great Cob Island.)

Once through the 'gate' into the Tollesbury South Channel, you should find it mainly buoyed along its N side with about five SHBs (the number varies), each showing a flashing light, but there is also the third of the PHBs, No.6, to take note of on the edge of the Nass about 200 yards up the channel. No.6 marks a hard, drying sandy knoll on the Nass, but, although the buoy itself can dry out, once the tide is flooding there is usually deeper water close to it, so tend to pass close to this buoy, remembering that the wind can blow it over the shallows.

At the last SHB, usually No.11, the channel turns sharply to starboard in a NW direction into a reach known as The Leavings, which used to be an anchorage for local fishing smacks, but now sees the beginning of the Tollesbury moorings. Follow the line of these moorings, being very careful of depth if tacking outside

Final approaches to Tollesbury Marina along Woodrolfe Creek

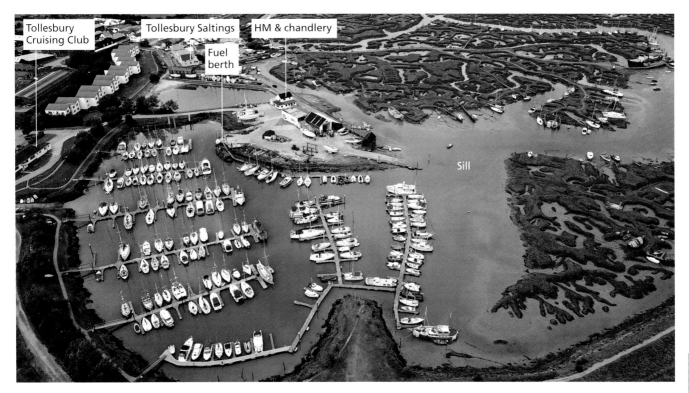

Tollesbury Marina

the line of starboard hand withies, and Woodrolfe Creek will open up to port. You will see the landmark white blocks of flats over the saltings, together with the masts in the marina and a red light vessel, which is HQ for the Fellowship Afloat Charitable Trust.

There is a landing place half way up the Leavings on the S side, which gives access to a walk along the seawall into Tollesbury. It can be used at most states of tide.

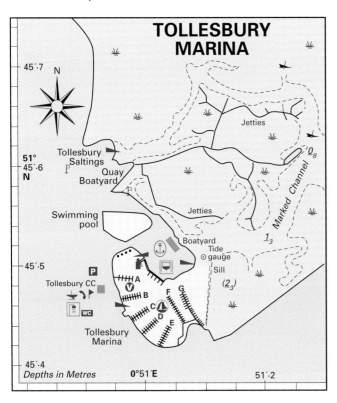

There is a tide gauge, marked in feet, on the S bank of The Leavings before you reach Woodrolfe Creek entrance, showing the depth over the marina sill; in the

TOLLESBURY MARINA   CM9 8SE

Contact
VHF Ch 80 Callsign *Tollesbury Marina*
Harbourmaster ☎ 01621 869202/868471
Email hm@tollesburymarina.com
www.tollesburymarina.co.uk
Access HW-1½hr to HW+1
Fuel Diesel at berth below crane
Facilities WC, showers, laundry, WiFi, swimming pool, tennis courts
Water On pontoons
Electricity On pontoons (chargeable)
Gas Calor and Gaz
Chandler On site
Provisions In town (10 minutes)
Pharmacy and doctor In town
Post Office In town
Boat repairs 20-T boat lift and cranes, three slipways up to 30T. Also 8T crane at Tollesbury Saltings (see text)
Scrubbing posts In marina
Slipway Contact marina office
Engineers Volspec nearby
Telephone At Tollesbury CC
Pub/Restaurant Tollesbury CC on site, pub in town
Clubs Tollesbury Cruising Club ☎ 01621 869561
www.tollesburycc.co.uk
Tollesbury SC ☎ 01621 869406 *Email* principal@tollesburysc.com
www.tollesburysc.com
Transport Buses to Maldon, Colchester, or Witham
Taxi ☎ 07788 480542

late afternoon it can be difficult to read with the sun in your eyes, so if in doubt call the marina for guidance.

Off the mouth of Woodrolfe Creek are some white conical mooring buoys, for use when there is not enough water to get into the marina.

There is a second tide gauge, on the N bank of Woodrolfe Creek just inside the entrance, again marked in feet. The creek dries and has a narrow, winding channel, but further up it is marked with a few port and starboard buoys, mostly lit Fl.R.5s or Fl.G.5s. The line of moorings also gives guidance as to the best water.

As you pass the light vessel to starboard and approach Tollesbury Marina the entrance is clearly seen to the left of an old black weatherboard granary shed beside the Woodrolfe Boatyard slipway. An arm of water also turns sharply to starboard along Tollesbury waterfront, but it should not be followed without current advice unless previously inspected at LW. It gives access to the self-styled 'natural marina' run by Tollesbury Saltings, where mud berths for visitors may be available on request, accessible close to HW.

Tollesbury Saltings ☎ 07521 318155
www.tsl-online.co.uk

A final tide gauge, also marked in feet, is painted on a hefty green starboard hand post sited on top of the sill, immediately outside Tollesbury Marina, to show the depth over it, which is about 2m at HWS and 1·5m on neaps. The sill is hard, uneven concrete.

On entering the marina, the fuel berth is hard round to starboard towards the boatyard crane. The first pontoon you pass on entering is G, with A down the far end. Visitors are allocated empty slots on any pontoon. There are bookable scrubbing posts beyond pontoon A.

BRADWELL

When entering the Blackwater the outstanding landmark is Bradwell Power Station on the S shore, close to which lie Bradwell Creek and Bradwell Marina. The distance diagonally across the Blackwater deep water channel from the Nass Bn to the isolated power station breakwater, which has 2FR(vert) lights at each end and can often look like a ship from a distance, is a shade under 1½M.

A cable beyond the W end of the breakwater there's a NCM beacon (Q), the Bradwell Beacon, which carries a depth gauge indicating depths in feet at the marina entrance. To enter Bradwell Creek and the marina, leave the beacon to starboard and head in between the red buoys to port and withies to starboard. Shoal patches have been noted near the beacon and close to the third red buoy, so be very careful if entering at LW±1½hr. The tide can run strongly across the approach channel with the buoys being pushed across the bank or into the channel, making it narrower than ever. The depth will vary frequently until well into the marked channel and it is best approached on a rising tide (especially at springs). Better depths have been found on the side of the channel marked by the buoys.

In recent years, greater depth of water has actually been found outside (E of) the buoyed channel, so if you need to enter or leave near to LW this may be worth a try but check our website for up to date information and watch the echo sounder.

At the last PHB bear to port and head for a green conical SHB. The line to this buoy is shown by a pair of leading marks on the seawall – two small red triangles

Right SHB and leading marks *Below* leading marks on seawall

Bradwell NCM beacon

Approaching the entrance to Bradwell Marina

Bradwell marina and approaches

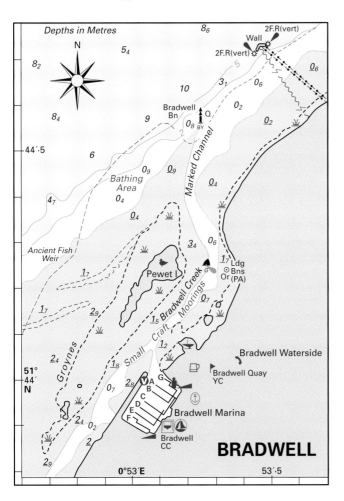

against a white painted patch on the wall. These marks have been adjusted for a change in the channel and are not always easy to make out; binoculars will help. Leaving the SHB very close to starboard, turn hard to starboard and follow the lines of moorings into Bradwell

BRADWELL MARINA   CMO 7RB

Contact VHF Ch 80
Callsign *Bradwell Marina*
Harbourmaster ☎ 01621 776235/776391
Email arthur@bradwellmarina.com
www.bradwellmarina.com
Access HW ±4½hr
Fuel Diesel and petrol berth at base of tower
(0830–1700). Tight turning space
Facilities WC, showers, laundry, separate WiFi on each pontoon, chemical toilet emptying point
Water Taps and hoses on pontoons
Electricity On pontoons
Gas Calor and Gaz
Provisions Bradwell Community Shop and PO (☎ 01621 776274, www.bradwellshop.co.uk)
Boat repairs 45-T boat lift, self-launch slipway (contact marina)
Engineers Althorne Marine Services ☎ 07904 329236
Pub/Restaurant Marina bar-restaurant on site
Green Man ☎ 01621 776226, at Waterside
King's Head ☎ 01621 776224, in village
Clubs Bradwell CC www.bradwellcruisingclub.co.uk
Bradwell Quay YC *Email* honsec@bqyc.org.uk www.bqyc.org.uk
(HQ near the Green Man)
Transport Weekday buses to Burnham-on-Crouch
Taxi ☎ 01621 741199, 784878

Creek. Best water is between the innermost line of small boat (drying) moorings and the S line of bigger boat moorings. Here the tide runs very strongly through the creek.

To port will be seen the remains of Bradwell Quay and some scrubbing posts (belonging to the nearby Bradwell Quay YC) beside a public slipway. Off the end of it is a large red beacon that must be left on your port side. Shortly beyond is a single red PHB. Turn to port around this and the marina entrance is open ahead between red and green piles, but remember the tide sets swiftly across the approach.

Pass between the piles and, unless directed elsewhere, the main visitors' berth is on the hammerhead berth dead ahead (row A) with a secondary berth on the hammerhead next to it to starboard (row B). The fuelling berth is ahead on the starboard side of the high jetty beneath the blue and white marina tower.

The marina's entrance channel can be navigated by shallow draught vessels at all states of neap tides, but at springs all craft must take care and time their entry for 90 minutes or so after LW. The marina itself is dredged to a general 6–8ft (1·8–2·4m).

It is sometimes possible to borrow a mooring in Bradwell Creek, but anchoring is not advisable. When picking up a mooring, be aware of the strong tide.

The marina is in the hamlet of Bradwell Waterside, which has one pub and no shops. There is a useful community-run shop and PO in the village of Bradwell-on-Sea, a 20-minute walk away.

If holidaying and staying at Bradwell, it is worth the walk, either by way of the sea wall or through the village, to visit St Peter's on the Wall (www.bradwellchapel.org). Established by St Cedd in 654AD, it is an extremely simple but calm place of worship, perhaps the oldest surviving church building in England.

Bradwell to Thirslet

When departing Bradwell Creek, be sure to round the beacon, leaving it to port, before turning up river. Due W an unlit SCB guards the end of the remains of Tollesbury Pier on N bank. It is then tempting to make directly towards Osea Island, which appears dead ahead, but between Bradwell and the island lies Thirslet Spit on the N side of the main channel. It is marked by the Thirslet SHB (Fl(3)G.10s), which, when finally located, is quite obvious,

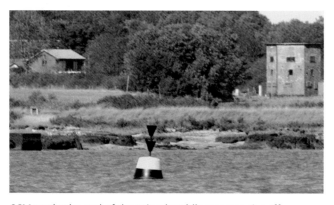

SCM marks the end of the ruined paddle steamer pier off Tollesbury

The wreck buoys in entrance to Goldhanger Creek and E of Osea

especially as the Radio Caroline pirate ship the *Ross Revenge* lies at anchor on the transit, so spotting it can be difficult.

Thirslet Spit is made of extremely hard sand and is steep-to on its river side. Many, many vessels have grounded on it as they make their way straight up or down the Blackwater. A dog-leg around it is essential, so steer for the moorings at Stone rather than directly towards Osea. (When returning down river, from Osea, keep the old Bradwell power station buildings fine on your port bow, after passing close outside the Stone moorings, until past Thirslet.)

Thirslet Creek runs NW from the spit buoy and can provide a sheltered anchorage when the sand banks are uncovered. However, once the banks are awash it becomes rather exposed.

Opposite Thirslet, on the S shore, St Lawrence Bay is an area popular with PWCs and water-skiers.

STONE

On the S shore ½M above Thirslet is Stone with a long shingle beach, many moorings and several large, highly active fleets of racing dinghies that criss-cross the entire river from Stone Sailing Club.

Stone Sailing Club CM0 7NF
☏ 01621 779344 when open
www.stonesailingclub.org.uk

Tides run fast through the moorings and it is best to shape a course to pass outside them all.

Stone to Osea

A further ¾M up river, across on the N side, the small No.1 SHB marks the end of Goldhanger Spit and the entrance to Goldhanger Creek. The spit extends from the E end of Osea Island and the Creek cuts NW towards the village of Goldhanger with an arm breaking away to run behind Osea Island towards The Stumble, eventually rejoining the main river and actually making Osea an island. If you choose to sail this area, look out for the isolated danger buoy, approximately 5 cables N of Goldhanger No.1 SHB, marking two wrecks.

A charted causeway runs from Decoy Point on the mainland to West Point on Osea Island and can be crossed by most craft about an hour either side of HW springs. A suitable deeper gap on the causeway is usually indicated between two withies.

There are oyster layings in Goldhanger Creek making it difficult to find an anchorage. Like Thirslet, it only offers shelter once the banks are dry. Several small craft do lie at the head of the creek where there is also the Goldhanger

Osea Island anchorage E of the old pier. The island is a luxury holiday resort

Small craft anchored at the top of Goldhanger Creek

SC (www.goldhangersailingclub.org.uk). If your boat can take the ground comfortably then there is a landing and Goldhanger village with its pubs, The Chequers Inn and The Cricketers, a reasonable walk away.

Across on the S shore at Stansgate there are more moorings and the Marconi SC. There is a free visitor mooring, A0, the western-most mooring on the outer row, if you wish to visit the club. The outer three rows of moorings are all-tide.

Marconi SC CM0 7NU
☎ 01621 772164 when open
Email info@marconi-sc.org.uk
www.marconi-sc.org.uk

NW of Stansgate, at the W end of the Marconi SC moorings, there is the Marconi PHB (Fl(2)R.3s), which doesn't always stand out too well. It is placed in good water, but at a point where the river channel narrows and it should be left to port for safety. The area between Stone and the anchorage E of Osea pier, particularly around the Marconi buoy, is frequently choppy and can be disturbingly rough with wind against tide.

Osea

The remains of the pier at Osea still carries 2F.G(vert) lights that act as a useful guide. There's good depth and holding E of the pier, off which are a couple of sizeable moorings, with the shell beach of Osea a popular place for walking and picnicking. Note however that the island is privately owned and you may not be welcomed above the HW mark. At LW, deep draught boats must beware The Barnacle shoal patch a cable E from the pier.

There's good holding if you set the anchor properly and shelter from N winds, in addition to offering a pleasant place to stretch your legs ashore or swim off the beach – and children can paddle about the anchorage in dinghies, practising their boat handling skills.

E Mayland Spit marks the entrance to Lawling Creek and is a PHM for the main river – leave to S on entering

Lawling Creek

South from Osea is the No.2 Mayland Spit PHB (Fl.R.3s), which marks the S side of the main river channel, but also the W side of the entrance to Lawling Creek. This creek runs SW to Maylandsea and the Blackwater Marina (see plan on page 86).

Enter Lawling Creek by leaving the Mayland Spit buoy to starboard (it is a PHB for the river only) and steer to leave the SHB Lawling Creek No.1 (Q.G.6s) to starboard. From there, leave No.3 Mundon Point (Q.G.4s) to starboard and No.2 (Q.R.4s) to port, altering course to about SW towards No.4 Mayland Creek (Q.R.6s) off the entrance to Mayland Creek. Continue to No.6 (Fl.R.4s) from where the Harlow (Blackwater) SC will lie ahead and the moorings offer a guide to the channel up to the Blackwater Marina.

There is a sheltered anchorage on the S side of Mundon Stone Point but be careful, the mud bank inside the headland is extensive. The small knoll of sand that forms the headland is often used for barbeques by visiting club cruises and is also a frequent perch for herons and cormorants.

Opposite Mundon Pt is the entrance to the drying Mayland Creek, which has a number of moorings in it.

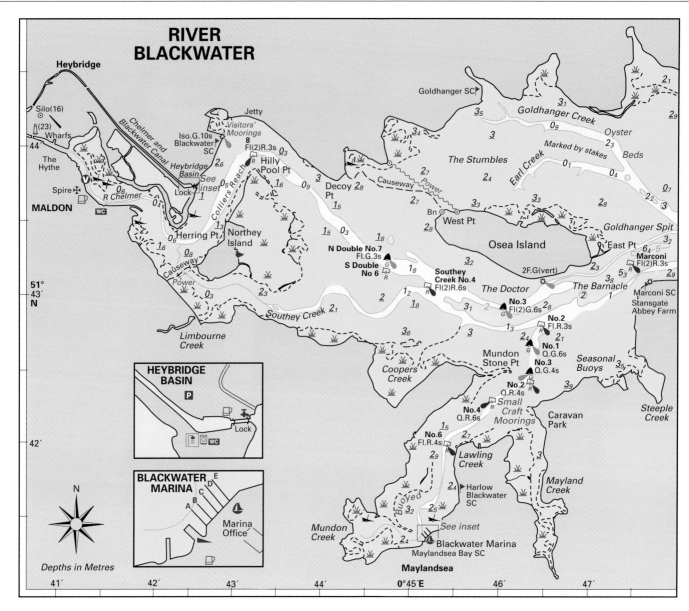

Map: River Blackwater

RIVER
BLACKWATER

Heybridge

Silo(16)
(23)
Wharfs
44
The Hythe

Spire
MALDON
WC

R Chelmer
0.6
0.4

Herring Pt

Causeway
Power
0.3

Chelmer and Blackwater Canal

Heybridge Basin
See inset
Lock

Colliers Reach

2.6
0.5
1

Limbourne Creek

1.6
0.8

Northey Island

2.3

Southey Creek
2.1

Coopers Creek

Jetty
Visitors' Moorings
Iso.G.10s
Blackwater SC
8
Fl(2)R.3s
0.3

Hilly Pool Pt

Decoy Pt
2.8
1.5
1.6
0.9
0.5

1.3
1.5
1.8

N Double No.7
Fl.G.3s
S Double No 6
G
R
1.8

Southey Creek No.4
Fl(2)R.6s
1.2
2
1.8

Goldhanger SC
3.5
3.4

The Stumbles
2.4

Causeway
Power

2.7
Bn
2.8

West Pt

3.3
3.2

Osea Island

2.0
No.3
Fl(2)G.6s
3.1
3.6
3

Goldhanger Creek
0.9
3

Marked by stakes
0.1
2.4

Earl Creek
0.4

Oyster Beds
2.3
2.2
0.7
3

2.8

Goldhanger Spit
3.2
East Pt
6.4
5

Marconi
Fl(2)R.3s
2.9

2F.G(vert)
The Doctor
(2)
The Barnacle
2.3
1
3.8
5.3

2.8
No.2
Fl.R.3s
1.3
2.4
2.1
No.1
Q.G.6s
Mundon Stone Pt
No.3
Q.G.4s

Seasonal Buoys
3.5

3.9

2.9

Marconi SC
Stansgate Abbey Farm

51°
43′
N

51°
42′

Depths in Metres

N

HEYBRIDGE BASIN
P
Lock
WC

BLACKWATER MARINA
E
D
C
B
A
Marina Office

No.2
Q.R.4s
Small Craft Moorings

No.4
Q.R.6s
1.5

No.6
Fl.R.4s
2.9

Lawling Creek

Buoyed
3.2
2.5

Harlow Blackwater SC
2.4
3

Caravan Park

Mayland Creek

Steeple Creek

Mundon Creek
2.4

See inset
Blackwater Marina
Maylandsea Bay SC

Maylandsea

41′   42′   43′   44′   0°45′E   46′   47′

About a mile in from the entrance, on the E bank, where there are more moorings, stands the Harlow (Blackwater) SC.

Harlow (Blackwater) SC CM3 6AG
☎ 01621 740300
Email publicity@harlow-blackwater-sc.co.uk
www.harlow-blackwater-sailing-club.co.uk

The club has 35 swinging moorings – the boats on them are afloat at HW ±2hr – and a launching ramp that has water at similar times.

From HBSC you can see the Blackwater Marina on the port hand, but you must approach by continuing to follow the winding line of moorings carefully until you reach a final green SHB (a beige-coloured canvas-

The 'green' box buoy

Harlow (Blackwater) SC

BLACKWATER MARINA
CM3 6AL

Contact
VHF Ch 80
Callsign *Blackwater Marina*
Harbourmaster ☎ 01621 740264
Email info@blackwater-marina.co.uk
www.blackwater-marina.co.uk

Access HW±2½hr
Fuel Diesel
Facilities WC, showers
Water Taps and hoses on pontoons
Electricity On pontoons
Boat repairs Slipway, 18-T travel hoist, 15-T crane. Dry dock, engineers, rigging
Slipway Contact marina
Gas Calor and Gaz
Provisions In village, five minute walk
Post Office In village
Pub/Restaurant On site and takeaways in village
Taxi ☎ 01621 741621

Maylandsea Bay SC

covered box mark, so not always obviously green), lying N of the marina, from where the pontoons are clearly visible ahead. These are drying pontoons that can only be reached at HW±2hr, but there are also 100 marina owned all-tide moorings laid to about half way down the creek.

The final approach is from the (green) box buoy in a curve marked by a series of recently laid PHMs, toward the pontoons in a direct line with the slipway on the right. 'A' pontoon is beside the slipway; 'E' is at the seaward end.

Above the marina the creek narrows rapidly and dries completely, but there is an active club, the Maylandsea Bay SC, just upriver. The club manages a few drying moorings (owned by Maldon DC) for its group of cruising members.
Maylandsea Bay SC CM3 6AL
☎ 01621 740470 when open
Email sec@maylandseabay-sc.org.uk
www.maylandseabay-sc.org.uk

Lawling Creek to Heybridge
From Osea, leave No.2 PHB (Fl.R.3s) to port and No.3 the Doctor SHB (Fl(2)G.6s) to starboard. The water along the Osea Island shore looks inviting, but beware the Doctor flats, which have caught the keel of many a yacht trying to take a short cut inside the buoy.

At the Doctor SHB the river turns NW and the next buoy is the No.4 PHB (Fl(2)R.6s) marking the entrance to Southey Creek. This creek winds away W behind

Blackwater Marina at the top of Lawling Creek

RIVER BLACKWATER

Saltcote SC adjacent to the old granary whose twin black towers are a good reference point

Northey Island to rejoin the main Blackwater River opposite Herring Point. It is a broad expanse of water at HW, but quickly narrows and dries as the tide ebbs. You can sail behind Northey on a good tide but beware the hard causeway between the island and the mainland at the SW corner.

Just above Southey Creek a pair of buoys, the Doubles, mark a distinct narrowing of the fairway, which shoals to less than 1m at LWS. The SHB, No.7 North Double, is lit (Fl.G.3s) and marks the rejoining with the main river of the arm of Goldhanger Creek that has gone around the N side of Osea Island across the Stumble.

The river now runs up to Heybridge between the NE shore of Northey Island to port (site of the Battle of Maldon in 991 AD) and Mill Beach, which stretches from Decoy Point, at the mainland end of the causeway across to Osea Island, up river to Heybridge. The channel off Mill Beach is narrow and there's little water at LW, although at HW on a big spring tide Northey Island now largely floods.

There are moorings all along the Mill Beach foreshore, but the main marks to look ahead for are the towers of the old granary, with the tiny Saltcote SC on the shore beneath, and the Blackwater SC (a long white building with a black roof set behind the seawall), which shows an Iso.G.10s light at night.

The club has a large number of drying moorings, a concrete launching ramp and a floating wooden pontoon that cruisers can go alongside at HW.

Blackwater SC CM9 4SD
☏ 01621 853923
Email secretary@blackwatersailingclub.org.uk
www.blackwatersailingclub.org.uk

Off the BSC the channel turns SW around the No.8 PHB (Fl(2)R.3s) Hilly Pool Point off the N tip of Northey Island. We found little depth off this buoy at LW in 2018. As its name implies, the river bed here is uneven, but best water is found towards the mainland (W) shore.

Blackwater SC at Heybridge; here the river turns SW

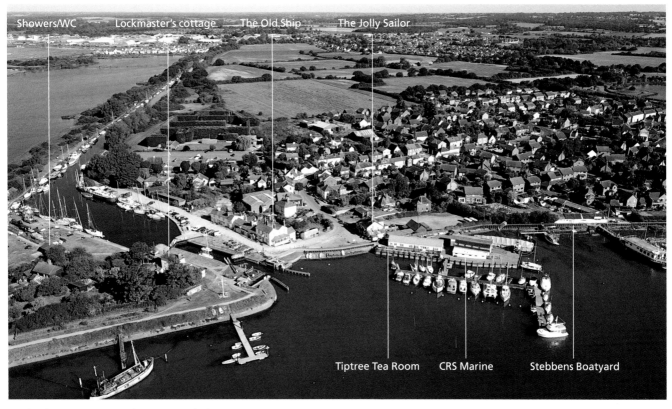

Showers/WC   Lockmaster's cottage   The Old Ship   The Jolly Sailor

Tiptree Tea Room   CRS Marine   Stebbens Boatyard

Heybridge Basin is a popular watering hole

Heybridge Basin lock

Heybridge Basin

Half way along Colliers Reach, so-called from the days when colliers brought up here, lies Heybridge Basin, the seaward end of the Blackwater & Chelmer Navigation, a canal running inland to Chelmsford. The basin is a traditional wintering berth for yachts but has also become a popular summer stopover. Its popularity means that prior booking is virtually essential.

Drying moorings extend along the foreshore between the Blackwater SC and the Basin lock, but not much further. The entrance to the lock is readily identifiable by a large clump of trees and white buildings with a space (the lock) between them. It is usually difficult to tell whether the lock gates are open or shut until directly in line with them as a red traffic light on the left hand side

HEYBRIDGE BASIN   CM9 4RX

Contact
VHF Ch 80
Callsign *Heybridge Lock*
Lock Master Grant Everiss ☎ 07712 079764
Email grant.everiss@waterways.org.uk
www.visitmaldon.co.uk/heybridge-basin
Access HWS -2hr, HWN -1hr;
0600-2000 May-Sept, 0800-1700 Oct-April, as tides demand
Facilities WC, showers, laundry
Water Taps, hoses
Electricity At shore points – tokens from Lock Office
Boat repairs Stebbens Boatyard ☎ 01621 857436 / 07974 530269
CRS Marine ☎ 01621 854684 / 07850 543873
Cranes 18-T at basin, 7-T at CRS Marine
Pub/Restaurant The Old Ship ☎ 01621 854150
The Jolly Sailor ☎ 01621 854210
The Tiptree Tea Room on seawall ☎ 01621 854466
Provisions Basics from small shop at rear of the Jolly Sailor, open in pub hours ☎ 01621 854210
Transport Bus to Maldon (infrequent)
Taxi ☎ 01621 855111, 355095

isn't used anymore. Having made contact with the HM on arrival you will be called in order to enter the lock.

The approach channel begins at the small Lock Reach SHB and is marked by a curving line of withies to be left close on your port side. There are depth gauges on either side of the lock entrance (shown in metres on the left, in feet on the right) and the lock is worked for about two hours before HW. There is almost always plenty of knowledgeable help with mooring lines once in the lock. Visitors should berth in the basin as directed. The Lock Master's cottage and office stands on the port side of the lock.

Once berthed in the Basin it is a pleasant dinghy trip up the canal (which has a 4kn speed limit) to land at a pontoon behind Tesco's supermarket in Maldon to re-provision. There is also a group of useful shops at Heybridge, reached by walking or cycling about 1M up the towpath and turning right along the road that crosses the canal. These include smaller supermarkets, a pharmacy, PO and small restaurant/takeaways.

In 2018 new lock gates were installed along with a new hydraulically operated cassion outer gate, which virtually doubles the lock's capacity. Major dredging to deepen, widen and straighten the approach channel was also carried out.

As an alternative to locking into the Basin, CRS Marine has drying pontoon moorings just outside the lock on the N side of the entrance, albeit with similar access times to the Basin, and some swinging moorings in the river.

Heybridge to Maldon

From Heybridge Basin, Colliers Reach continues SW to Herring Point, where the Blackwater becomes the River Chelmer, and turns NW once more, then W, and winds up to Maldon. A few smacks may be anchored opposite Herring Point in the bight off the end of the mole, but they dry out soon after HW.

Leave Herring Point No.9 SHB to starboard and keep following the red and green buoys as the channel first twists to the N, close to the E shore, then back W past the end of the Promenade (mole). Maldon YC (www.maldonyc.org.uk) stands on the W shore just S of the Promenade. A large yellow/black post with a yellow X topmark stands a short way along the promenade marking the inner end of a concrete launching ramp.

Lines of drying moorings outside the channel on both the Prom foreshore and the opposite bank, together with the channel buoys, give a good indication of the deep water. A sharp turn to starboard at the No.19 final SHB brings you onto a course parallel and close to the beginning of Hythe Quay. Beware Thames barges motoring to and from the Quay around tide time,

MALDON   CM9 5HN

Contact
River Bailiff ① 01621 875837 (office at Hythe Quay)
① 07818 013723
Email rivers@maldon.gov.uk
www.visitmaldon.co.uk
Access MHWS ±1hr to visitors' pontoon at Hythe Quay
Water Tap
Chandler Marinestore, North St ① 01621 854280
Gas Calor and Gaz at Marinestore Chandlers
Provisions In town
Post Office In town
Pharmacy and doctor In town
Boat repairs Various yards along North St and Downs Road including Shipways Boatyard ① 01621 854280 15-T crane, slipway, 20-T winch; Hedgecock's ① 07836 715685, 15-T crane.
Rigger TS Rigging ① 01621 874861 www.tsrigging.co.uk
Pub/Restaurant Queen's Head ① 01621 854112
Jolly Sailor ① 01621 853463
Many others in town
Club Maldon Little Ship Club ① 01621 854139 (Open weekends, Weds/Fri evenings)
www.mlsc.org.uk
Maldon YC
Email info@maldonyc.org.uk
www.maldonyc.org.uk
Taxi ① 01621 850850, 855111

because they need the full width of the deep water to manoeuvre, particularly if they are to be turned to berth at the quay with their heads downstream.

Visitors should lie alongside the floating pontoon set parallel to the N end of the Quay and be prepared to dry out, unless their visit is to be very swift at HW. There is no charge for the occasional overnight stay alongside this pontoon, though a charge may be made for longer stays. It has perhaps 2·5m at HWS and 1·0m at HWN.

Above the Hythe Quay, boatyards and mud berths line the W bank right up to the road bridge at the Fullbridge, but there are likely to be few available berths. A drying berth may be available on the upstream side of

One of several Thames Barges based at Maldon rounding Herring Point SHB on its way downstream

Approach to Maldon

the first pontoons belonging to Shipways Boatyard (see box), which is immediately above the Queen's Head pub and has Marinestore Chandlers on site. It's advisable to call first and enquire.

Maldon town climbs the hillside with the spire of St Mary's church standing clear above the masts of barges lying in their permanent berths at the Hythe, while further upstream and to the right are the grey buildings of the old timber yards and flour mills. This was once a thriving port with smacks lining the foreshore along the prom, barges being repaired at Walter Cook's yard (where the blocks are still used by barges), and barges and coasters coming and going to the mills, plus a number of busy boatbuilding yards above the town and a sailmaker in between. Today the barges at the Hythe are used for corporate and private charters, and yachts and motor boats fill the mud berths that line the bank from the Hythe right up to the Fullbridge. However, the commercial traffic and smacks have gone, although several yards are still busy with yachts.

Maldon Little Ship Club stands behind the Quay and the Jolly Sailor and Queen's Head pubs serve the needs of thirsty sailors. The River Bailiff has his office at the

Visitors can lie alongside the Hythe Quay floating pontoon for short stays at high water

seaward end of the Quay close to Walter Cook's old black shed. The whole Quay has been 'sanitised', but there is still an East Coast air that thickens as you move up river through the various boatyards, where the charm of mud and old wooden boats still persists.

Looking upstream to the end of navigation on the Blackwater/Chelmer at Fullbridge

12. RIVER CROUCH

⊕ **Landfall waypoint**
51°41'·8N 001°08'·3E
Just S of Swin Spitway SWB
Charts
Imray 2000 series, Y17
Admiralty SC 5607, 3750
Tides
Burnham-on-Crouch HW Walton +0042
Crouch Harbour Authority
Harbourmaster ☎ 01621 783602
Email info@crouchharbour.org.uk
www.crouchharbour.uk

Main hazards

The Whitaker Channel, leading in towards the River Crouch, runs roughly NE-SW between Foulness Sand (on the S side) and the Buxey and Ray Sands (on the N side). All of these sandbanks are extremely hard and present a serious hazard to any vessel grounding in rough weather. The buoyage in the channel is excellent with marks at frequent intervals – and all of them lit.

There is shoal water between the Swin Spitway and the Whitaker Beacon, across the eastern tail of the Swallowtail bank, and the Swallowtail itself dries between points S of the Swallowtail No.2 and No.4 buoys. The channel between the Buxey Sand and the W end of the Swallowtail is narrowing but is still deep.

Tides are strong, but follow the courses of the channels without too much set across the sands.

Watchkeepers must keep a lookout for both inbound and outbound ships using the main channel along the S side of the River Crouch.

There are speed limits on different stretches of the Crouch and these are clearly indicated by marked buoys.

Approaches

From NW, N and NE From the Rivers Colne and Blackwater, and the Wallet, the normal route will be through the Spitway, which is the shallow channel running between the Wallet and the Swin. Identify and pass comfortably close to both the Wallet Spitway (L.Fl.10s Bell) and Swin Spitway (Iso.10s Bell) SWBs before turning WSW towards the Swallowtail route, or heading S for the Whitaker Channel.

As an alternative to the longer haul out to the Spitway, shoal draught boats coming from the Colne or Blackwater may slip through the shallow inshore Ray Sand (Rays'n) Channel. This runs between the Buxey Sand and the Dengie Flats. It is a passage recommended only on a rising tide, above about half tide, and with a close watch kept on the depth sounder. Recent information may be found at www.crossingthethamesestuary.com.

Starting from the Knoll NCB, reach the Swire Hole with its rapidly changing depths, then head WSW until the Buxey Bn bears S. Then alter course to about SW, leaving the Buxey Beacon ½M or so to port. While making towards the tall pylons on Foulness, look for the unlit Raysand North SWB (a pillar mark). Then turn S towards a second unlit SWB, the spherical Raysand Middle, and beyond it an unlit spherical yellow buoy

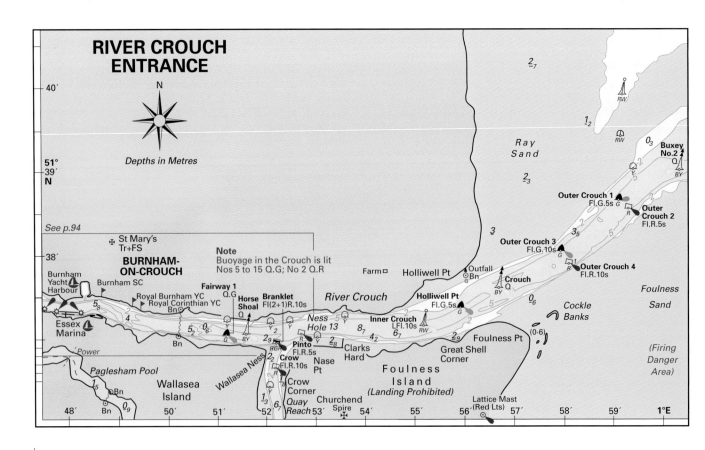

which lies on the northern edge of the Crouch. Once in the deeper water, head SSW towards the Outer Crouch No.1 and No.2 buoys.

Alternatively, a shallow draught boat can cut the corner more when on passage from the Blackwater. From Sales Point, round the tip of St Peter's Flats then shape a course of about 185°, leaving both of the outer wrecked target vessels about 1M W. After passing the Buxey Bn, which should be about 1M E, head a little more W (around 195°) and make towards the Foulness pylons, to find the SWB pillar and finally turning S as before towards the second SWB and the unlit yellow buoy.

From E, S and SE Coming in from the E means navigating through the off-lying sand banks towards the Inner Whitaker SCB (VQ(6)+LFl.10s) before heading SW into the Whitaker Channel.

From the River Thames or the North Kent coast, the navigator will again have to work through the sands before carefully crossing the NE end of the Whitaker Spit, which in recent years has been slowly growing to the NE.

Note that the NE extent of the Shoeburyness Outer Firing Danger Area covers almost the entire drying area of the Foulness Sand.

Entry

From the Inner Whitaker SCB, the Whitaker Channel runs SW for almost 9M to the Crouch NCB (Q) at Shore Ends. The deeper buoyed channel lies along the edge of the Foulness Sand with good water all the way, although care must be taken in the region of the Sunken Buxey where there is a kink in the channel between Buxey No.1 SCB (VQ(6)+L.Fl.10s) and Buxey No.2 NCB (Q).

The alternative route is along the Buxey side, although it does have one area of shallows. From the yellow Swallowtail No.1 (Fl.Y.5s), pass two more lit yellow special marks, then through a gate formed by the Swallowtail No.4 (Fl(2)Y.10s) and the Buxey Edge SHB (Fl.G.10s); cross shallows to pass the Swallowtail W WCB (VQ(9)10s) and the Sunken Buxey NCB (VQ), joining the main channel at the twin Outer Crouch buoys.

The Crouch NCB (Q) marks the start of the River Crouch itself. There is often a sizeable seal colony hauled out on the Foulness Sand shortly before Shore Ends, which makes a fine sight.

River Crouch
(via Whitaker Channel)

Crouch Q

Outer Crouch 4 Fl.R.10s — Outer Crouch 3 Fl.G.10s

Outer Crouch 2 Fl.R.5s — Outer Crouch 1 Fl.G.5s

Buxey No.2 Q — Buxey No 1 VQ(6)+LFl.10s

Whitaker 8 Fl(4)R.10s — Whitaker 7 Fl(4)G.10s

Whitaker 6 Fl(3)R.10s — Whitaker 5 Fl(3)G.10s

Whitaker 4 Fl(2)R.5s — Whitaker 3 Fl(2)G.5s

Whitaker 2 Fl.R.5s — Whitaker 1 Fl.G.5s

Inner Whitaker VQ(6)+ LFl.10s

245° 230° 245° 260° 245° 260° 265°

⊕51°40'·70N 001°09'·2E

River Crouch
(via Swallowtail/Sunken Buxey)

Crouch Q 245°

Outer Crouch 4 Fl.R.10s — Outer Crouch 3 Fl.G.10s

Outer Crouch 2 Fl.R.5s — Outer Crouch 1 Fl.G.5s

Sunken Buxey VQ. 230°

Swallowtail W VQ(9)10s 250°

Swallowtail 4 Fl(2)Y.10s — Buxey Edge Fl.G.10s 225°

Swallowtail 3 Fl.Y.15s 240°

Swallowtail 2 Fl.Y.10s 250°

Swallowtail 1 Fl.Y.5s

⊕51°41'·8N 001°08'·3E

Buxey Beacon NCM

Shore Ends to Burnham

From the Crouch NCB the river runs westwards past the Holliwell Point SHB (Fl.G.5s) and the Inner Crouch SWB (LFl.10s) for about 2¾M to the mouth of the River Roach, which opens S. A further PHB (Fl.R.5s), Pinto, lies over a wreck E of the Roach entrance. On the W side of the Roach entrance is the red/green/red Branklet 'preferred channel' buoy (Fl(2+1)R.10s), which marks the mud spit out from Wallasea Ness and must be left to port when heading for Burnham or to starboard if heading into the Roach.

Inner Crouch SWB

Looking upstream close to the Horse Shoal NCB. The wharf in the background is due to be removed in late 2019

From the Branklet buoy a slight dog-leg around the Horse Shoal NCB (Q) should keep you in a dredged section up to the Fairway No.1 SHB (Q.G), but there is some doubt about whether this is still a necessary diversion. From Fairway No.1 (marked 'F1') the marked deep-water channel runs onwards along the S shore of the Crouch, beyond Burnham town and the marinas. However, once the lines of moorings are reached there is good water anywhere across the river – but be aware of the tide, it can easily run at up to 3kn. Be careful also, when beating up river, not to stray into the breaks in the Wallasea Island sea wall opposite the whole Burnham waterfront. These breaches, made to create a wetland nature reserve on the island, have submerged obstacles in them to prevent navigation and the ebb pours out strongly through the gaps.

BURNHAM

Approaching Burnham-on-Crouch, the first of the long lines of swinging moorings on the N side of the river starts at the Rice & Coles boatyard, identified by a crane on the seawall and a landing pontoon. A group of four large yellow spherical buoys, a short way downstream, marks the crossing point for high voltage power cables and no attempt should be made to anchor nearby.

Anchoring is also prohibited anywhere in the Fairway and is to be avoided anywhere within the moorings.

Outside Burnham Week (usually the last week of August) there are moorings available up and down the river. These are looked after by the various boatyards and yacht clubs, which also have their own landing pontoons.

The first landmark for Burnham is the big white building of the Royal Corinthian YC. This club welcomes visitors on its all-tide pontoon – if you would like to use it or one of its several visitor moorings, call the club secretary (Open for food Weds and Fri evenings, all day Sat, Sun until early pm).

Royal Corinthian YC
☎ 01621 782105
www.royalcorinthian.co.uk

From there, amongst the housing along the river are the Royal Burnham YC, The Anchor, The White Harte, Prior's boatyard, and finally the Burnham SC before reaching Burnham Yacht Harbour. It's an interesting waterfront steeped in history, but is steadily changing as older sites are taken up with modern housing. However, it is still a centre for shopping, chandlery, sail and boat repairs or maintenance. A ferry service runs from the Town Quay (by the Anchor pub) across the river to Wallasea at Essex Marina in summer (for details see information panels).

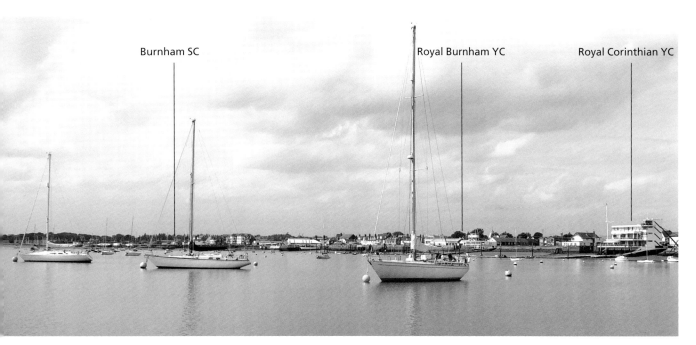

Burnham SC | Royal Burnham YC | Royal Corinthian YC

Burnham waterfront and moorings with Royal Corinthian YC and pontoon at far right

Burnham Yacht Harbour

The harbour is cut into the N shore of the Crouch, just up river from Burnham town, with a yellow pillar mid-channel buoy with an X topmark (Fl.Y.5s) off the entrance. It is important to pass close to this buoy, because the entrance channel is dredged through mud banks that dry.

From this offing buoy, head in towards a big blue-grey shed and pass between a pair of large metal posts, red (Fl.R.10s) to port and green (Fl.G.10s) to starboard.

There is no designated visitors' berthing, so call ahead and, if arriving late, request codes for the gate to the pontoons and the door to the ablutions block.

From the entrance, turn to starboard for pontoon row A and to port for row H. Berth numbers are on ends of fingers with low numbers close to the shore and high numbers near the river. Some fingers, particularly in row A, are shorter than the boats occupying them, which can make spotting the numbers difficult.

BURNHAM YACHT HARBOUR   CM0 8BL

Contact
VHF Ch 80
Callsign *Burnham Yacht Harbour*
Harbourmaster ☎ 01621 786832
office ☎ 01621 782150
Email admin@burnhamyachtharbour.co.uk
www.burnhamyachtharbour.co.uk

Access 24hr

Fuel Diesel berth on row 'F', landward end close to boat lift. Tight turning space

Facilities WC, showers, laundry, WiFi (free)

Water Taps and hoses on pontoons

Electricity On pontoons. Charged per night

Gas Calor and Gaz from chandler

Chandler Marinestore, on site, ☎ 01621 783090
www.marinestore.co.uk

Boatyard Boat repairs, 35-T travelift, 100-T slipway, all services

Sailmakers Lonton & Gray 01621 786200
www.lontonandgray.com

Provisions At Co-op (Fiveways), about 10 minutes walk up road from marina, or in town, about 15 minutes walk.

Post Office and pharmacy At Fiveways (near Co-op, see above)

Pub/Restaurant Swallowtail on site, many in town

Pharmacy At Fiveways near Co-op

Ferry Crossings to Essex Marina in season ☎ 07704 060482
www.burnhamferry.co.uk

Trains Direct to London

Taxi ☎ 01621 783007, 784878

Entrance into Burnham Yacht Harbour

Burnham Yacht Harbour

Essex Marina and Wallasea

On the S shore of the Crouch, slightly upstream from the Burnham Yacht Harbour, is Wallasea Bay with the Essex Marina, whose pontoons run parallel to the river. At the W end of the bay is the Baltic Wharf, which is a busy shipping wharf and watchkeepers must keep a sharp eye out for vessels manoeuvring in the main channel.

Approaching the marina is more a case of not passing it by. A pair of outer and inner pontoons run parallel to the river with entrances at both ends and a linking walkway between them and the shore in the middle. Riverside berths (along N side of arm 'A') are alongside the main pontoon, while all others are on fingers, every berth having a finger on both sides. Contact the marina office for berthing instructions and ask whether to enter from downstream (east) or upstream (west) end.

Wallasea to Althorne Creek (Bridgemarsh)

Above Wallasea and the Baltic Wharf the river turns NW through Cliff Reach with shallows along the N shore, so it's wise to leave Fairway buoys 13 and 15 Croshaw, both Q.G, to starboard. Here the Fairway ends, off Creeksea, and the river scenery becomes more rural and interesting when compared to the reaches below Burnham.

ESSEX MARINA   SS4 2HF

Contact
VHF Ch 80
Callsign *Essex Marina*
Harbourmaster ☎ 01702 258531
Email info@essexmarina.co.uk
www.essexmarina.co.uk
Access 24hr
Fuel Diesel and petrol from barge at W end beside boat lift
Facilities WC, showers, WiFi
Water On pontoons with hoses
Electricity On pontoons
Gas Calor
Chandler Marinestore, on site. ☎ 01702 258094
www.marinestore.co.uk
Boat repairs 70-T travel-lift, slipway
Pub/Restaurant Essex Marina YC restaurant/bar, open to all, closed Mon.
Ferry Crossings to Burnham town quay in season
☎ 07704 060482 www.burnhamferry.co.uk
Trains Rochford (4M away) for London
Taxi ☎ 01702 200200

Approaching the downstream ends of the two
Essex Marina pontoons

Offices Walkway Fuel berth

Essex Marina

The NW section to Althorne Creek and Bridgemarsh Marina, known as Cliff Reach because of the 40-50ft cliffs along the N shore, offers one of the few places in the Crouch with any shelter from NE winds. Anchorage can be found under the cliffs, but there are some foul patches along the low water line. If the wind goes into the W it can be very uncomfortable here and a move to anchor under the opposite shore may be worthwhile.

Ada Point and the entrance to Althorne Creek

Throughout Cliff Reach and indeed most of the succeeding reaches, the best water lies about midway between the banks, but keep towards the outsides of bends as there are often spits and shoals off points and headlands.

To port at the top of Cliff Reach is Black Point where the main river bends back SW and Althorne Creek runs off to the N behind Bridgemarsh Island (no landing allowed). Althorne Creek is the location of Bridgemarsh Marina.

Bridgemarsh Marina

Any intending visitors should call first as spaces are limited.

A large red beacon (Fl.R.5·5s) labelled Ada Point, off the E tip of Bridgemarsh Island, is the first sign of Althorne Creek. If entering the creek, leave this beacon to port and, as the entrance opens up, follow the line of red can buoys leading in around the bend W to the marina hidden behind the island. Approaching the marina the end of the main pontoon is directly ahead. A sign indicates that the fairway continues to port along

The pontoons of Bridgemarsh Marina seen from innermost channel buoy

BRIDGEMARSH MARINA CM3 6DQ

Contact
Office ☎ 01621 740414 / 07422 517024 (manager)
or 07753 315919 (Deputy)
www.bridgemarshmarina.co.uk
Access HW ±4hr
Facilities WC, showers
Fuel Diesel in cans
Water On pontoons
Electricity On pontoons
Gas Calor (Butane and Propane)
Boatyard Minor repairs, slipway, 9T crane, boat storage, scrubbing posts.
Pub/Restaurant Club Nautico bar/restaurant, on site
Transport Railway station, 1hr to London, 10 minutes Burnham.
Taxi ☎ 01621 783007, 784878

Approaching Fambridge pontoon from downstream

the S side of this pontoon. Least depth is less than 1·0m at the pontoon but the bottom is mud.

A separate, second pontoon stands beyond the first, on the far (W) side of the yard's slipway.

ALTHORNE TO FAMBRIDGE

From Ada Point the main river takes a dive SW past the yellow Canewdon racing mark (summer), then W along the S shore of Bridgemarsh Island, which floods on spring tides, through Easter Reach and NW through Raypits Reach before returning to a W'ly course with Shortpole Reach passing the W end of Bridgemarsh Island. (Circumnavigating Bridgemarsh Island by way of Althorne and Bridgemarsh Creeks is possible near HWS with a fair wind and a very shallow draught boat or dinghy, but there's an old ford to cross and the channel is tortuous, so it's quite an adventure.)

North Fambridge Yacht Station

A little over 1M above Bridgemarsh Creek (the W end of Bridgemarsh Island) there are lines of moorings at Fambridge, with the North Fambridge YC and North Fambridge Yacht Station on the N shore. The Station is a

120m long floating pontoon outside the North Fambridge YC clubhouse for visiting boats to lie alongside. This and the moorings are operated by the Yacht Haven (see below). Posts at each end of the pontoon are lit Fl(3)G.4s. Anchoring is only advisable above or below the moorings, but there is good depth. Astonishingly, the NFYC clubhouse, at the top of the ramp up from the pontoon, was designed by Brunel for use as a field hospital in the Crimean War!

As you approach Fambridge from downstream (E), you only see the end of the visitors' pontoon and may not appreciate its length until you are much closer. Berthing is available along both sides (1·2m least depth), as directed, but it can be crowded, so call ahead for a berth. (Phone is usually more effective than calling on Ch 80.) Alternatively, if you have found a berth, visitors can pay the flat rate berthing fees at the Ferry Boat Inn. If manoeuvering upstream of the visitors' pontoon, be aware that depths shallow rapidly inside the first line of moorings.

Note The North Fambridge Yacht Station and the Fambridge Yacht Haven are under joint management, hence the duplication of some contact and website details.

North Fambridge yacht station, looking downstream. Note the shoaling area immediately upstream of the pontoon

NORTH FAMBRIDGE YACHT STATION CM3 6LR

Contact
VHF Ch 80
Callsign *Fambridge Yacht Haven*
☎ 01621 742911
Email fambridge@yachthavens.com
www.yachthavens.com/fambridge
Access 24hr to moorings/pontoon
Facilities WC, showers, WiFi (free with code)
Water Hoses on pontoon
Electricity On pontoon
Gas Calor and Gaz from marina
Boat repairs Slip and 25-T hoist
Club North Fambridge YC www.nfyachtclub.co.uk
Email admin@nfyachtclub.co.uk
Pub/Restaurant Ferry Boat Inn at top of yard ☎ 01621 740208
Transport Railway station 1M in village, trains to London or Burnham (complimentary drop-off service provided)
Taxi ☎ 01621 850850, 855111, or ask in office

Fambridge Yacht Haven (Stow Creek)

A little over ½M upstream from Fambridge, Stow Creek branches off to the N with Fambridge Yacht Haven at the top. A lit yellow buoy is in the river off the entrance. In the mouth of the creek there's a beacon, known as Stow Post (Q(4)Y.8s), showing a 4kn speed limit sign. This should be left to port when making for the marina, despite some charts still suggesting it should be left to starboard, and there is a small green buoy on the E side of the entrance.

The ¼M channel is dredged, straightforward and is marked with small red and green buoys, all with reflective tape. There is a pair of lit (2Ldg.F) leading mark posts at the N end and you should find least depths of 1·5–2m. There is a substantial building on the skyline beyond that appears directly above the leading posts when on track. As soon as the marina opens up to starboard you can turn sharply in along the long pontoon, the fairway being on the S side. The fuel berth is just over halfway along.

Office   Slipway   Fuel berth   Yacht station

Stow Creek

Looking SE over entrance to Fambridge Yacht Haven

Leave post to port

Lit leading posts

Approaching Stow Creek

Turning into the Haven Marina

FAMBRIDGE YACHT HAVEN   CM3 6LU

Contact
VHF Ch 80
Callsign *Fambridge Yacht Haven*
Office ✆ 01621 740370
Email fambridge@yachthavens.com
www.yachthavens.com/fambridge
Access 24H
Fuel Diesel berth; petrol by jerry can or available for boats on trailers
Facilities WC, showers, laundry, WiFi (free with code)
Water Hoses on pontoons
Electricity On pontoons
Gas Calor and Gaz
Chandler Small stock on site
Provisions Basics available in clubhouse – see below
Boat repairs Slip and 40T boat hoist
Pub/Restaurant West Wick YC clubhouse/café/bar on site (closed Mondays) www.ww-yc.co.uk
Ferry Boat Inn, N Fambridge ✆ 01621 740208;
Transport Railway station 1M in village, trains to London or Burnham (complimentary drop-off service provided)
Taxi ✆ 01621 850850, 855111, or ask in office

STOW CREEK TO BRANDY HOLE

Just W of Stow Creek the main river turns SW past a small red buoy, while an arm called Clementsgreen Creek carries on W, but is not navigable for cruisers. The SW stretch of the river, called Brandy Hole Reach, has a SHB 'Brandy Hole' halfway along, and sees the Crouch becoming much narrower and shallower. A notice warns against anchoring above this point because of shellfish beds. Moorings here and beyond mostly dry at LW, although some remain afloat in Brandy Hole Bay, a designated water-skiing area, and near the landing pontoon on the S shore where the river once more turns W. The lines of moorings extend for over a mile up stream to Fenn Creek and beyond.

The old Brandy Hole Yacht Station no longer exists as a single entity, because the boatyard, with its slipway and pontoon, is now in different ownership from the building that was once the yacht club. The latter is now an event venue. If planning to visit the area, phone ahead to the moorings business as they may be able to meet you at the

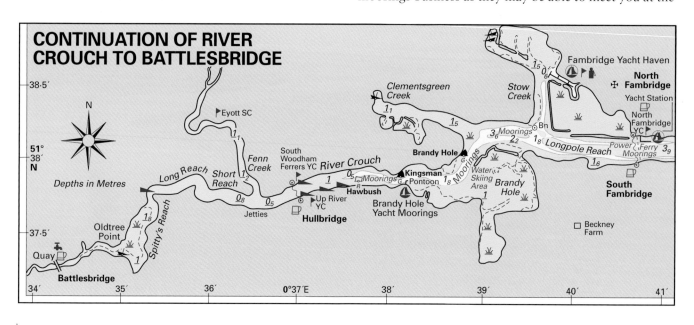

CONTINUATION OF RIVER CROUCH TO BATTLESBRIDGE

Approaching the Up River and South Woodham Ferrers clubs

BRANDY HOLE MOORINGS   SS5 6QB

Contact
☎ 01702 231496 or 07788 470718
Email info@brandyholemoorings.co.uk
www.brandyholemoorings.co.uk
Access HW ±4hr
Facilities Moorings, slipway, boat repairs,
canvas work
Landing At pontoon, but shoreside access gate may be locked;
contact Brandy Hole Moorings
Provisions At Co-op, Hullbridge, 20–30 minutes walk
Post Office Ferry Road, Hullbridge
Pub/Food The Smugglers Den (walk up river along sea wall)
☎ 01702 233428

The pontoon at Brandy Hole Moorings, and the restaurant beyond

(usually locked) gate off the pontoon. They will usually make room on the pontoon for you to stay if you are happy to take the ground.

Brandy Hole to Battlesbridge

The channel meanders on upstream through moorings, the deeper route marked by two unlit buoys, the Kingsman SHB and beyond it, the Hawbush PHB. We are now so far up river that HW is half an hour after Burnham, yet there are some very active clubs and large numbers of moorings.

The Up River YC has a private slipway and a clubhouse with bar, kitchen and changing rooms, plus moorings in the river. Both the dinghy and cruiser fleets are very active right through the season.
Up River YC SS5 6PA
www.upriver.org.uk

The South Woodham Ferrers YC stands on the N bank near the ford just E of Fenn Creek and opposite the Up River YC. The club has cruiser moorings, workshops and a large concrete slipway. There are showers and toilets in the clubhouse.
South Woodham Ferrers YC CM3 5WP
☎ 01245 329464
www.swfyc.com

From Fenn Creek the river runs west for a short distance, through moorings and past houses with shoreside moorings on the S bank. Occasional yellow buoys beyond the last mid-river moorings appear to suggest the best water, although the bottom seems fairly flat. From there, the river follows a winding, reasonably wide route until the final bend at Oldtree Point when the old mill buildings and antiques centre at Battlesbridge come into view; here, the banks suddenly close in and space to manoeuvre becomes severely restricted.

Battlesbridge

A visit to Battlesbridge is certainly an adventure. There is perhaps enough water on a high tide for a boat drawing 1·5m to get here for a swift pint in the local pub, but do not linger when the tide turns, and think about how you are going to turn round as soon as you arrive.

There is a private small craft landing stage on the S bank just before the bridge, where boats of up to 20ft can lie free of charge for a maximum period of 3hr. The ground at the small craft landing is fairly flat, but the mud at the opposite N wall slopes outwards and lying there with bilge keels would mean leaning out at an alarming angle, while a single keel boat would need to be leant inwards rather carefully to avoid rigging and guardrail damage. Beware also of a substantial horse in midstream, which is all ready to catch your keel as you turn the boat to head down river. With so little room to turn, only undertake the manoeuvre at or (better) just before HW.

Perhaps the best advice for any newcomer is not to plan on staying over a tide, or perhaps even visit at all, unless you have first reconnoitred by road at LW and sized up the situation.

Battlesbridge at LW, looking downstream from the bridge

13. RIVER ROACH

⊕ **Waypoint**
51°37'·0N 000°52'·3E Just E of Branklet buoy
Charts
Imray 2000, Y17
Admiralty SC5607, 3750
Tides
Paglesham HW Walton +0040
Rochford HW Walton +0050
Crouch Harbour Authority
Harbourmaster ☎ 01621 783602
Email info@crouchharbour.org.uk www.crouchharbour.uk
Roach Sailing Association
Secretary ☎ 07836 344508 *Email* roach@eastcoastpilot.com
www.roachriver.org.uk/rsa

Main hazards

There are two ways of entering the Roach and the only notable hazard is the entry via the Havengore Bridge, which requires good weather and shallow draught, plus permission from the live firing range officials. Otherwise, there are no real hazards within the Roach, provided you follow the channels and avoid spits extending from offshoot creeks.

There are a lot of fishing boat movements in the river, so anchorages need to be chosen with care to avoid obstructing fairways.

There is an 8kn speed limit in the Roach, reducing to 4kn in the creeks and through the Paglesham moorings.

Approaches

The Roach can be entered either from its junction with the Crouch or directly from the sea across the Maplin Sands, then through the Havengore lifting bridge and the inside creeks.

The flood tide in the creeks between Paglesham and the Havengore initially runs S towards and under the bridge, until at around HW-2 or less the Broomway covers; the current then reverses, flowing N under the bridge and along the creeks. The reverse happens on the ebb, the current initially flowing S, then reversing when the Broomway uncovers.

Section 1 of this chapter deals with the approach and entry from the Crouch, and the details of the river as far as Paglesham.

Section 2 describes the approach and entry from the sea across the Maplin Sands through the Havengore Bridge, and then on northwards through the creeks to join the Roach near Paglesham.

Section 3 describes the upper reach of the Roach from Paglesham to Rochford.

SECTION 1: FROM ROACH ENTRANCE TO PAGLESHAM

Approach from the Crouch

When approaching from the Crouch, make for the red/green/red Branklet 'preferred channel' buoy (Fl(2+1)R.10s) ½M E of the Horse Shoal NCB (Q), but remember to leave it on your starboard hand – the Branklet Spit is extensive.

Entry from the Crouch

Leave the Branklet preferred channel buoy close to starboard at the entrance in order to keep off the mud bank spreading out from Nase Point on the E shore. Then keep to the middle of the channel, favouring the outside of bends. There are racing buoys, but once past the Crow PHB (Fl.R.10s) further channel marks do not resume until approaching Paglesham.

Branklet to Paglesham

Unlike the Crouch, there is shelter to be found within the Roach from all wind directions. The first useful spot is in Brankfleet at the N end of Quay Reach, just within the mouth of the river, under the W shore, where there is fair depth close in under the sea wall and good holding. Be sure to remain N of the yellow racing buoy Jubilee, because this is positioned off a bay that dries out.

A few boats are occasionally moored on the E side of Quay Reach near a landing on Foulness Island, charted as 'The Quay'. The landing is none too clean and somewhat slippery, but gives access to the hamlet of Church End. It is all MOD land, so you must keep to the footpath, then road, and the walk is about a mile.

Right The Branklet buoy at the Crouch/Roach junction
Far right Landing spot in Quay Reach

The curving N entrance to Yokesfleet Creek, where a quiet shallow anchorage can be found inside

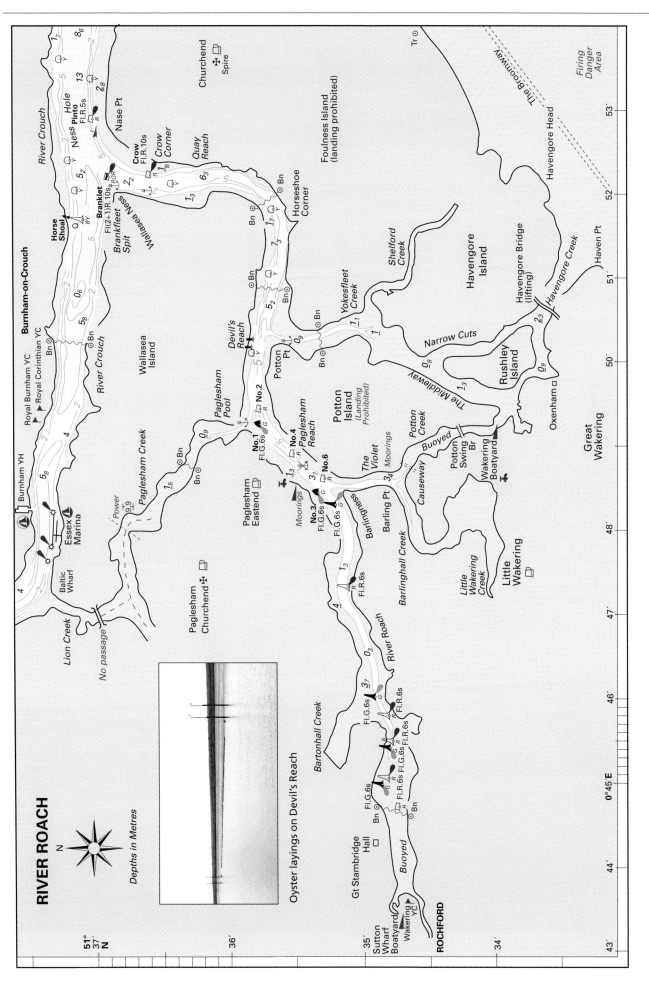

RIVER ROACH

Depths in Metres

Oyster layings on Devil's Reach

River Crouch

River Crouch

Burnham-on-Crouch

Burnham YH

Royal Burnham YC

Royal Corinthian YC

Baltic Wharf

Essex Marina

Power

Lion Creek

No passage

Horse Shoal

Brankfleet
Fl(2+1)R.10s

Wallasea Ness

Brankfleet Spit

Wallasea Island

Crow Fl.R.10s

Crow Corner

Quay Reach

Nase Pt

Ness Pinto Fl.R.5s

Hole

Churchend
Spire

Horseshoe Corner

Bn

Bn

Bn

Bn

Bn

Devil's Reach

Paglesham Pool

Paglesham Creek

No.2

No.1
Fl.G.6s

No.3
Fl.G.6s

Paglesham Eastend

Paglesham Churchend

No.4

Paglesham Reach

No.6

Moorings

The Violet

Potton Pt

Yokesfleet Creek

Foulness Island (landing prohibited)

Shelford Creek

Havengore Island

Havengore Bridge (lifting)

Havengore Head

Havengore Creek

Haven Pt

The Broomway

Firing Danger Area

Tr

Narrow Cuts

Rushley Island

Oxenham

Great Wakering

The Middleway

Potton Island
(Landing Prohibited)

Moorings

Potton Creek

Causeway

Buoyed

Potton Swing Br

Wakering Boatyard

Little Wakering Creek

Little Wakering

Barling Pt

Barlingness

Fl.G.6s

Barlinghall Creek

River Roach

Bartonhall Creek

Fl.R.6s

Fl.G.6s

Fl.R.6s

Fl.G.6s

Fl.R.6s

Fl.G.6s

Fl.R.6s

Fl.G.6s

Fl.R.6s

Fl.G.6s

Bn

Bn

Gt Stambridge Hall

Buoyed

Sutton Wharf Boatyard

Wakering YC

ROCHFORD

N

51° 37' N

36'

35'

34'

43'

0° 45' E

44'

46'

47'

48'

50'

51'

52'

53'

The S entrance to Paglesham Pool or Creek

Underwater power cables cross the river at the S end of Quay Reach where the channel bends sharply W. Keep to the outside of this bend where a yellow racing buoy 'Roach' indicates the deepest water. A short way on, in Devil's Reach, more cables cross and immediately afterwards Yokesfleet Creek opens off S to run down the E side of Potton Island. Another sheltered anchorage can be found just inside the entrance under Potton Point, but beware the mud banks on either side of the entrance.

On the N side of the main channel close W of the Yokesfleet Creek mouth there are oyster layings on a substantial floating structure between pairs of lit posts. Similarly, beware some possible layings on the Potton side a little further on.

It's at this point that the river turns SW into Paglesham Reach. On the corner, a narrow creek branches off NW, confusingly known as both Paglesham Creek and Paglesham Pool. There's a small, sheltered anchorage just inside the mouth, protected by the withied mud spit off the western point, but it's best found below half tide with a close eye on the echosounder. The gutway is very narrow. A shoal draught boat should be able to lie afloat here at LWS. There is a landing about 100m above the pill box on the point, a timber walkway laid directly on the saltings, from where it is possible to walk to the Plough and Sail pub at the top of the lane above the boatyard.

Plough and Sail ☎ 01702 258242
www.theploughandsail.co.uk

Also on the corner are fairway buoys No.1 (Fl.G.6s) and No.2, which start the buoyed channel through the Paglesham moorings. This fairway is used by many fishing vessels going to and from their moorings up the river and anchoring is prohibited. Boats wishing to anchor must do so either above or below the lines of moorings and set a riding light. The Roach Sailing Association (see RSA contact details at start of this chapter) manages most of the moorings downstream from the hard, and visitors may use any vacant ones with permission.

The old black, timber shed of what for years was Shuttlewood's yard will be seen on the N side, together with a pontoon landing and hard. Landing on the pontoon is not encouraged (indeed in 2018 its owners were not maintaining it and it appeared to be in a poor state) though it's unlikely you will face objections if going ashore by dinghy; you may choose instead to use the hard immediately adjacent to the downstream side of the black shed. The RSA also manages a short stretch of shoreline immediately upstream of the old yard, including a short jetty, and you are welcome to land there near HW if you wish. Look for the bow section of a small boat on the salting, pointing skywards.

It is under the mud of the Paglesham foreshore that the remains of HMS *Beagle* are believed to have been found. Darwin's famous ship was pensioned off after her third voyage, a survey of Australia, and used for some years as a Customs watch vessel in the Roach. Then she

Looking upstream at Paglesham from above the RSA-managed moorings

MAPLIN SANDS

APPROACHES TO
HAVENGORE CREEK

Depths in Metres

was sold for scrap in 1870 and what are believed to be her remains have been discovered in the Paglesham mud, together with possible parts incorporated in the structure of Shuttlewood's black shed.

The pontoon and the hard at Paglesham, a huge houseboat obscuring most of the black shed

SECTION 2: THROUGH THE HAVENGORE BRIDGE TO PAGLESHAM

Approaches to the Roach across the Maplin Sands

The main barrier to entering via the Havengore Bridge is the depth on the Maplins, particularly over the Broomway, which is an ancient raised track that dries about 4m, so has only about 2m over it at HWS (on a big tide) and often as little as 0·5m at neaps. On an average spring tide, boats with as little as 1–1·5m draught may still touch as they cross the Broomway and, sensibly, should only attempt it in smooth sea conditions. A local saying has it that when there's 5m height of tide at Southend, there's 5ft over the Broomway. It seems to be a reasonable equation, but monitor the PLA's broadcasts detailing actual tidal heights, which include Southend, on Ch 69 at H+15 and H+45, to discover any significant variation from the predicted height.

The approach across the sands requires good weather and a suitably high tide, plus permission from the Shoeburyness Firing Range Officer (Ch 72 *Shoe Base* or ☎ 01702 383211) before setting off across the sands towards the Havengore Bridge. Maximum recommended

Blacktail W beacon, in deep water 3½ miles SE of Havengore Bridge

Looking NW in Havengore Creek, the bridge beyond the two SWBs

draught for using this 'overland' approach (or exit) is 1·5m, even at HWS. The Shoebury ranges are used on most weekdays from 0600-1630 (1230 on Fridays), although permission to cross them may be granted if circumstances permit, with 24hr notice to the Range Officer. The bridge is manned every day HW±2hr (daylight hours only) and may be lifted on request. It has bars hanging beneath it and there is no room nor indeed permission for any craft to pass without the bridge being lifted. Contact the Bridge Keeper (VHF Ch 72 *Shoe Bridge* or ☎ 01702 383436) to confirm opening – but be

warned, it has been prone to breakdown in recent years. The ECP website usually carries news of any outages in its News section, and warnings may also be included in HMCG's MSI broadcasts.

There are two suggested routes for the first part of the passage towards the bridge across the Maplin Sands shown on the chartlet on page 105. Start either route no earlier than HW-1½hr. Watch the depth constantly and keep your boat speed down, because uncharted obstructions do exist on the sands although these routes are used frequently by leisure craft. Contact the Bridge Keeper when about 1½M away.

The first route, for boats approaching from E, starts close to the Blacktail West beacon and requires a course made good NW for 2·8M to reach the vicinity of the SE end of a line of three large steel posts. These posts are not usually charted, the area to head for is at approximately 51°32'·70N 000°52'·50E as shown on the chartlet on page 105.

The second route begins close to the S Shoebury SHB (Fl.G.5s). If early, and the weather is quiet, the 'artificial island' close NW provides a waiting anchorage in a gully on its W and N sides. Recent charts may show that this island (an experiment in land reclamation) does not cover, but it appears to be eroding quickly. From the island, a course of 006° made good for 1·7M will bring you to a charted wreck shown on the chart as an unlit IDM. Leaving this mark a good 25m to port, turn onto a course of about 065° for 0·45M towards the area mentioned above at 51°32'·70N 000°52'·50E.

There are (in 2018) three heavy posts in a generally straight line leading 320° and the bridge will be seen some 1·5M distant, bearing 305°. Leave each post to starboard. The third post reached differs from the other two in that it has cross-pieces attached all the way up, and is close to the Broomway, where the shallowest water may be expected.

After this final post, look approximately NW close to the eastern side of Havengore Creek entrance where you should see a small conical Safe Water Buoy. Be aware there is an unmarked submerged wreck 50m to stbd of the rhumb line from the post to this buoy. As you reach the buoy, look towards the bridge and you should see a tall withy - leave this to port before reaching another SWB and beyond it a starboard-hand withy.

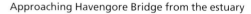

Approaching Havengore Bridge from the estuary

From here, head along Havengore Creek towards the bridge, finding the deeper water towards the east side of centre. Ignore a group of poles seen across the channel to port, on the S side near Haven Point.

Caution Be aware also that withies in this whole area, as in similar places, do come and go over time as they collapse or are knocked down, and eventually replaced. That any withies and buoys are there at all is due solely to the voluntary work of Roach Sailing Association members.

HAVENGORE

Contact
Havengore Bridge ① 01702 383436
Range Officer ① 01702 383211
VHF Ch 72
Callsigns *Shoe Base* (Range Officer);
Shoe Bridge (Havengore Bridge keeper)
Range activity information is often included in MSI broadcasts
Range Information
https://shoeburyness.qinetiq.com/public-safety/information-for-mariners.aspx

Havengore Bridge

The bridge is much larger than might be expected and is heavily used by MoD traffic, but the Keeper will do his best to accommodate yachts wishing to pass through, after consultation with the Range Officer if the range is active. Traffic lights show clearly when to proceed through the open bridge. If the tide is still flooding, you may find it running hard beneath the bridge. Yachts in particular should keep to the E side passing through the bridge to ensure enough air draught.

Once through the bridge, Rushley Island lies immediately ahead. Boats heading for the Crouch and Paglesham will generally take the right fork, Narrow Cuts, and that is the recommended route N for those not thoroughly familiar with these waters. The left fork leads to the S ends of both the Middleway and Potton Creek.

You may find it helpful to view online aerial photography of the area as this can give a good idea of the route to take for the best water. These are all creeks for exploration on the last of a rising tide with plenty of time to retreat before being stranded, but they do have an air of muddy secrecy that can be appealing.

Route inbound from the Bridge via Narrow Cuts

Though drying, Narrow Cuts, as its name implies, is a narrow, dug channel that gives the best route between the Havengore Bridge and the Middleway and Yokesfleet Creek beyond, and onwards to the Roach. It is marked with withies, but they are infrequent so do follow them carefully - at HWS the expanse of water seems wide because the saltings each side are covered all the way to both sea walls. In particular, note that nearing the N end of Narrow Cuts the best water is very close to the eastern sea wall, from a point where a red beacon stands on the wall with railings and steps down.

Reaching the junction with the Middleway, be aware of the extensive mud spit that stretches out from the western corner. Turn NNE to continue towards the Roach along Yokesfleet Creek.

Yokesfleet Creek

Shortly after joining the Middleway and heading NNE, two others branch off SE. The first is the dammed New England Creek; the second is the narrow and drying Shelford Creek which is a dead end. The Middleway becomes Yokesfleet Creek, swinging NNW and on to its junction with the Roach. A good anchorage can be found in the last half-mile or so, and also close under Potton Point, with shelter from all but N or S winds.

Reaching the Roach, be aware of the long spit of mud extending from Potton Point as you turn into the river. Turn west here, upstream, to reach Paglesham after about a mile, or east towards the Crouch.

Routes inbound from the bridge via the Middleway and Potton Creek

Taking the left fork westwards after passing inbound through Havengore Bridge, you should find occasional withies leading you past the west side of Rushley Island, the best water generally following the outside of the bends. After about half a mile you will see pontoon moorings ahead at the S end of Potton Creek, where the Middleway also begins - if following the shallow Middleway, turn north with the better water favouring the west side to meet the junction with Narrow Cuts described above.

Continue WNW instead to enter Potton Creek, with the pontoon moorings on your port side. Potton Creek can be used by boats with as much as 2m draught, but only near HW on a good tide. The bottom along this stretch is fairly flat with no defined gutway, as the pontoons and cranes of Wakering Boatyard at Bullman's Wharf come into view.

There is good water up to the yard, over 3m at HWS. Great Wakering village is a good mile's walk from the yard.

WAKERING BOATYARD   SS3 0DA

Contact
① 01702 219422
Email wakeringboatyard@outlook.com
www.wakeringboatyard.co.uk
Access HW±2hr
Facilities WC
Electricity On pontoons (limited)
Water
Slipway
Services Boatyard storage with water and electricity available, tradesmen, 7·5T-hoist, 20T-crane, salvage

Potton Creek northwards, approaching Wakering Boatyard

Continuing N'wards beyond the yard, Potton Bridge comes into view. This swing bridge will operate on demand, HW±2hr, call VHF Ch 72 *Potton Bridge*, ☎ 01702 219491. The deepest water from hereabouts follows a gutway, well marked by withies and buoys. Pass through the bridge on its east (Potton Island) side to reach a port-hand withy soon after. Continuing N along the marked channel, Potton Creek crosses a ford, which is very hard and raised about 2ft above the river bed. It should be approached with caution, and above half tide.

Soon after the ford, after a narrow gate between a PHB and a withy, a branch off to the SW is reached, Barlinghall Creek which meanders narrowly and muddily up towards Little Wakering. Continuing N instead, along The Violet, another half mile brings you to the Roach, heeding the No.6 PHB which marks a long spit reaching out from Barling Ness. Paglesham is then in view to starboard, close downstream.

Potton Bridge swings open for us, heading N. The starboard side has the best water

SECTION 3: FROM PAGLESHAM TO ROCHFORD

Paglesham to Rochford

The final stretch of the Roach up to Rochford begins a short way above the last of the Paglesham moorings, at fairway buoys No.3 (Fl.G.6s) and No.6, N of Barling Ness. The main channel of the Roach continues W above Barling Ness. There is good water with up to 1·5m at LW as far as the old Barling Quay on the S shore, but then it shallows considerably and, sensibly, can only be explored close to HW. That said, boats of up to 1·5m draught do make it up the next 1½M towards Stambridge Mills on the top of the tide. Pilotage in this section was made easier in recent years with the laying of new lit buoyage for much of the route.

The buoys encountered first on the way upriver are brightly coloured plastic pillar buoys about a metre high, each lit Fl.6s in their respective colours. The first of these, Blackedge, is a SHB just beyond the entrance to the Violet. The channel is wide and reasonably deep here and the second buoy, the Barling PHB, is ¾M further on, as the river bends to the SSW just before the old Barling Quay. The Bartonhall SHB is a further ¾M upstream, opposite Bartonhall Creek. The Mucking PHB closely follows, then a few hundred yards beyond and round the next river bend to W and then WNW, there are two 'gates' of buoys, closer to the N shore, the Lower Rochford PHB and SHB, then Top Rochford PHB and SHB. Between the two gates, you may see 8kn speed limit reminder buoys with lollipop topmarks.

The channel swings to port after passing between the Top Rochford pair, and from here the best water is marked by a succession of eight port- and stbd-hand

SUTTON WHARF · SS4 1JU

Contact
☎ 01702 546147
Email suttonwharf@outlook.com
www.suttonwharfboatyard.com
Slipway 50T/80ft limit
Crane 35T-hoist
Berthing Pontoons, alongside and swinging (all drying)
Electricity Water
Repairs Including upholstery
Yacht Club Wakering YC ☎ 01702 542545
www.wakeringyachtclub.com *Email* wakeringyc@gmail.com
Open Fri evenings and Sunday lunch times, bar only

buoys, all lit QR or QG. These are laid and maintained by local organisations. You may also see a few withies, and the RSA advises that any you find should be stbd-hand withies.

The river makes its final bend to starboard (towards the old Stambridge Mills) at the last of the SHBs, Sutton Wharf No.1 QG.

Opposite, to port, you will see the Wakering YC pontoons which are lit 2R(vert) on their ends. The club has drying berths alongside the walk-ashore pontoons with water (and possibly electricity if pre-booked) and space for visiting shoal-draught boats. ☎ 07703 774686 in advance for visitor berth availability.

Following the river to starboard, round the SHB, the large Sutton Wharf Boatyard lies to port. The yard has pontoon and quay berths and other services.

Sutton Wharf and Wakering YC, at the head of the Roach

14. CANVEY AND LEIGH

Charts Imray 2100, C1, C2
Admiralty SC5606
Honorary Port Pilot Rob Scriven ☏ 07860 828048
Email canvey@eastcoastpilot.com

This chapter is in two sections – the first describes the north and east aspects of Canvey Island, and nearby Leigh-on-Sea, while the second describes Holehaven on the west side of the island.

Note There is no water-side marine fuel available anywhere in this whole area.

1. LEIGH, EAST CANVEY AND BENFLEET

⊕ **Landfall waypoint**
51°30′·95N 000°42′·90E Close S of Leigh SHB
Tides HW Sheerness

Hazards

Apart from Ray Gut itself and parts of Hadleigh Ray, this entire area, including many moorings, dries soon after half ebb. Potentially extremely uncomfortable in strong E winds unless in the creeks. Only attempt entry on a rising tide and only in a shoal draught boat.

Entry

The unlit Leigh SHB marks the entrance to Ray Gut, which gives access to Benfleet, Smallgains and Leigh Creeks, and lies ½M 290° from the end of Southend Pier (2F.G.13m8M). Apart from the pierhead, there are no lit marks at all in this area.

It is unlikely that you will find enough water to pass the Leigh buoy much earlier than HW-4. Benfleet YC's members' rule of thumb for getting right up Benfleet Creek from here is that the Marsh End Sand should already be covered and the tide rising. There is excellent information available including recent survey and guidance notes on the Benfleet YC website, www.benfleetyachtclub.org. Details particularly in Benfleet Creek itself can change from year to year.

From the Leigh buoy, head NW and pass through a red buoy, then a pair of R and G buoys during the first ½M, the channel curving slightly to port. Then turn onto about 290° as you head for the large fishing boat moorings in deeper water in Hadleigh Ray. About 0·9M further on, small buoys, some lit, leading off generally NW show the entrance to Leigh Creek.

LEIGH-ON-SEA

Leigh Creek is marked with lit buoys, the lights on some being unreliable; there is a port/stbd pair at its start, then port-hand buoys only. It has an exaggerated S-bend, first to right then left, as it passes outside the large cluster of

Leigh Marina   Victoria Wharf   Bell Wharf   Leigh SC

Leigh-on-Sea waterfront from the E, at LW

LEIGH MARINA   SS9 2ES

Contact
☎ 01702 479009
www.leighmarina.co.uk
Facilities WC, showers
Electricity On pontoon
Water On pontoon
Boatyard Slipway, crane, 13-T travel hoist,
engineer, repairs.
Also Mike's Boatyard Repairs, 6-T crane ☎ 01702 713151
Clubs Leigh SC ☎ 01702 476788 www.leighsailingclub.org;
Essex YC ☎ 01702 478404 www.essexyachtclub.co.uk
Email mail@essexyachtclub.co.uk
Leigh MBC ☎ 01702 714858 www.leighmotorboatclub.com
Pub/Restaurant Several close by
Transport Bus station, trains to London
Taxi ☎ 01702 334455, 861998

yacht moorings, and is quite narrow. For a trip ashore to the interesting Old Leigh or beyond, you could consider staying afloat in Hadleigh Ray and taking the dinghy into the creek. There is a small and basic set of drying pontoon moorings at Leigh Marina with some facilities, at the W end of the waterfront reached by closing the waterfront and following the narrow gutway past the town.

Instead of Leigh Marina, you may find room to dry out alongside Bell Wharf (W side has flat mud) or against the E side of Victoria Wharf, although both can be busy with fishing boat movements and there was no room at all when we visited in 2018. Alternatively, it may be better to request a spare mooring from one of the two clubs in the town. Leigh SC is based in the old railway station behind Bell Wharf, and the Essex YC is based in the old minehunter *Wilton* 200 yards to the E where there is also a drying pontoon on the ship's E side with fresh water available. The two clubs' moorings are

Leigh-on-Sea from the E, the final creek buoy in the foreground

Essex YC from the same point, their pontoon lying along the far side of the *Wilton*

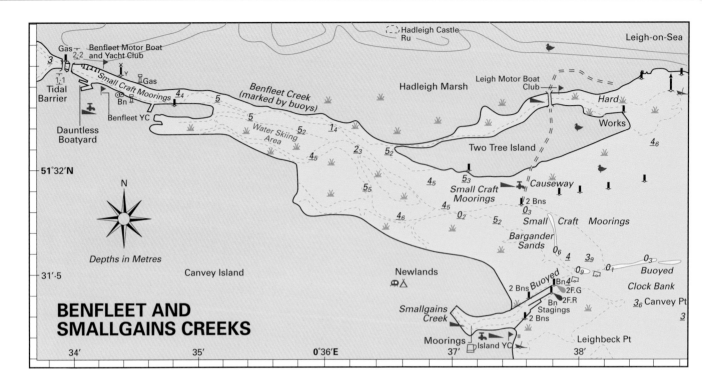

mostly on firm flat mud where a bilge-keeler should stand upright, but do ask the club(s) for local advice, especially if you choose to anchor instead, as there are occasional holes and gullies. It is not advisable to try to walk ashore at LW.

Leigh Creek meanders on behind Two Tree Island to its road bridge, where you will find Leigh Motor Boat Club based in an old barge (see page 111 for contact details).

Smallgains Creek

The Island YC stands on the very E point of Canvey, close by an old Roman dock and pottery on the S shore of the drying Smallgains Creek, an inlet at the E end of Canvey Island, and looks out SE across the Estuary. It has a forest of wooden staging moorings along the S shore of the creek with some more on the N side near the entrance.

To reach the club, continue W along Hadleigh Ray past the entrance to Leigh Creek, following the large fishing boat moorings along the S side in the deeper water.

Smallgains Creek, looking W from above its entrance

Approaching Smallgains Creek

Monitor the depth constantly. Pass the club's yellow waiting buoy (dries at LWS), then follow the channel WSW between lit PHBs and SHBs and posts to the entrance to Smallgains Creek and enter between the wooden piers, the eastern ends of which are lit 2FR (vert) and 2FG (vert). Just inside the entrance there is a short, steep slipway up onto the S staging, which is suitable for tenders.

The deeper water follows the N shore once inside, past two green buoys, then crosses to the S after the creek bends to port – two green posts in the water and a pair of leading mark posts on the S bank show the crossover route. From there, follow the S shore one boat's length off the sterns of moored craft.

There's a broad club-owned slipway on the S shore and immediately before it is a visitors' pontoon, alongside Brinkman's Wharf, which is the quayside area where IYC stores boats and gear. Some visitors choose to pick up a mooring out in the Ray – anchoring there is not advised because of clutter on the bottom – and land by dinghy. However, the club says that visitors will always be found a space.

Just upstream from the IYC slipway is the start of AW Marine's extensive staging and pontoon moorings, all drying, where you may be able to find a visitor berth on request. Half way along the S shore is the main slip, opposite which, on the N side, is another slip serving boats on that side of the creek.

ISLAND YACHT CLUB SS8 7TX

Contact
① 01268 510360
Email admin@islandyachtclub.org.uk
www.islandyachtclub.org.uk (includes sketch chartlet)
Access HW±1hr
Facilities WC, showers, visitors' pontoon, slipway
Taxi ① 01268 681999

Island YC visitor pontoon and slipway

AW MARINE 'The Marina' SS8 7TJ

Contact
① 01268 680606
Harbourmaster ① 07900 517906
Email awmarine@btinternet.com
Access HW ±1hr
Facilities WC, showers
Slipway 40-T cradle
Boat repairs Shipwright on site
Services Electrical, electronic, engineering, rigging services to order
Café On site
Taxi ① 01268 681999

Benfleet Creek

At the W end of Hadleigh Ray, a narrow buoyed channel heads off NW towards Two Tree Island and becomes Benfleet Creek. The Benfleet YC stands on the N shore of Canvey Island, E of the tidal barrier across Benfleet Creek, and has moorings in the creek. The creek and its approaches dry, so if you are unfamiliar with the creek and are trying to reach the club, a rising tide is essential, as is shoal draught. You should phone ahead for advice about a mooring or a place on the slipway and refer to the comprehensive guidance notes and diagrams on Benfleet YC's website.

There are two routes from the Hadleigh Ray roughly NW towards a pair of starboard hand posts with conical tops. Between them there are shallows and a sand horse. The N route was once buoyed, but is no longer. The S route, known locally as 'The Hole' is deeper and the preferred route, and can be found by following the line of moorings, which include two belonging to BYC. When nearing the two green-topped poles, turn WNW to leave them close on your starboard side.

These two starboard hand posts mark the end of a wide concrete causeway/slipway extending S from Two Tree Island where there is water available. The island is a nature reserve and is 20 mins walk from Leigh Station.

Leaving the posts at the end of the causeway close to starboard, turn W and leave more moorings close to

BENFLEET SS8 0QT

Contact
① 01268 792278
Email secretary1@benfleetyachtclub.org
www.benfleetyachtclub.org
Open every day with food available, hours vary
Tides HW Sheerness +0010
Club Benfleet YC
Facilities WC, showers, slipway
Water From club
Chandlers (both close outside club gate):
Dauntless Yacht Centre ① 07771 944288
www.dauntlessyachtcentre.co.uk
Email info@dauntlesstachtcentre.co.uk
Essex Marine (mainly engine spares) ① 01268 795554
Boatyard Dauntless Boatyard ① 01268 793782
www.dauntlessboatyard.com *Email* info@dauntlessboatyard.com
Toilets, slipway, travel hoist 20T/46ft, crane 18T, boat repairs and engines
Gas Calor and Gaz from Camping & General (20 minute walk)
① 01268 692141
Pub/Restaurant In south Benfleet, 10 minute walk
Taxi ① 01268 556666

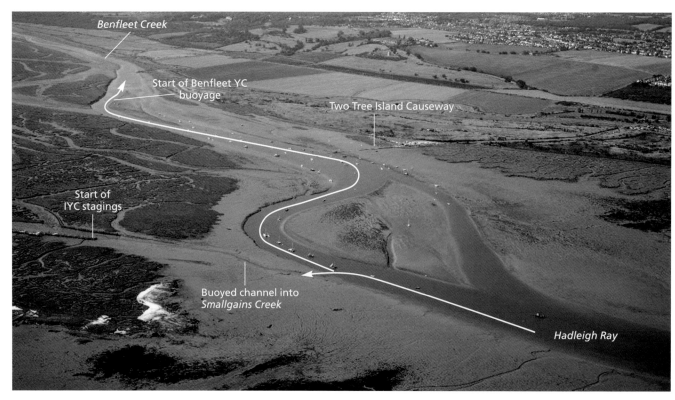

Passage from Hadleigh Ray to Smallgains Creek and Benfleet Creek shown clearly at LW *Patrick Roach*

Passing the beacons on the end of Two Tree Island

Approaching Benfleet YC

The head of Benfleet Creek

starboard, aiming for a large yellow/white buoy in the distance towards the S side of the creek, before reaching the first Benfleet YC large SHB just beyond it. Then follow the R and G buoys (all these buoys are numbered and belong to the club, but be aware there are also a few yellow or white racing buoys, which do not mark the channel) as the channel meanders from one side of the creek to the other, eventually guiding you close to the N bank where you pass the start of the club's moorings on your port side. Just past the start of the stagings, take particular care to follow the buoyed dogleg from the N bank to the S bank – there is a submerged cliff of mud to catch you if you carry straight on. The channel on this dogleg is quite narrow. After crossing over, continue

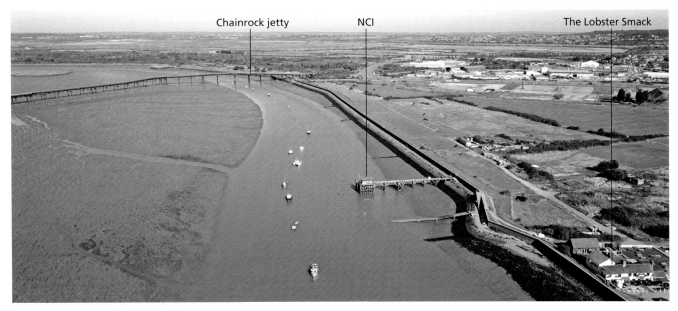

Chainrock jetty   NCI   The Lobster Smack

Holehaven Creek, from overhead the entrance looking N

upstream along the S side until the clubhouse and slipway show on the port bow. Pontoon moorings lie parallel to the shore just beyond the slipway.

On the N shore, opposite BYC, are the moorings of Benfleet Motor Boat and YC (① 01268 753311), actually a pub which may also be able to help out with a berth although in generally even shallower water.

Note that even the locals will not leave Benfleet Creek once the tide is ebbing – always leave with some flood left. The ebb runs so fast that if you touch, you will almost certainly not get off.

2. HOLEHAVEN CREEK

HOLEHAVEN CREEK

⊕ **Landfall waypoint**
51°30'·50N 000°33'·19E (close S of creek entrance)
Tides HW Sheerness +0010

Holehaven is a possible venue to wait for the tide when on passage up or down the Thames. Its shallow entrance may limit its usefulness on upstream passages. A dinghy trip ashore is possible.

Hazards and approach

There is little depth in the entrance at LWS. Heavy commercial traffic passes the entrance and has to be crossed on arrival and departure because all small craft in this part of the Thames must use the south side of the river, whether bound up or down stream.

Final approach to Holehaven Creek entrance will need to be made from a point on the opposite shore when traffic permits.

Entry

The entrance, close downstream from the London Gateway Container Port, is not obvious until close to and the access channel is narrow with little water at LWS. There are large mooring buoys on the E side, large

HOLEHAVEN   SS8 0NR

Possible local advice from the NCI
Contact
① 01268 696971
VHF Ch 65 Callsign *National Coastwatch Holehaven*
Fuel Petrol station 1M
Pub/Restaurant See text

ships may be lying moored to the E of these. Enter close to these buoys. Once over the bar and about 200m inside, it deepens to about 2·5m least depth. The line of moored fishing boats is on the W edge of the best water. The gutway appears to be very narrow in places.

Anchor toward the S end (not amongst moorings) or you may be able to borrow a mooring – all are private, and there are no visitors' moorings. Beware of stone groynes on the E side.

Two cables in, there is a slipway to starboard (with a starboard hand post at its outer end), which is steep at its inshore end where dinghies can land. Just beyond is the old HM's office on a pier, now occupied by the National Coastwatch Institution. The NCI Station volunteer staff may be able to give advice or, out of hours, ring the PLA Duty Officer ① 01474 562215.

Behind the wall here is the Lobster Smack pub (① 01268 514297) with its popular restaurant; the pub is mentioned by Charles Dickens in *Great Expectations*.

The deep water runs on for another ½M before reaching the disused Chainrock Jetty, which has 11m air draught clearance. If access N is required by boats that can't pass beneath the jetty, follow the drying gutway that starts just W of the jetty to join the deeper water again behind Coryton.

The channel meanders on inland, marked by lit PHBs and used by barges, to a junction where the drying East Haven Creek wanders away NE towards Benfleet beneath a tidal barrier (2·8m) and a fixed road bridge (3·1m). Alternatively, the equally shallow Vange Creek can be followed NW beneath another tidal barrier (8·8m) then through small boat moorings to Wat Tyler Country Park.

15. RIVER THAMES

⊕ **Landfall waypoint**
51°29'·56N 000°52'·61E Close N of Sea Reach No.1 North

Charts
Imray 2100, C1, C2
Admiralty SC5606 1185, 1186, 2151, 2484

Tides
HW Sheerness; HW London Bridge

Port of London Authority (PLA)
☎ 01474 562200 www.pla.co.uk
www.boatingonthethames.co.uk

London VTS
Callsign *London VTS*
VHF Ch 69 (PLA seaward limit to Sea Reach No.4)
Ch 68 (Sea Reach No.4 to Crayfordness)
Ch 14 above Crayfordness including the Thames
Barrier Control Zone

HM Coastguard
London Coastguard Ch 16 (Shell Haven to Teddington)
☎ 020 8312 7380 or call *UK Coastguard* on Ch 16

Thames Barrier Control
VHF Ch 14 Callsign *London VTS*   ☎ 020 8855 0315

Main hazards

Large ships, floating debris, shallows on the bends, fast river buses upstream from Woolwich. As on any river, substantial floating debris can be encountered and a good lookout should be kept. There are many large mooring buoys, some now lit with a fixed blue light, but others unlit.

Approaches

The pair of Sea Reach No 1 buoys marks the seaward end of the dredged channel into the River Thames and is the gateway to the centre of the deep water shipping channel.

Small craft should stay outside this main channel and make their approach to the Thames following the edges of the drying shallows, staying well out of the way of commercial shipping to comply with the PLA's General Direction 39, which states: *'The Master of a sailing vessel or vessel less than 20m in Length Overall shall ensure that the vessel keeps out of the way and does not obstruct or impede the operation or safety of any vessel approaching, leaving or manoeuvring on or off any berth or ship facility on the Thames'.*

Sea Reach to Tower Bridge: General information

A first trip up the Thames from out in the Estuary may seem daunting, but it's straightforward and should be an interesting experience to be enjoyed and remembered. The Port of London Authority (PLA) is responsible for navigational safety and related matters on the tidal Thames and publishes a useful River Thames Recreational Users Guide, available as a booklet or downloadable from its recreational website, www.boatingonthethames.co.uk.

Southend Pier to East Blyth buoy

E Blyth (Q)
Cross Main Channel
0·97M 220°
W.Leigh Middle Q.G
Leigh
Southend Pier 2F.G
2·8M 262°
⊕51°30'·80N 000°43'·30E

RIVER THAMES – SEA REACH

Depths in Metres

See plan

The river passage begins at the two Sea Reach No.1 buoys, although the PLA's Lower River Sector actually starts at the pair of Sea Reach No.4 buoys Fl(2)5s(sync) R and G respectively, N of the Medway entrance.

Passage planning

When planning your passage there are five particular areas of importance:

1. Will you have enough time?

The tides run strongly in the river, reaching 4kn in places at springs, and if you want to run the whole way to St Katharine's in one 'hit', the 40M can be readily achieved with a boat speed of 4-5kn – HW London Bridge is about 1hr later than at Sheerness.

Conversely, the trip down river gives only about 5hr of fair tide. However, the combination of the tide plus 5kn of boat speed should still see you off the Medway by LW if you set off downstream from Tower Bridge at HW-1 (London Bridge).

With the need to depart upstream at LW, the Queenborough moorings and Stangate Creek anchorage are ideal spots to wait for the tide. A good time to leave Queenborough is 1-1½hr before LW Sheerness.

A possible alternative point of departure is Holehaven (see 'Canvey and Leigh' chapter) on the western edge of Canvey Island. It's 8M up river from the Nore Swatch and that allows a later start – check the charted depths at the creek entrance, though, to ensure you can leave when required.

You could also break the journey using moorings at several locations, described in this chapter.

2. Will the Thames Barrier be open?

The Thames Barrier is closed regularly for testing, as well as in times of flood risk, and the Barrier Duty Officer should be contacted when planning the river passage to ensure closure is not planned for the day of your trip. Test closure dates are published in advance by the PLA and can also be accessed via the 'Thames Updates' page at www.eastcoastpilot.com. When the Barrier is closed, other flood gates are closed too, for instance sealing off Embankment Marina (Gravesend).

3. Which side of the river should you use?

It is a PLA requirement that the first part of your upstream journey has to be made along the S shore to stay clear of the commercial installations at Canvey, Coryton and the London Gateway Container Terminal, and well south of the buoyed Yantlet Channel and outbound Yantlet Secondary Channel. Note that you may encounter ships coming downstream in this Secondary Channel, which means they will be S of the buoyed main channel!

Despite this widely known requirement, the authors have frequently seen skippers of leisure craft not complying with it. Skirt the shallows on the south side, stay out of trouble and stay safe.

If leaving from Holehaven, cross immediately to the S side when safe to do so. If inbound from NE, cross to the S side of the estuary from W Leigh Middle SHB (Q.G) heading SW towards E Blyth NCB (Q), as shown on charts.

Further up, in Lower Hope Reach, resume the starboard side of the river and stay to starboard for the rest of your journey upstream.

Outbound, it is again a PLA requirement to stay on the S shore throughout, crossing NE, if necessary, only between the pairs of Sea Reach Nos.4 and 5 buoys. This crossing point is also clearly charted.

The ebb tide roars past the Broadness buoy, near Gravesend

London Gateway container port

4. Have you got enough fuel?

It should be noted that there is only one location on the Thames between the Estuary and Tower Bridge where you can readily take on fuel alongside through a hose and that is at the fuel barge just downstream from St Katharine Docks. There is no fuel available at Queenborough. The nearest in the Medway is at Gillingham.

5. Have you booked a berth?

Note that visitors are generally only accepted at the five London marinas – Gallions Point, West India, South Dock, Limehouse, and St Katharine's – if they have booked a berth in advance. The marinas are usually busy and often full, especially in high season. You may be asked to show proof of third party insurance on arrival. Incidentally, you may well be visited by the police making routine security checks at any London marina, if not on the river itself.

VHF Communications

The river is heavily used by commercial traffic, large and small, and a constant radio watch on the appropriate London VTS channel is sensible. Like any port controllers, the harbourmasters who man the VTS communications are primarily there for commercial

shipping, but will always help leisure sailors with advice and guidance in a professional manner. If in doubt, ask, but remember that good and succinct radio procedure will smooth the way if you do talk to them.

Information is broadcast by *London VTS* on Ch 14 and 69 at H+15 and H+45, and on Ch 68 at H and H+30.

If you have a AIS transceiver on board, it is doubly important to monitor VTS because they can specifically identify you and may wish to contact you.

Finally, a point about distress calls on the river – because virtually everyone is monitoring the correct *London VTS* frequency, a distress call made on that frequency rather than the conventional Ch 16 would be instantly heard on many craft. The PLA Harbourmasters and London Coastguard, who sit in the same room at the Thames Barrier Control Centre, tell us that this is now common practice.

Medway to Gravesend

For the passage to London, leave Queenborough at LW-1 to 1½hr and route by way of Grain Hard SHB (Fl.G.5s) and Grain Edge SHB (unlit) to the Nore Swatch PHB (Fl(4)R.15s). Shoal draught craft will cut this corner slightly with care.

From Nore Swatch, make good about 295° through the Swatchway S of Nore Sand, past the Mid Swatch SHB (Fl.G.5s) and 290° to the W Nore Sand PHB (Fl(3)R.10s). Between these buoys, inshore, there is an arc of orange buoys marking a firing range off the shore of Grain. Just W is a wandering gutway marked with a conical beacon that leads into Yantlet Creek, a possible stopover for shoal draught boats able to take the ground.

Continuing past the Yantlet Flats, towards the E Blyth NCB (Q), the small town of Allhallows is prominent on Grain. From there the N and S shores close in, and it starts to feel more like a river than an estuary.

Take care with the depth along this stretch – the shallows on the S shore push further to the N. The huge London Gateway container port stretches along the N shore beyond Holehaven.

Coalhouse Point – do not pass the beacon inshore between the yellow buoys!

Marina and Gravesend SC

Approaching Gravesend

Embankment Marina entrance   Gravesend SC and pontoon   Gutway to marina

Embankment Marina and Gravesend SC near LW

The entrance to Holehaven Creek (see page 115) opens on the N shore about ¾mile before you reach the Mid Blyth NCB (Q). The creek can be hard to make out from afar, but the entrance is just W of the four commercial jetties on Canvey.

About 3M further on, once past the Cliffe Fleet (Q.R) and Lower Hope (Fl.R.5s) PHBs, the river turns S into Lower Hope Reach (The Lower Hope). The shore to port is flatter and shallower around the bend, so do not cut the corner.

The deep water channel here is much narrower and it's time to change sides of the river. Look for a gap in the traffic, watching astern for small, deep-laden coasters typically using the same inshore course and plan to reach the W side beyond Mucking No.5 SHB (Fl(3)G.10s).

The river now bends to starboard round Coalhouse Point, with its curious tower that looks exactly like a giant box-kite, into Gravesend Reach. Rounding the bend just inside the Ovens SHB (Q.G Bell), a line of yellow buoys stretches from the shore out to the S end of the first of six groynes, all marked with posts and lit Fl.G.2·5s. It is essential to leave them all to starboard. Pass close N of Tilbury SCB (Q(6)+LFl.15s) to keep clear.

Once in Gravesend Reach, Gravesend town is in sight ahead on the S shore. Large tugs moor along the shore off the Embankment Marina and the Gravesend SC, both of which can be hard to spot. The clubhouse is about 500 yards before the town proper and is a low building with a white flagpole. There is a long apartment block behind to the SW. The gated entrance to the marina faces NW and is immediately adjacent to the E side of the clubhouse and, like several locations on the tidal Thames, also has a floodgate.

RIVER THAMES

GRAVESEND

Tides HW Sheerness +0025

THE EMBANKMENT MARINA   DA12 2RN

Contact
Harbourmaster ☎ 01474 535700
Email info@theembankmentmarina.net
www.theembankmentmarina.net
Access HW-1hr to HW via lock gate,
0800–2000 1 April–31 October;
1000–1600 1 November–31 March
All locking by prior arrangement
Max length/beam 27m/6m/2m
Facilities WC, shower, pump-out
Water, Electricity On quayside
Slipway For small boats only, inside marina
Club Gravesend SC ☎ 07506 367699
Email secretary@gravesendsc.org.uk
www.gravesendsc.org.uk

The gates at Embankment Marina

The Embankment Marina is in the old basin of the Thames and Medway Canal, built early in the 19th century to carry munitions from the Thames to the naval dockyards at Chatham. The canal was never successful, was soon superseded by the railway (which actually uses the canal tunnel near Strood), and much of it has been filled in. The marina, dredged to 1·5m over soft mud, is basic but it is a potentially useful stop, although limited by access – only the inner lock gate survives and so it is only opened near HW on free flow. The approach to the entrance is along a gutway which runs NW-SE from the deep water, and through the bridge. Phone in advance to arrange a visit.

Gravesend SC (details above) has no visitor moorings, but will always try to allocate you a vacant club mooring if you ask – maximum length 36ft. The club has a useful but drying pontoon attached to the frontage and parallel to the gutway (this alignment is useful on your approach), which affords brief access to dry land without ladders at around HW. The club also may be able to help with launching craft up to 20' and one ton.

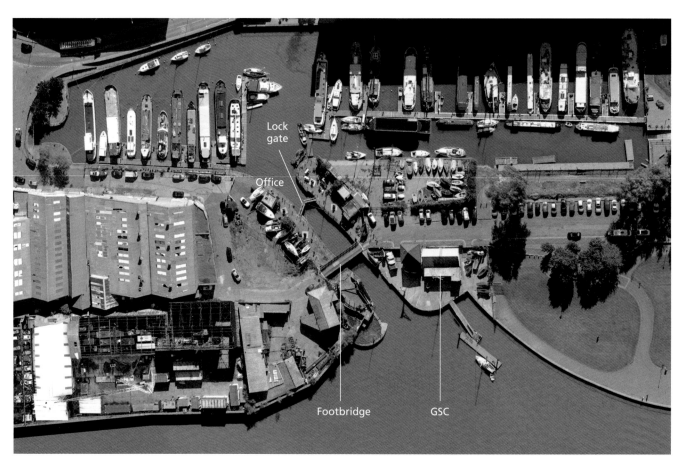

Lock gate

Office

Footbridge   GSC

Embankment Marina

The Port of London Authority (PLA) has a number of local moorings, large yellow cans laid off and just up river from GSC, which may be available for a small charge. A PLA launch (the PLA offices are just up river) may call to collect mooring fees and give advice. There is also a sturdy wooden all-tide ramp at the W end of the promenade (300 yards W of GSC) where you can land from a dinghy.

It is also possible, only if booked in advance, to moor on the large pontoon joined to the downstream end of the public Town Pier (this is the second pier you come to upstream from the marina and GSC). It is a very substantial metal-sided pontoon, and can be subject to wash from passing ships – be sure to arrange adequate fendering even though you will probably be berthed on

GRAVESEND PONTOON

Contact
☏ 07949 750236 or 07798 885332
www.gravesendpontoon.co.uk
Email alan.kew@btinternet.com
Access 24H
Electricity, water On pontoon
Pub/Restaurant Many in town
Transport Trains to Medway Towns and London.
Taxi ☏ 01474 369369, 353535, 535455

DA11 0BG

the inside. Shoreside access is via the Town Pier. A berth here is bookable with Gravesend Pontoon Ltd, which also manages three swinging moorings immediately downstream from the pontoon.

Gravesend town pier and its pontoon

Moored off Thurrock YC

Greenhithe moorings and slipway

Gravesend itself is an interesting town steeped in history with pleasant riverside walks. Sadly there is still an air of dereliction about the land E of the marina gate, in contrast to the splendid esplanade to its west.

Gravesend to Erith

As you continue westwards passing the town of Gravesend, the Tilbury cruise ship and ferry terminal are seen on the N side. A small ferry runs across the river here from the Town Pier.

The shipping activity continues, especially on the N shore, as you leave Gravesend Reach and turn gently to starboard into Northfleet Hope. (Incidentally, a 'fleet' is an area of shallow water and 'hope' means a small bay and the anchorage off it.) Round this corner, facing W, is the entrance to Tilbury Lock, used by merchant ships – your listening watch on Ch 68 will help with news of movements. There is a container ship terminal to starboard by the lock entrance, followed by a large grain

terminal, which can be an unpleasant source of dust in a N wind. Also this area can be choppy in strong winds as the currents swirl around the bend.

Up ahead to starboard, as development thins out on both shores, is Thurrock YC, identifiable by three large grey and white tower blocks close by and yachts moored in the river near the end of the club's landing stage. Visitors' moorings may be available by arrangement. The club is now in a fine building ashore, but was once in the ancient Gull light vessel whose light mast stands at the head of the slipway. The club is open most weekdays until 1600, weekend lunchtimes, and Thursday evenings. The moorings are well sheltered from the N.

Thurrock YC RM17 6JF
☎ 01375 373720
www.thurrockyachtclub.org.uk

After Thurrock, the river turns SW for a mile or so in St Clement's or Fiddler's Reach and a modern housing development at Greenhithe covers the S bank with woods behind. Towards the W end of the modern housing there are a few PLA-owned moorings close inshore, some usually unoccupied - as at Gravesend, a PLA launch may call to collect mooring fees. There is a charted sturdy wooden slipway S of the moorings where you can land by dinghy. The interesting historic part of Greenhithe is all close to the top of this ramp, fronted by the ancient Pier Hotel (no longer a hotel), which includes a restaurant (DA9 9NN, ☎ 01322 382291). There is a corner shop and a large superstore, both about a 10-minute walk, and a railway station very close to the river with trains to London and the Medway Towns.

The huge QEII road bridge (53m) dominates the view ahead as the river turns NW into Long Reach. Here the tide can run well in excess of 3kn under the bridge and you have 17M to go to Tower Bridge.

Beware of ships manoeuvring at busy berths on the N shore below and above the bridge. In the far distance, large wind turbines can be seen at Dagenham and to port is the prominent concrete blockhouse of the Dartford Creek Tidal Barrier.

Rounding Crayford Ness to port (where you must switch your listening watch from Ch 68 to Ch 14), Erith YC, a large building with a sloping roof, is conspicuous ahead on the S shore with many yacht moorings close by.

Erith Yacht Club

The club welcomes visitors and offers a useful stop if you are running out of tide on passage between London and

The QEII Bridge

Erith YC - drying pontoon by clubhouse, slipway and jetty to the right

the Estuary; there is likely to be a vacant mooring for monohulls up to 35ft on request – contact the secretary using details below. Be aware that 2·1m below the surface there are bridles between adjacent moorings in each line. Larger boats can anchor just upstream, where holding is good in mud. You will be able to lie for a short time alongside the pontoon in front of the clubhouse – this has about 3·5m depth (max) and dries – but the club cannot accommodate overnight stays on it.

Immediately upstream of the clubhouse is a long concrete jetty, its end marked by a red post, on which you can land from a dinghy at LW.

About ¾M further upstream (beyond the substantial commercial jetty and close to two tower blocks) is the charted town causeway, where you can also land by dinghy, with a large supermarket close by. There is a smaller supermarket a short walk from the club.

ERITH YC   DA8 2AD

Tides HW Sheerness +0030
Contact
VHF Ch 37
Callsign *Erith Yacht Club*
☎ 01322 332943,
Hon Secretary ☎ 07946 068358
Email secretary@erithyachtclub.org.uk
www.erithyachtclub.org.uk
Open Sundays all year, Weds lunchtime, Fri evening
Facilities WCs, showers
Max length on moorings 11m
Water/Electricity On tidal pontoon
Fuel 1M away at garage
Provisions See text
Transport Buses pass club gate; trains from Erith.

Gallions Point Marina lock gates are beyond the lattice tower on the N shore of Gallions Reach

Lock gates

Erith to Thames Barrier

Continuing up river, the environment once again becomes industrial with an enormous landfill site on the N shore at Rainham Marshes and the Ford motor works at Dagenham beyond, around Jenningtree Point. On the S shore opposite Fords, a structure like a beached whale is actually a sewage works.

Rounding Cross Ness point into Barking Reach and passing the modern sprawl of Thamesmead to port, a huge illuminated sign board stands on the N shore in front of stacks of shipping containers. This is the downstream signal station for the Thames Barrier. It displays the London VTS VHF Channel and phone number, and the CEVNI symbol for '*Stop as required by regulations*'.

The sign is 3M from the Barrier; after another ¾M as you round Margaret Ness, call '*London VTS*' at the Thames Barrier Navigation Centre on VHF Ch 14, and announce your position and intentions. Keep it brief – wait for a pause in the constant radio traffic then say for instance: "*London VTS, yacht 'XXXX', Margaret Ness, upstream, permission to pass through the Barrier please.*" You will usually be given the all clear and told which span to pass through. Small craft may be asked to call again when you have the Barrier in sight.

Beyond Margaret Ness, in Gallions Reach you will find the gated entrance to Gallions Point Marina to starboard. The entrance is not at all obvious from a distance, but is 400m upstream of a lattice radio mast on

The downstream sign board for the Thames Barrier

RIVER THAMES

Gallions Point Marina lock gates

GALLIONS POINT MARINA   E16 2QY

Pre-booking essential for visitors
Tides HW London Bridge -0015
Contact
VHF Ch 80
Callsign *Gallions Point Marina*
Harbourmaster ☏ 020 7476 7054
Email info@gallionspointmarina.co.uk
www.gallionspointmarina.co.uk
Locking hours 1000-1645 weekdays, 0900-1645 weekends
Access HW±5hr
Max length/beam 22m/7·6m
Facilities WC, showers, pump-out
Slipway In marina
Water On pontoons and quay
Electricity On pontoons
Gas Calor (berthholders only)
Engineer On site
Provisions Retail Park to N; shops to W in N Woolwich; both 10 minute walk.
Transport Docklands Light Railway (Gallions Reach). Buses. London City Airport

the N shore. Note that if the Thames Barrier is closed, as a flood precaution or for testing, this marina will be inaccessible, because there is a floodgate outside the lock that is always operated at the same time.

There are shallows to be aware of on the N side of the final approach if near LW. There are no buoys or waiting pontoons. Advance booking is required and we have often found the place full.

The lock is a modern one built into the original huge lock that gave entry to the Royal Docks and takes a maximum length of 22m. The operator will be on your port side on entry and will usually pass down lines.

Being close to the end of the City Airport runway, the location is subject to aircraft noise, except at night (2230-0630) and from 1300 Saturday to 1230 Sunday.

Vessels on passage down stream from the non-tidal Thames often use Gallions Point Marina as a stopover to wait for the tide. It is also handy for visiting the ExCeL

exhibition centre, close by. This part of the old docks is undeveloped and much of its hardware – huge capstans and bollards, for instance – remains and is kept smart, and there is much wildlife around too.

The river sweeps past Gallions Point with Woolwich to port, turning W into Woolwich Reach. Just ahead are the Woolwich Ferry terminals, large grey rectangular buildings standing on each shore. The two ferries (if both are operating) cross the river frequently, but they will use Ch 14 to give warning and will respond to a call on the radio if confirmation is needed.

The Thames Barrier

The Thames Barrier, less than a mile from Woolwich Ferry, displays clear lights on each bascule to indicate which span (gap) to use: the lights form a green arrow pointing in from each side of the span in use, and a red 'X' either side of spans that are closed.

Charts show the designation of the spans (B to G with C, D, E and F most frequently used), also see the diagram on page 121. When you are told which span to use, London VTS will use the letter, e.g Foxtrot Span. These letters are not marked on the barrier itself.

Provided you are on the starboard side of the river, the green arrows will be obvious – they have a narrow beam and would not be visible to anyone travelling up stream on the incorrect side of the river (as we understand sometimes happens). Do not approach within ¼M of the Barrier unless you are on passage through it and, if you have a working engine, you are required to use it, not sail through. If in any doubt, do not hesitate to contact the TBNC, where your query will be handled with courtesy.

Thames Barrier Navigation Centre (TBNC)

Contact
VHF Ch 14
Callsign *London VTS*
☏ 0203 260 7711

Green arrows

Approaching the barrier, lined up for the designated span

THAMES BARRIER TO GREENWICH

Greenwich Yacht Club

Less than 1M above the Barrier, the grey building of Greenwich YC stands on stilts against the S bank. The club welcomes visitors and is open on Tuesday evenings and at weekends. A call to the Harbourmaster may result in permission for an overnight stop or short stay on a mooring among the trots some way upstream, or possibly against the all-tide pontoon in front of the clubhouse if you are less than 13m LOA. The pontoon has water and electricity and least depth about 1·7m. At night, the pontoon is lit 2F.R.(vert). The pontoon can be badly affected by wash from passing barges.

Just beyond the elegant white towers that carry a cable car system across the river, modern apartment blocks and the huge white dome of the O2 now dominate the scene, virtually filling the Greenwich Peninsula at the end of Bugsby's Reach.

Greenwich YC pontoon

GREENWICH YACHT CLUB · SE10 0BW

Tides HW London Bridge -0010
Contact
VHF Ch 37
Callsign *Greenwich Yacht Club*
Enquiries ☎ 020 8396 0321 ext 0
Harbourmaster ☎ as above ext 31
or 07415 682823
Email harbourmaster@greenwichyachtclub.co.uk
www.greenwichyachtclub.co.uk
Open weekends and Tues evenings
Facilities (when club open) WC, showers
Water On pontoon
Electricity On pontoon
Slipway Yes (public but a fee for parking at GYC)
Provisions Shops 20 minute walk
Transport Underground (N Greenwich) and Cable Car, 20mins

Beside the O2, on Blackwall Point, is the upstream-facing signal station for the Thames Barrier, identical to the one downstream at Barking and serving the same function – from here you will call '*London VTS*' again on your return journey.

A point of interest to starboard is London's only lighthouse, on Trinity Buoy Wharf, once used for testing and training at this former maintenance site for Trinity House.

Once past the Dome and into Blackwall Reach, the Greenwich Meridian is crossed and the massive office

Greenwich YC

RIVER THAMES

Trinity Buoy Wharf and its training lighthouse

blocks of Canary Wharf stand out to starboard. Over on the W side of Blackwall Reach, through an impressive blue-painted lifting bridge, lies the West India and Millwall Docks complex; this includes marinas in Poplar Dock and Blackwall Basin, as well as extensive quayside moorings in West India Dock.

Access to Blackwall Basin and Poplar Dock involves an air draught limit of 5·2m, passage through a lock and five more bridges after the blue bridge and is not normally possible at all during business hours.

Furthermore, neither generally offers visitor moorings.

However, West India Dock, which covers a huge area behind the lock normally has visitor moorings available, but only for pre-booked groups of six or more boats. It is popular for club visits and also regularly accommodates superyachts, Naval visits and tall ships. On approach to West India, having booked in advance, contact the dock office on Ch 13 when about 10 mins away.

The lock is immense, hence the preference for fleets rather than single leisure boats. Berthing beyond is

The West India Docks area

The Blue Bridge, gateway to West India and Millwall Docks

against the S wall, which has a low timber 'rubbing strake' that may be awkward for any less able crew members on boats under 30ft with low freeboard. The dockside has water, power and toilets, but is in a public area without the security normally offered by a marina.

The nearby Museum of Docklands (E14 4AL, ☏ 020 7001 9844) is well worth a visit.

Upriver of the entrance to West India, beware of shallows on the inside of the bend as the river swings round Saunders Ness to reveal the glorious buildings of the Royal Naval College at Greenwich and the National Maritime Museum, together with the legendary tea clipper Cutty Sark.

> From here onwards, the river is usually made uncomfortably choppy by the wash from barges and coasters, as well as the many pleasure boats and very fast river buses that ply the waterway. Great care should be taken when working on deck – prudent skippers should now consider preparing fenders and shorelines, wherever is their destination.

Greenwich to Tower Bridge

After Greenwich the river turns N into Limehouse Reach and, half way up on the W side, is London's largest marina, the 200-berth South Dock Marina at Rotherhithe.

South Dock Marina

Inbound to the marina, call the lock office when passing Cutty Sark. Advance booking is required. The entrance is just downstream from Greenland Pier, a large pontoon with a white painted and roofed ramp to the shore. This pier is a frequent stop for the fast river bus services and the area is often very choppy, especially in a breeze. It is

WEST INDIA AND MILLWALL DOCKS

Tides HW London Bridge -0010

1. WEST INDIA VISITOR MOORINGS
(Canal & River Trust)   E14 9ST

Contact
VHF Ch 13
Callsign *West India Dock Control*
Marine Control (manned 24/7) ☏ 020 7987 7260 or 07710 175280
General enquiries ☏ 0303 0404040
www.canalrivertrust.org.uk
Visitor moorings Fleets of about six or more only; pre-booking essential
Access HW±4hr between 0700-1900 (but small craft schedule to arrive around HW)
Facilities WC, showers
Water Quayside
Electricity Quayside
Gas Calor or Gaz available nearby
Pub/restaurant Many in area
Provisions Shops at Canary Wharf
Transport South Quay (Docklands Light Railway), Canary Wharf (Tube), Buses

2. BLACKWALL BASIN
(Canal & River Trust)   E14 9SF

Visitor moorings not generally available
Contact for entrance See West India details above
www.canalrivertrust.org.uk

3. POPLAR DOCK MARINA
(British Waterways Marinas Ltd)   E14 8EG

Visitor moorings not generally available
Contact for entrance See West India details above
Contact for office See Limehouse Marina details, page 129/130
www.bwml.co.uk/poplar-dock-marina

possible to wait on the inside of the Greenland Pier pontoon – there's enough length for a 34-footer N or S of the ramp – but it can be very rough indeed there and boats must be well fendered and not left unattended. Alternatively, there are usually lighters moored downstream of the entrance and you may be able to hang off one of these. You may choose instead to wait on idling engine just downstream of the lock.

Beware of strong cross currents when entering the lock. Inside, there are permanent looped lines hanging down on each side of the lock and, if you can moor starboard side to, the lock keeper may also be able to pass lines.

Fast ferries and choppy conditions, both hazards for small craft

Approaching South Dock Marina

Inside the lock at South Dock

This marina is unique among the London destinations in that it is on the S bank of the river; many Thames visitors seem to pass it by, but its public transport connections are very good indeed, it is particularly close to the attractions of Greenwich and there is good local shopping. There is a sailing centre with a slipway in the adjacent huge Greenland Dock, once a centre for the whaling trade.

South Dock Marina

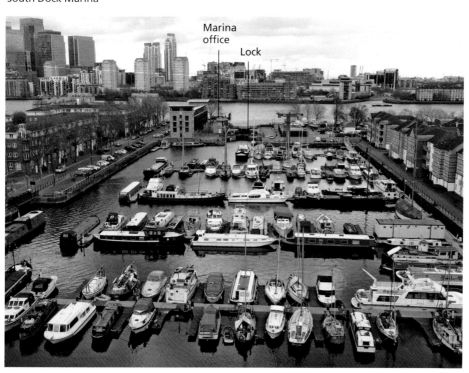

SOUTH DOCK MARINA   SE16 7SZ

Pre-booking essential for visitors
Tides HW London Bridge -0010
Contact
VHF Ch 37, 80
Callsign *South Dock Marina*
Lock office ☎ 020 7252 2244
Email southdockmarina@southwark.gov.uk
www.southwark.gov.uk/leisure-and-sport/south-dock-marina
Access From 0700-1900 (0800-1700 Sundays and Bank Holidays) when tide allows: nominal 2m+ over the sill from HW-2½ to HW+1½hr
Max length/beam 27m/6·4m
Facilities WC, showers, pump-out, WiFi near office, laundry
Water On pontoons (use own hose)
Electricity On pontoons
Gas Ask in office
Slipway At adjacent Surrey Docks Water Sports Centre ☎ 0844 893 3888
Crane 18·5T (20T without spreaders)
Boatyard For boat owners' use 0800–1800 weekdays, 0900–1400 weekends (but no noise on Sundays). Many boatyard trades available locally: ask at the office
Pub/restaurant Many close by
Provisions Small supermarket 150m from SW corner; many shops at Surrey Quays Retail Centre (10min walk)
Transport Buses; Rotherhithe, Surrey Quays and Canada Water Tube stations (15 minute walk). River bus.

The area is very quiet, and wildlife abounds here. If you like country walks, then a visit to the park and Russia Dock Woodland created in the old Surrey Docks, running N-S across the Rotherhithe peninsula, will be both a surprise to newcomers and a delight to all. Find the road called Onega Gate on the N side of Greenland Dock and head N.

From South Dock Marina, the river runs ½M N before another turn to port. On the N side of the bend is one of the most popular destinations for cruising yachtsmen, Limehouse Marina.

Swinging road bridge and lock gate beyond, waiting pontoon on stbd side (see text re limitations of pontoons)

Limehouse Marina

The entrance actually faces SW and can be hard to identify from downstream. It comes after a tall apartment block that towers above others along this stretch and has a small painted turret on its roof. There is a white flagpole by the pub just W of the entrance. Strong cross tides at the entrance can make it very choppy in a breeze.

Access is through a swinging road bridge and then a lock. Advance booking is required and insurance details may be requested. Traffic lights apply – Red, Red/Green (stand by) or Green. If your boat is canal-capable, you must hold a CRT licence to enter.

There are two waiting pontoons accessible HW±1½hr (both dry), one before and one behind the road bridge, both with shore access, but beware that you cannot return to the outer one after going ashore. Particularly in a SW wind, waves can funnel into the entrance and cause the pontoons to heave around quite violently. Fenders must be set very low if using them. Once through the bridge and on the inner pontoon, a vessel is effectively trapped, so it may be better to wait out in the river until able to enter.

The lock has mooring lines hanging vertically against the walls around which you can loop your own lines, and the office is in the building to port by the basin entrance. To starboard is the headquarters of the Cruising Association, where visitors, even if non-members, may use the bar and restaurant in the evenings. There are also several good restaurants close by in Narrow Street, including The Narrow (① 020 7592 7950), a pub owned by Gordon Ramsay, and plenty of other eating opportunities a few minutes' walk away in Commercial Road.

Limehouse Marina is another convenient and quiet base for visiting London with good facilities and supplies available nearby, plus good transport links. The Rotherhithe road tunnel entrance is close by.

When returning to the river from the marina, skippers are well advised to make a long sound signal, because approaching traffic heading upstream cannot be seen.

Approaching Limehouse Marina from downstream

The waiting pontoons – no access to outer one from shoreside

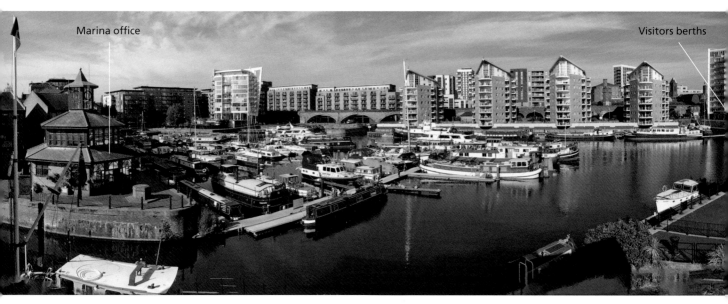

Marina office

Visitors berths

Limehouse Marina, the office to the left. Visiting groups may be berthed together in the far corner to the right on 'H' pontoon

LIMEHOUSE MARINA

E14 8EG

At the time of going to print, Limehouse Marina and all other BWML-owned marinas had just been sold. It is therefore possible that some of these details may change. Watch the Thames updates section of the ECP website.

Pre-booking essential for visitors

Tides HW London Bridge -0010

Contact
VHF Ch 80
Callsign *Limehouse Marina*
Lock office and bookings ☎ 020 7308 9930, 07766 774726
Email limehouse.marina@bwml.co.uk
www.bwml.co.uk/limehouse-basin-marina

Access HW±4hr, 0800–1800 April–September, 0800–1600 October–March. Other times between 0500-2200 may be possible on request with 24hr advance notice

Max length/beam 28m/7·5m

Facilities WC, showers, launderette, WiFi, pump-out

Water On pontoons, use own hose

Electricity On pontoons, uses prepaid cards from office

Chandlery A few chandlery items in the office

Repairs Ask in lock office

Provisions Shops nearby and in Commercial Road, 5 mins walk

Pubs/restaurants In Narrow Street nearby and Commercial Road, 5 mins walk

Club Cruising Association ☎ 020 7537 2828 www.theca.org.uk

Transport Docklands Light Railway from Limehouse Station, just NW of the marina; Buses on Commercial Road

Beyond Cuckolds Point, opposite Limehouse, the river turns SW into the Lower Pool, passing the famous Prospect of Whitby pub to starboard. The next bend to starboard has the headquarters of the River Police on the N shore and brings Tower Bridge into sight ahead in the Upper Pool with The Shard (306m high) dominating the scene beyond.

Hermitage Community Moorings

Three cables W of the Police HQ, there is a substantial set of pontoon moorings joined to the N shore by a walkway. This is Hermitage Community Moorings, a not-for-profit location established mainly for large traditional river barges, many of which are residential. There are two visitor berths on the downstream end of the outermost pontoon, one inside the pontoon, one on the outside. Minimum depth on the inside berth is approximately 1·0m LAT (beam and tide dependant, see details below) and the bottom is hard – there is more water on the outside berth, but it could be very uncomfortable in a small modern lightweight boat especially during day time, even though the pontoons are very substantial and deaden some of the chop. The usual facilities are provided.

The moorings are a very short walk from St Katharine's and have the obvious benefit of being in the river itself and not behind a lock gate. Advance booking is advised. Initial contact is best made by phone. Special rates apply for historic vessels. There is paperwork available at the visitor berths in an 'honesty box' for weekend use when the place is unmanned, when

Limehouse lock – CA HQ at the end to the right, the marina office opposite on the left

Approaching Hermitage Moorings – the visitor moorings are at the near ends of the outside pontoon

HERMITAGE COMMUNITY MOORINGS   E1W 1NG

Pre-booking advised for visitors
Tides HW London Bridge
Contact
☎ 020 7481 2122 (weekdays only 1000-1700)
www.hcmoorings.org
Email manager@hcmoorings.org

Access Outer berth: all-tide, least depth 2·1m.
Inner berth: restricted near LW, least depth 1·0m at
point 5m inshore from pontoon
Facilities WC, showers, pump-out
Water On pontoon
Electricity On pontoon
Fuel As St Kats
Provisions As St Kats
Pubs/Restaurants As St Kats
Transport As St Kats

Fuel barge between Hermitage Moorings and St Kats

St Katharine Docks

On upstream from the fuel barge, the entrance to St Katharine Docks (widely known as St Kats) is on the N shore just short of Tower Bridge.

This marina enjoys a splendid position, almost in Central London and within walking distance of many attractions, and its looks and ambience make it a tourist attraction in itself. Its prices do reflect this, although the period rates can be much better value than daily rates. It is very popular and often completely full, especially when one of the frequent large events is being hosted in the Central Basin. Advance booking (at least a week ahead in mid-season) is essential; nonetheless it may be worth calling the day before if you decide to try at short notice.

Access is through a large lock from about HW-2hr to about HW+1½hr, although this depends on the height of tide. Locking times are published on the St Kats website. Report in by VHF when you are 5 minutes or so away.

There are waiting buoys SE of the entrance. These are rather close together and the inshore row has only 1·2m least depth. The waiting pontoon shown on some older charts is no longer available. Call ahead and ask about possibly using St Katharine's Pier just upstream of the entrance if wanting an overnight waiting berth on the river.

At busy times, waiting outside for the lock can be hard work for helmsmen as they cope with stemming the strong current, avoiding other boats waiting to enter and

Hermitage visitors' berths. Note the swell on this windy day

members of the 'co-op' can help out if needed. If arriving at night, the visitor berths are either side of the downstream post, which carries 2F.G lights.

Just upstream of Hermitage Moorings, also on the N side, is the large black fuel barge *Heiko*. Be aware that the advertised operating times (see St Katharine Docks details) are approximate and the barge does not operate at all at weekends. If you require fuel, contact is preferred by phone (see St Katharine Docks details, page 132), or VHF Ch 14, and follow directions – you may be asked to moor on the N side of the barge to shelter from the chop.

RIVER THAMES

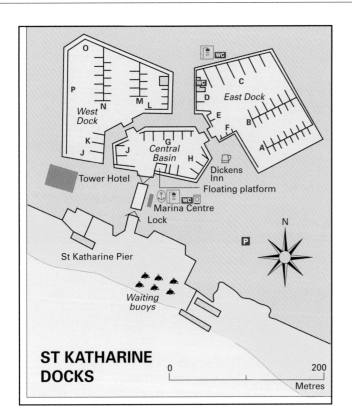

ST KATHARINE DOCKS
West Dock
East Dock
Central Basin
Tower Hotel
Dickens Inn
Floating platform
Marina Centre
Lock
St Katharine Pier
Waiting buoys

N

0   200
Metres

ST KATHARINE DOCKS   E1W 1LA

Pre-booking essential for visitors

Tides HW London Bridge

Contact
VHF Ch 80 (during locking times)
Callsign *St Katharine's*
Office ☎ 020 7264 5312
Email marina.reception@skdocks.co.uk
www.skdocks.co.uk/marina

Access Approx HW-2hr to HW+1½hr, Apr-Oct 0600-2030, Nov-Mar 0800-1800, but see marina website for exact daily times

Facilities WC, showers, launderette, pump-out (accessible from most berths)

Water On pontoons

Electricity On pontoons, separate charge

Gas Calor – ask in office; Gaz from fuel barge in river

Fuel barge At barge *Heiko* in river ☎ 020 7481 1774 or 07831 451260 VHF Ch 14, call sign *Heiko*.
Opening times: Mon-Fri 0630-1430, closed at weekends

Doctor Close nearby in Thomas More Street, ☎ 020 7488 3653

Pub/restaurant Many inside marina, more nearby outside. Popular street-food market, Fri lunchtimes.

Provisions Small supermarket outside to W, large one outside to E

Approaching St Kats lock. Best to moor stbd side to if you can

Almost a full lock. Note floating pontoon on the right

frequent large and noisy river ferries using the neighbouring pier. You will normally be called in individually by VHF, but sometimes there can be an unseemly rush into the inviting lock by the waiting skippers as soon as the traffic lights on each pierhead change. Inside the lock, the starboard side is preferred, where there is a floating timber pontoon with cleats at deck height. To port is the old stone wall with bollards and hanging chains. There is often quite a surge felt in the lock until the outer gate closes, and skippers may find it easier on arrival to secure a stern line first.

From the lock, you pass through a lifting road bridge into the Central Basin where suddenly all is still. There are two more basins, East Dock and West Dock, leading off from it through lifting footbridges.

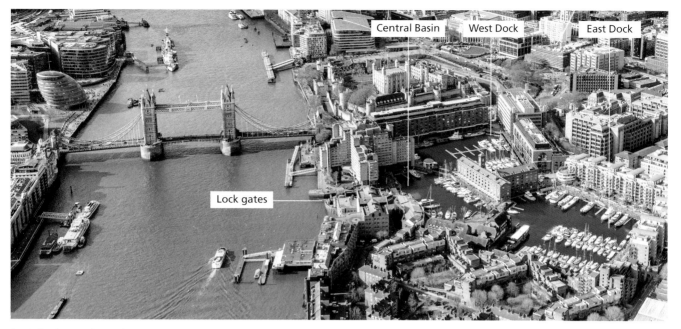

Central Basin   West Dock   East Dock

Lock gates

St Katharine Docks Marina

All berths are behind smart-card security gates. The whole area is usually beautifully kept and the marina is surrounded by trees, flower beds and hanging baskets. Although it's busy – there are many shops, cafes and restaurants and plenty of people walk through on their way to and from work – it can at times be uncannily quiet, although aircraft noise can intrude when the wind is in the east. The East Dock is certainly the quietest of the three.

You may be asked to show proof of insurance. Locking out on departure must be booked in advance.

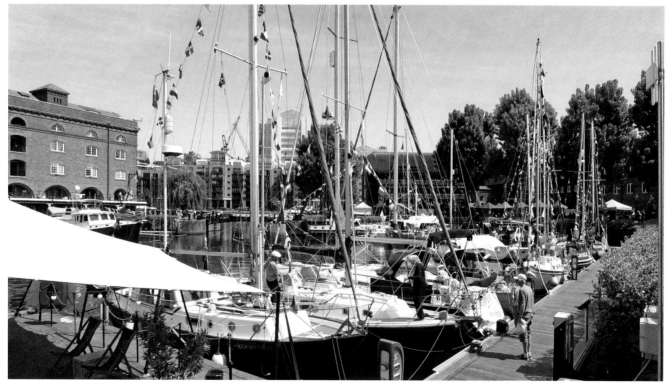

A group of visiting club boats in the central basin of St Kats

16. RIVER MEDWAY

⊕ **Landfall waypoints**
From E 51°27'·20N 000°45'·60E
Close E of West Cant PHB (Q.R)
From W (Thames) *and N:*
51°28'·36N 000°45'·55E
Close N of Nore Swatch PHB (Fl(4)R.15s)

Charts
Admiralty SC5606, 1834
Imray 2100, Y18

Tides
Entrance HW Sheerness
Chatham HW Sheerness +0009
Allington Lock HW Sheerness +0100

Harbour Authority (Peel Ports London Medway)

Contact
VHF Ch 74
Callsign *Medway VTS*
Harbour office Sheerness ☏ 01795 596596
Medway VTS Office ☏ 0151 949 6650/6418
For any additional leisure boating information, including a useful 'visitor chart', contact the Medway & Swale Boating Association, www.msba.org.uk

Main hazards

The lower part of the Medway is busy with commercial traffic, some of it large, and close attention should be paid to shipping movements. Listen to *Medway* VTS on Ch 74. Note that the VTS personnel are not based locally and have no direct view of the river, only through CCTV.

This traffic uses Sheerness Docks, close to the mouth of the river, Thamesport container terminal and a natural gas (LNG) terminal, both in Saltpan Reach, while other ships travel right up river almost to the fixed bridge at Rochester. The very large LNG tankers (often brightly coloured) have strict exclusion zone rules; again listen to Medway VTS.

There is a dangerous wreck (the *Richard Montgomery*) immediately N of the approach channel, 2M NE of Sheerness, in a total exclusion zone marked by yellow light buoys.

There can be overfalls by Garrison Point on the first of the ebb and there are many drying areas on both shores along the river, with some shore features completely covered at HWS.

THE MEDWAY

This chapter describes pilotage in the tidal Medway from the sea inland 25M to Allington Lock, although for most yachts the head of navigation will be the fixed bridge at Rochester, 13M upstream from Sheerness.

As a tourist destination the Medway Towns have much to offer with the Historic Dockyard Museum, modern shopping centres, Royal Engineers' Museum, Rochester Cathedral, castles and Dickensian festivals. Away from it all in the lower reaches of the river, there is fine sailing as well as interesting and peaceful creeks and inlets. The upper reaches beyond Rochester Bridge pass through an interesting mix of rural scenery, quiet villages and industrial history.

Approaches

From E Approach across the Cant shallows from the Spile buoy or along the S edge of the main shipping channel. Note that there is a 'secondary' shipping channel along the S edge of the main channel, marked on its S edge by yellow buoys, all Fl(2)Y.5s. Stay S of both channels, but avoid the shallows S of the West Cant buoy (Q.R) and an outfall marked by a small NCB (Q).

From N, NE or the Thames The Nore Swatch (Fl(4)R.15s) marks a convenient point from which to head S to the unlit Grain Edge buoy on the N side of the main channel opposite the West Cant, taking care to avoid the shallows of Grain Spit.

SHEERNESS

Contact
VHF Ch 74
Callsign *Medway VTS*
VTS office ☏ 0151 949 6650/6418

Sheerness is a commercial port and does not accommodate leisure craft. However, one small part of the original Royal Naval Dockyard remains, a small dock called the Camber, just S of the old fort and Port Office at Garrison Point. This dock is used by fast pilot boats and Sheerness RNLI lifeboats, but could be a place of refuge in an emergency with the consent of Medway VTS.

The Medway entrance from the NE

Garrison Point   Old Ferry Pier   Grain Hard SHB   Grain Tower

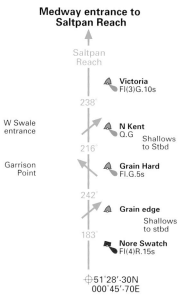

Entry to River Medway

Beware a disused ferry terminal jetty protruding N from Garrison Point – the ebb sets quickly E beneath it.

The Port Control building stands on top of the large fort on Garrison Point and displays a bright light (Fl.7s) warning of shipping movements. The light is directed up stream if traffic is inbound and to seaward if traffic is outbound.

Unless certain that there is no traffic, use the charted recommended leisure craft track on the W shore, from the No.11 SHB (Fl(3)G.10s) to Grain Hard SHB (Fl.G.5s). The ebb is also weaker on this side. Heading on towards the N Kent SHB (Q.G), take care not to stray onto the steeply shelving bank to starboard, especially W of Grain Hard buoy where there are charted obstructions including Grain Tower Fort.

Heavy shipping leaving the Medway is often escorted in this section of the river by large tugs, which can be unsympathetic to leisure craft close to the main channel.

Inbound, passing Sheerness Docks

Medway Entrance to Stangate

From the N Kent SHB, the entrance to the West Swale can be seen on the S side of the channel, marked by the Queenborough Spit ECB (Q(3)10s). See pages 168-171.

Once through the relative narrows of the entrance and into Saltpan Reach, which runs E-W, there is more scope for using the width of the river, shipping permitting. Off to starboard, on Horseshoe Point, the LNG terminal receives very large ships and further W stand the cranes at Thamesport container terminal. Stay at least 150m clear of the LNG terminal, 250m clear if there is a ship berthed there (these limits are rigorously enforced), and beware of very large ships turning opposite either terminal.

Bearing about 240° from the Victoria SHB (Fl(3)G.10s), the Stangate Spit ECB (VQ(3)5s) marks the W side of the entrance to Stangate Creek, the first anchorage in the Medway. A line of electricity pylons from the SE, ending immediately E of the entrance, is prominent. There are heavy mooring buoys along the S side of the main channel, E of Stangate entrance, which can be almost invisible at night and are often occupied by huge barges. The buoys are unsuitable for use by small craft.

Stangate and Sharfleet Creeks

Stangate Creek runs due S from the Medway for 1·6M from the Spit buoy and is a very popular and peaceful anchorage, but be sure to display a riding light at night as boats are often on the move there after dark. The bottom is mud and holding is generally excellent. The marshes each side teem with birdlife.

The ruined building on Burntwick Island (to starboard at entrance) once housed a steam engine to pull a defensive boom across the Medway. Evidence of much older settlements includes fragments of Roman pottery still found there.

Half-a-mile into the creek, after passing an unlit SHB with a wreck very close W of it, Sharfleet Creek turns off to the W and then NW into a horseshoe curve. This creek too is popular, although you need to choose your spot so as not to take the ground at LW and to avoid blocking the channel. There are no marks or withies. Parts of Sharfleet, once the best oyster grounds in the Medway, are very deep, and most of it has more than 2m at LWS. Many head for the deeper water on the W side of the 'horseshoe'. In a N'ly breeze, machinery noise can carry across from Thamesport, but otherwise this is a peaceful place. With shoal draught and a rising tide, the adventurous skipper can take a shortcut W across the Ham Ooze from Sharfleet to Half Acre Creek or to the Medway in Kethole Reach.

Stangate Creek continues S from its junction with Sharfleet Creek with good holding everywhere. Visitors generally bring up on the windward side of the creek, although the surrounding countryside is marsh and does

A typical evening in Stangate Creek

not give much shelter from strong winds near HW. The creek divides at its S end with the Shade to port offering another possible anchorage. Beyond the Shade, Funton Reach soon peters out into the drying areas of Funton Creek and Bedlams Bottom, graveyard of the famous racing Thames barges *Sirdar* and *Veronica*.

To starboard at the S end of Stangate Creek, immediately S of Slaughterhouse Point, there is a pool affording better shelter in a N wind. Some charts show

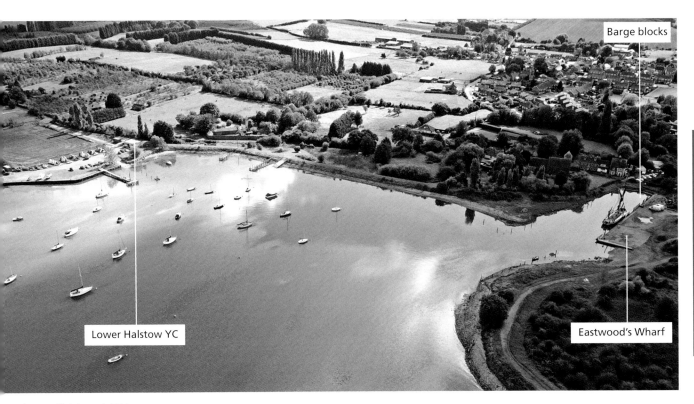

Barge blocks

Lower Halstow YC

Eastwood's Wharf

Lower Halstow at HW

this pool, and an area near the N end of Stangate, as 'explosives anchorages', but there now seems to be no reason for these to be charted, a leftover perhaps from the Medway's naval dockyards.

SW from this pool, Halstow Creek will take shoal draught boats right up to Lower Halstow on the tide, but note that the whole area dries.

LOWER HALSTOW

Lower Halstow is a peaceful village with an ancient church, a pub, a village shop and an old quay. The old Eastwood's Wharf, opposite the church and once used to load bricks onto barges, is a possible spot to visit if you draw little more than 1m, although you may find as much as 2m at springs. On entry, the best water is close to the W side until you reach the wall. There are no toilets and the usable section of wharf is sometimes largely occupied by the barge *Edith May*; rafting alongside her may be possible, but you may then not sit quite upright. If the wharf is empty, lie alongside it a few lengths in from the N end. The S section of wharf is unusable, because there are barge blocks there, marked by a warning notice. Anchoring off and going ashore by dinghy over HW is an alternative.

In the SE corner of the inlet is Lower Halstow YC (www.lhyc.org.uk), access HW±1½hr, with its many drying moorings, a short jetty and a slipway. To reach the club from Stangate, head SW midway between the E shore and the small islet and aim for the middle of the club moorings seen ahead. The jetty displays a fixed red light at night. Ask in advance if you can use a club visitor buoy. The bottom is generally quite flat with 2m at HW.

The barge *Edith May*, at Eastwood's Wharf

The drying moorings at Lower Halstow

Stangate Creek to Bishop Spit

N of the entrance to Stangate Creek, in Saltpan Reach, there is the Z2 NCB(Q) and, further N, the Z1 Isolated Danger mark (Fl(2)10s).

Pilotage W is straightforward, noting a second Isolated Danger (Fl(2)5s) on the S side of the main channel opposite Thamesport. Large ships turn in this area of Saltpan Reach.

Passing the No.12 PHB (Q.R), the river turns SW into Kethole Reach. Over to starboard, the drying Stoke Saltings was one of the areas in the Medway used by 19th century gangs of 'muddies', who, between two tides, could fully load a Thames barge with the blue clay used in cement making. An unlit SHB on the edge of the flats marks the start of Stoke Creek, another drying inlet with a small boatyard and moorings at its head.

Half way along Kethole Reach, the E Bulwark SHB (Fl(3)G.15s) and unlit W Bulwark PHB mark the extremities of the wreck of the 15,000T battleship HMS *Bulwark*, which exploded in November 1914 with the loss of over 700 lives. Here the disintegrating Bee Ness disused jetty juts out from the NW shore and on its SW side is the entrance to East Hoo Creek, a narrow anchorage running NW and carrying over 2·5m almost to its head in Damhead Creek.

If you venture into East Hoo Creek, another relic of WWI can be visited by dinghy near LW – the hulk of a WWI German U-boat lies north of Bee Ness jetty at about 51°25'·8N 000°37'·9E.

SW of the No.14 PHB (Fl.R.5s), a line of heavy mooring buoys stretches along the SE shore – these are virtually invisible at night. Just past the last buoy is the entrance to Half Acre Creek, marked on its W side by the No.16 Bishop PHB (Q.R), behind which lies the extensive and drying Bishop Spit.

Half Acre Creek

Running SW, Half Acre Creek provides a wide, deep water passage for a mile beyond the entrance. Keeping industrial buildings on Motney Hill on the bow, watch for cross-tides. The large tripod of the No.7 beacon is across the flats to port, in the area where a shortcut is possible to or from Sharfleet Creek near HW. Further on SW, some charts show a barge on the E side of the channel, but this has not been seen in modern times. At the Otterham Fairway SWB (Mo(A)10s), Half Acre Creek divides into three, as follows:

South Yantlet Creek runs off to starboard, curving NW following a string of unlit SWBs, numbered 1 to 3. Beyond the third of these is a drying area N of Nor Marsh island, which may be crossed with 2m after HW-3 towards the fourth and final red and white No.4 SWB pillar buoy. Best water is just S of this buoy. Continuing W for 2 more cables across mud that dries about 2·5m in places, the channel rejoins the Medway in Pinup Reach.

Otterham Creek runs S from the Otterham Fairway buoy for about 1·5M and is a buoyed but drying route to the boatyard at Otterham Quay, which is to port at the end, opposite a commercial wharf. Most tides will allow a 2m draught boat to reach the quay, a destination for boat repairs or storage, but with no provision at all for visitors.

OTTERHAM CREEK   ME8 7XE
Access HW±1hr
Boat repairs Otterham Creek Boatyard ☎ 01634 260250 or 07968 658688; 9-T crane and dry docks (max. length 80ft)
Engineers On site
Taxi ☎ 01634 233333, 666666

Bartlett Creek is the third, middle branch from the Otterham Fairway buoy and heads WSW past a prominent wreck to an unlit PHB, then W towards the Rainham Fairway PHB (Fl(2)R.5s) at the N end of the gutway of Rainham Creek.

Continue W from the Rainham Fairway PHB for a short distance with the distant Gillingham gas holder on the bow, then a gutway marked by occasional withies leads SW towards the unlit Mariners PHB off Horrid Hill.

The Mariners buoy is laid by Mariners Farm Boatyard, a friendly DIY boat storage venue popular for winter lay-up, where a drying mooring may be available. Beyond the buoy, look SW for two posts close to the shore, topped with coloured cans – swing to port around the first, then sharply to starboard around the second and follow a short line of moorings that leads towards a wide slipway. On approach, do not worry that few masts are in evidence – the yard is hidden behind high trees.

MARINERS FARM BOATYARD   ME8 7TL
Contact
☎ 01634 233179
www.marinersboatyard.co.uk
Email enquiries@marinersboatyard.co.uk
Access HW ±2hr
Facilities WC, 8-T crane
Water/electricity At yard
Provisions Short walk to Sharps Green or Lower Rainham
Taxi ☎ 01634 233333, 666666

With shoal draught and a rising tide, an alternative route from up river to Bartlett Creek runs SE from further up the River Medway opposite Folly Point, passing between a post and a red can to cross the causeway off the SW corner of Nor Marsh, then on SE past Horrid Hill to meet Bartlett Creek.

This remote and interesting area south of the main Medway channel is nationally and internationally important for many species of birds and is full of life in winter and summer.

Bishop Spit to Darnet Ness

Continuing up stream on the Medway past the entrance to Half Acre Creek, the main river runs W in Long Reach. It is safe to stay out of the main channel by skirting along its N edge, past SHBs No.15 (Q.G), No.17 (Fl(3)G.10s) and No.19 (Fl.G.5s). Beyond No.19, on the N shore, the long coal jetty of the now-demolished Kingsnorth Power Station was still standing in 2019. It was not clear if this will remain or be demolished too. The S shore of Long Reach shelves steeply, mostly covers at HWS, and frequently catches out the unwary on a falling tide.

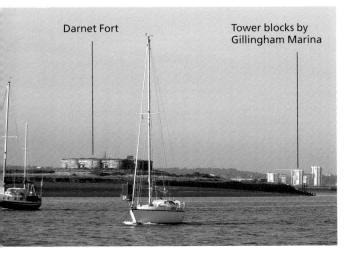

Darnet Fort · Tower blocks by Gillingham Marina

Yachts heading downstream past No.22 buoy at Darnet Ness

WHITTON MARINE
ME3 9LB

Contact
☎ 01634 250593
www.whittonmarine.co.uk
Access HW+/-1.5
Facilities WC, showers
Water, electricity On pontoon
Boat repairs Slipways, engineering
Pub, provisions In Hoo St.Werburgh, short walk.
Taxi ☎ 01634 251234

The final PHB in Long Reach, No.22 (Fl.R.5s), stands close to the N edge of Darnet Ness, a small island on the S side of the river where it turns SW into Pinup Reach with R beacon No.6 (Q.R) on its corner. A Palmerston Fort stands on Darnet Ness, built in the 1860s and once housing heavy muzzle-loading rifled guns for defence of the Naval dockyards at Chatham.

Middle Creek

At this bend, the adventurous shoal-draught skipper may choose to take the twisting Middle Creek that heads WNW by the No.1 Beacon, either to visit the boatyard at Whitton Marine or to circumnavigate Hoo Island, at suitable states of the tide. The channel is buoyed, but the buoys are not shown on all charts. Starting with a SHB

No.1, follow WNW to a PHB marked No.2, rounding this and turning SW, using the gas holder at Gillingham as a transit to find No.3 SHB. The channel then roughly follows the shape of Hoo Island about 50m off, turning NW towards No.4, an SCB in line with a distant church steeple.

At this point, with enough tide, you could carry on NW past No.5 PHB towards the Hundred of Hoo SC and Whitton Marine, which can usually find room for visitors alongside drying pontoons, and offers services including marine engineering.

Otherwise, continue W through some moorings towards the R and G posts close to the Hoo Island shore, which indicate a gap in the causeway between Hoo Island and the mainland.

From the R and G markers, head SW (initially staying close to Hoo Island shore – this stretch is the shallowest of the route) and join the Orinoco Channel, which leads either NNW to Port Werburgh, or SSE back to Short Reach in the Medway beside an unlit WCB (see page 142 for further notes about the Orinoco).

Lock gates   Fuel berth   Entrance to tidal marina

Approaching Gillingham Marina from downstream

Gillingham Marina lock gate, the fuel berth to the right

The drying tidal basin

The marina's locked basin

Darnet Ness to Gillingham Marina

If not entering Middle Creek but continuing up the Medway, head SW through Pinup Reach, where the shortcut through to South Yantlet Creek (see above) may be seen to port, before passing the No.25 Folly SHB (Fl(3)G.10s) and No.24 PHB (Fl.R.5s) off Folly Point. The channel is narrow here so take particular care with large traffic. An unlit G post stands on the SE corner of Folly Point to starboard and the shallows extend a long way S of Hoo Island – this island houses a fort matching that on Darnet Ness. Gillingham is now in clear view ahead with a prominent gas holder standing close S of Gillingham Marina.

Note The speed limit upstream from here reduces to 6kn.

At SHB No.27 (Q.G) and PHB No.26 (Fl(2)R.10s), the channel turns just N of W into Gillingham Reach and yacht moorings line both shores. Those on the N shore are close to shallows.

Medway Cruising Club and Segas SC are on the south bank, just beyond the next PHB, No.28 (Fl.R.5s). Both clubs are usually open at weekends. The Commodore's Hard public slipway stretches into the river between these two clubs and can be used to launch or recover dinghies and small craft.

Medway Cruising Club ME7 2SE
☎ 01634 856489
www.medwaycruisingclub.org.uk

Segas SC ME7 1TT   ☎ 01634 855365
www.segassailingclub.co.uk

Lock

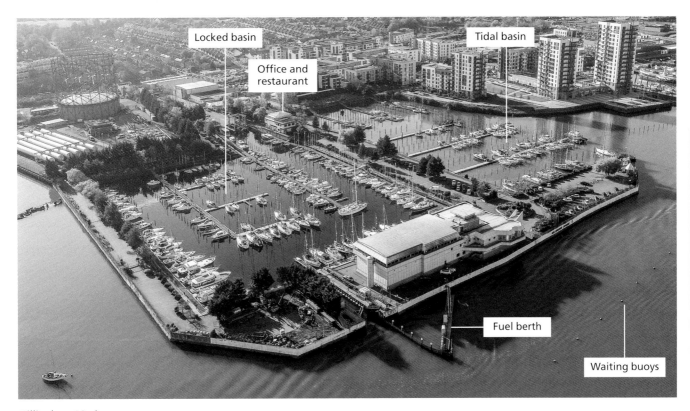

Gillingham Marina

Gillingham Marina

Immediately next to Segas SC is the high E wall of Gillingham Marina, which has two basins, one behind a lock, the other tidal. Viewed from the river, the lock gate is towards the downstream end of the N wall, to the left of the large pale-coloured building (a leisure centre) and the tidal basin is upstream, round behind the wall at the right hand end. The tidal basin dries to soft mud.

Berths should be booked in advance if possible. All berths in the locked basin are either alongside finger pontoons or stern to (preferably) against pontoons with the boat's bow secured between piles (like the Dutch 'box' system). Boats wishing to depart outside lock operating hours can be offered berths in the tidal basin. The marina office is in the large building at the S end of the wall between the two basins.

Locking is not 24hr (see marina details) but there is a row of waiting buoys in deep water in front of the marina wall. The lock has traffic lights. Vertical cables are set in the lock walls to put lines around, if you cannot reach the bollards at the top, and there are floating fenders on each side. Free flow is sometimes used near to HWS.

There is a refuelling pontoon on the river just upstream of the lock gate. It is angled out into the stream, which can make departure from it a little awkward on the ebb.

Immediately upstream from Gillingham Marina is a rectangular inlet known as Gillingham Pier, where there is a high wharf, plus a wide Victorian stone slipway and some pontoon moorings. The slipway runs down the

GILLINGHAM MARINA — ME7 1UB

Contact
℡ 01634 280022
www.gillingham-marina.co.uk
Email berthing@gillingham-marina.co.uk
VHF Ch 80
Callsign Gillingham Marina

Access Locked basin HW ±4½hr approx, 0600–2200 (summer) and daylight hours (winter)

Tidal basin HW ±2½hr approx

Max length/beam 16m/5·5m

Facilities WC, showers, launderette, pump-out, WiFi

Water On pontoons

Electricity On pontoons

Fuel Diesel and petrol from pontoon outside lock

Gas Calor and Gaz from office

Boat repairs Full service boatyard, 65-T and 20-T boat hoists

Engineer On site

Rigger Pier Rigging ℡ 01634 893303, Medway Slings (also canvas work) ℡ 01634 726400

Sailmaker Dolphin Sails agent on site

Chandler Outside marina gate ℡ 01634 283008
Email chandlery@gillingham-marina.co.uk

Provisions Supermarket, turn right outside marina, 2 min walk

Pub/restaurant The Quarterdeck marina bar/restaurant on site, hours vary. Pubs close by – directions from office.

Transport Buses outside. Trains to London, Ramsgate and Dover
Taxi ℡ 01634 818818, 575656.

Slipway between piles

Gillingham Pier moorings and slipway, the No.30 buoy in the foreground

centre of the inlet, and has piles leaning inwards along both sides. The area is operated by Medway Council and anyone wishing to use the slipway or moorings should contact the Piermaster first, via the Council on ☎ 01634 331153. The paddle steamer *Medway Queen* (with a new hull, but many original components within) is moored there permanently against the western wharf.

GILLINGHAM AND HOO TO ROCHESTER BRIDGE

At No.29 SHB (Fl(3)G.10s), which stands opposite Gillingham Marina, the river turns sharply NW round Hoo Ness into Short Reach. Watch out for shipping entering and leaving Chatham Docks through the locks on the W side of this bend.

Halfway along Short Reach, there is a small unlit WCB on the edge of the shallows to starboard. This marks the W end of the route behind Hoo Island (see section on Middle Creek above); the Orinoco Channel leads NNE from the WCB, branching to port to the Port Werburgh entrance, and starboard to join Middle Creek. Port Werburgh, the collection of residential barges and lightships seen on the N shore, has absorbed the old Hoo Marina, and does not accept any visiting craft. However,

Medway YC and its all-tide pontoon

Hoo Ness YC remains on the shore there, with its drying jetty and slipway accessed through Port Werburgh's entrance, and can host club visits by prior arrangement using its swinging moorings in the river.
Hoo Ness YC ME3 9TW ☎ 01634 250052
www.hooness.org.uk

The Orinoco is withied, but some are metal and all are covered at HW, when it would be safer to cross the surrounding flats where you should find 1·5m.

Continuing NW along Short Reach, Cockham Woods are ahead on the N bank and, to port, lies St Mary's Island. St Mary's was once part of the Chatham Naval Dockyard and is now a major waterside housing development, the shore lined with modern houses. Numerous yacht club moorings line the S side of the channel, spreading to the N shore once past the No.30A (Fl.R.2·5s) and No.31 (IQ.G) buoys. Beyond No.31, the dinghy sailors' Wilsonian SC stands on the shore, followed, as Cockham Reach bends to port, by Medway YC's headquarters beneath the woods on the N bank at the apex of the bend.

Medway Yacht Club

Medway YC can often provide a mooring for visitors on request, at a small fee. Visitors are welcomed and may use the clubhouse and facilities, including the bar and restaurant. There is an all-tide pontoon jetty for landing by dinghy, also a trot boat service, although during midweek you may be allowed to moor overnight on the hammerhead, where there is a fresh water tap.

MEDWAY YACHT CLUB   ME2 4XB

Contact
☎ 01634 718399, 0900–1630 Monday–Saturday
www.medwayyachtclub.com
Email office@medwayyachtclub.com
Trot Boat Callsign *Invicta* on VHF Ch 37, operates 0900– 1800 (Saturday and Sunday), 0930 (out to moorings) and 1630 (collection from moorings) on weekdays.
Restaurant Wed-Sat, Sun evenings also lunch Sat and Sun.

Upnor SC clubhouse and moorings

Upnor Castle

Lock entrance to Chatham Marina

Looking E inside the marina entrance, fuel berth on the right immediately inside

Upnor Sailing Club

Upstream from Medway YC is the all-tide landing for Upnor SC where, as at Medway YC, it may be possible to borrow a mooring on request. Its clubhouse is set in a row of cottages behind the sea wall and close by are two large pub/restaurants, the Pier and the Ship, both popular with yachtsmen.

Upnor SC ME2 4UY
☎ 08446 645049
www.upnorsailingclub.co.uk

The Pier ☎ 01634 717317
The Ship ☎ 01634 290553

The river continues SW in Upnor Reach, where Upnor Castle sits on the W bank. In 1667, cannon fire from here failed to stop the Dutch raiders under Admiral de Ruyter, who sank 16 ships of the Royal Navy.

On your port side, across the river from Upnor Castle, you will find the lock gate entrance to Chatham Maritime Marina, built in the old No.1 Basin of the Naval Dockyard.

Chatham Maritime Marina

The tide runs hard directly across the entrance, which is fairly narrow – the lock widens once inside. Always seek permission before entering. Care needs to be taken not to end up going sideways into the lock. Check the tidal flow and apparent strength before entering and leaving. Inside the lock there are floating pontoons on each side with cleats at deck level. There are traffic light controls and sometimes the lock runs free-flow near to HW with the inner road bridge raised.

This 412-berth marina has the usual facilities – it is popular and often full at peak times. The lock can be very busy indeed during summer weekends. Its surroundings have undergone major regeneration from dockyard days with housing and businesses springing up. It can be an attractive venue for those cruising with children on board - on its doorstep there is a growing number of family restaurants plus an outlet shopping mall (which includes eating places, but closes quite

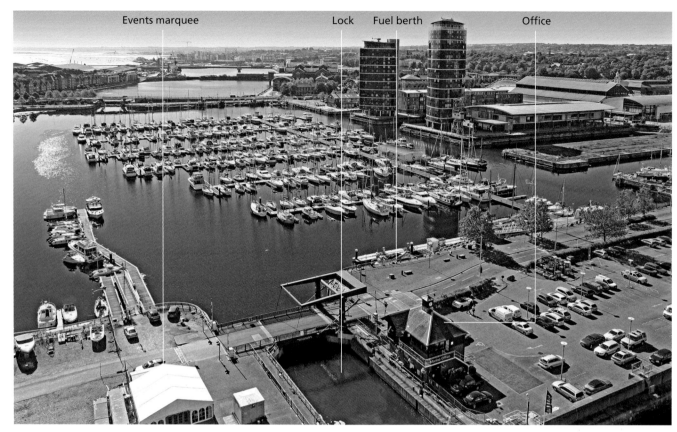

Events marquee   Lock   Fuel berth   Office

Chatham Maritime Marina

CHATHAM MARITIME MARINA   ME4 4LP

See plan on page 139

Contact

VHF Ch 80

Callsign *Chatham Marina*

☎ 01634 899200

www.mdlmarinas.co.uk/mdl-chatham-
maritime-marina

Email chatham@mdlmarinas.co.uk

Access 24hr (1·5m over cill at LWS). Possible (rare) limited access at top of HWS

Facilities WC, showers, launderette, WiFi

Water On pontoons

Electricity On pontoons

Fuel Diesel and petrol inside immediately to starboard once inside

Gas Calor and Gaz

Rigger As Gillingham Marina, above

Boat repairs 16-T crane in yard

Sailmaker see Gillingham Marina details

Chandler Pirate's Cave ☎ 01634 295233 (across river at Frindsbury, requires transport; Volvo Penta agent); Gillingham Marina Chandlery (30-min walk)

Pub/Restaurant Several nearby

Provisions Supermarket nearby

Transport Trains - Chatham or Rochester stations, services to London, Ramsgate and Dover

Taxi ☎ 01634 222222, 840840

early), a multi-screen cinema, and even a gin distillery. More housing development was underway on the marina's N side in 2018/19.

The town centre is several miles away, but there are bus stops on the SW side of the marina with regular services until late evening.

Close the W shore of the river and opposite the marina lock, swinging moorings that extend upstream belong to the Royal Engineers Yacht Club. The REYC are happy to let visitors use any spares, although any dinghy trip ashore has to be upriver to the old Dockyard mast slip, or downriver to Upnor. Contact ☎ 07486 875298 or 07870 433039 to enquire.

Just up river from the marina, enormous sheds stand on the E shore. These are relics of the old naval dockyard, covered slipways where ships were once built and maintained, but now part of a vast museum, the magnificent Historic Dockyard (☎01634 823800 https://thedockyard.co.uk for opening times), which is rated as one of Britain's major tourist attractions. If you are visiting Chatham Marina, ask in the office for details of any special offers on entrance to the museum, which is a 15-minute walk away. Rope making is one of the many fascinating items to be seen, still being done in the traditional way on a 'rope walk'. Naval ships were built here from the late 1500s (including HMS *Victory*) and continued right up to the days of modern submarines, the last of which, HMS *Ocelot*, is one of the ships on display.

CHATHAM TO ROCHESTER

Upstream of the marina on Chatham Reach, on the E shore, is a long floating pontoon, Thunderbolt Pier, running parallel to the stream and connected to the shore at its N end. There, Victory Moorings runs as a berth holders' facility but may have room for visitors, although only if pre-booked.

Victory Moorings, at
Thunderbolt Pier

Sun Pier all-tide pontoon

Victory Moorings
☎ 07785 971797
Email asm-victory@hotmail.co.uk

Continuing along Chatham Reach beyond Victory Moorings, you will see in the distance the blue-painted Sun Pier on the S side as the river turns sharply round to NNW at Chatham Ness. In Rats Bay, on your port side below the pier, there is a row of moorings which may possibly be available to overnight stops. Three are swinging moorings, three fore-and-aft, and three larger 'ship' moorings.

Beyond these, brief landings for shopping or crew changes at Sun Pier should be possible, if there is space on its 70ft steel landing pontoon, which has electricity and water and at least 2·5m on its outside at LWS (queries to Medway Council ☎ 01634 338122). Set your fenders high if you stop here. There is a token system for access to and from the shore.

Unless you are intending to pass beneath Rochester Bridge, the final stretches before you reach it have little to offer the visitor other than perhaps an interesting sail or motor.

The covered slips at the Historic Dockyard - a must see for visitors to Chatham

Note The shallows of the Chatham Ness Shoal – the deeper water in Limehouse Reach is towards the W side for the first half of its length. Much of the W bank of this reach has new walls, the old industries above having been cleared away in preparation for the new builds of the extensive Medway Towns regeneration scheme getting underway.

Nearly a mile further on, having run up Limehouse Reach and turned SW again into Bridge Reach, Strood Pier on the NW shore is also unfortunately not available to visitors. A very large Russian-built Foxtrot-class submarine has lain rusting on the river here for some years, but in 2018 appeared to be undergoing some restoration – quite a sight.

Just upstream, the fixed Rochester Bridge carries road and railway across the river with an air draught of 5·4m at HWS. Best water is on the starboard side, but there is negligible water under and immediately beyond the bridge at LW and easy passage is only feasible for motor cruisers or shoal draught yachts that can drop their rigs. You are unlikely to meet any large commercial craft under the bridge, but monitor Medway VTS on Ch 74 to be sure.

ROCHESTER TO ALLINGTON

General notes

Navigation beyond Rochester Bridge is best done on the flood from about half tide onwards and is very largely confined to motorboats with only a handful of small yachts to be seen. A journey along the full 12M to Allington Lock needs careful timing in relation to your boat's draught and overall height, not only to ensure adequate depth as you progress, but also to arrive at Aylesford Bridge while there is still enough air draught to pass beneath it (minimum 2.2m) and then to arrive at the lock during operating hours. Departure from Rochester at about HW-3½hr (Allington) can work well. As a double check on the HW time at Allington Lock, it is about one hour after HW Sheerness.

Although the river banks have a busy industrial past – and there is certainly clutter on the bottom in some stretches – you are unlikely to encounter any small cargo ships of the type that once ran up to the paper mill wharves.

The lock keeper at Allington (see details at end of this chapter) will be happy to help with advice on request.

Rochester to the M2 Bridge

Immediately above the bridge there are jetties and pontoons on both sides of the river. If on the move near LW, the W arch under the bridge has the best water, moving across to midstream 100m above the bridge. Over on the port side beneath the towering ruin of Rochester Castle is Rochester Pier (ME1 1QN), a public pontoon that may be used for short daytime stops (requires a token, bought on the jetty, to return from shoreside – queries ☏ 01634 338122). Access is locked overnight from sunset to 0700.

Next, also on the Rochester shore, are the extensive pontoon moorings of Rochester Cruising Club. This club welcomes booked club visits and can also take individual visitors. It has diesel available for members, and visitors too provided they are staying overnight. The ancient keep of Rochester Castle looms behind the club which is in a great location as a base for local sightseeing.

Rochester Cruising Club ME1 1QN
☏ 01634 841350 www.rochestercc.co.uk

The first jetty to starboard belongs to Strood Pelican Cruising Club, which doesn't normally accept casual visitors. Immediately beyond Rochester CC, beware of shallows midstream if near LW. The next club reached is to starboard - Strood YC, some of whose moorings are on an all-tide pontoon and some beyond on the drying saltings. Visiting boats can be accommodated, up to 40ft LOA – apply in advance using the form provided on their website.

Strood YC ME2 2AH ☏ 01634 718261
www.stroodyachtclub.uk

The river curves to the S and, ahead on the port side, in front of a mass of modern housing, are the remains of the slipways of the old Short Brothers seaplane factory, dating back to 1917 and now used as the base for the local rowing club.

Past Wickham Point, the river again turns SW towards the huge bridges of the Medway Crossing.

Rochester fixed road and rail bridges, air draught 5·4m

Rochester Pier is the first landing beyond the fixed bridge

Rochester Cruising Club on the shore beneath the castle

Looking downstream from overhead Strood YC

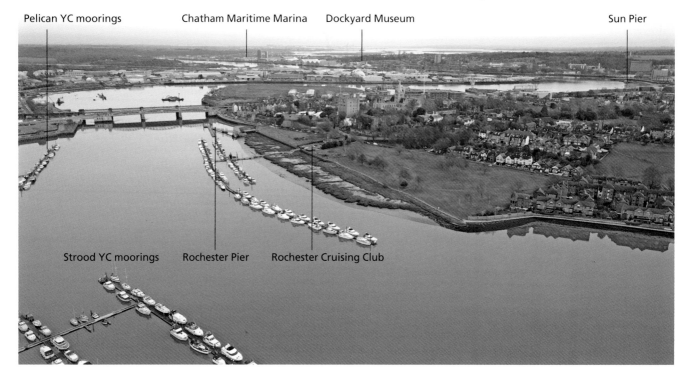

Pelican YC moorings   Chatham Maritime Marina   Dockyard Museum   Sun Pier

Strood YC moorings   Rochester Pier   Rochester Cruising Club

Strood YC moorings and clubhouse on the west bank

MEDWAY BRIDGE MARINA ME1 3HS

Contact
① 01634 843576
www.medwaybridgemarina.co.uk
Email info@medwaybridgemarina.co.uk
Fuel Diesel and petrol
Gas Calor and Gaz
Facilities WC, showers, WiFi, slipway
Water On pontoons
Electricity On pontoons
Chandler On site
Café/Restaurant Café/bar on site www.thesovereignbb.co.uk
Shipwrights and Engineers At marina with 25-T hoist.
KMS Medway Engineers ① 01634 845380 within marina
Boatyard Full boatyard services at Beacon Boatyard
(ME1 3JN, outside marina gate). 7-T crane. ① 01634 841320
www.beaconboatyard.co.uk
Provisions Shops in nearby Borstal village
Transport Buses in Borstal village
Taxi ① 01634 848848

Just short of the Crossing, on the S shore, is the sprawling Medway Bridge Marina where advance booking is requested. There is a mix of all-tide, half-tide and mud berths, engineers, a chandler and, in a 1930s Rhine cruising ship, a café that also offers bed and breakfast www.thesovereignbb.co.uk. Fuel here is the last on the river before Allington Marina, beyond Allington Lock. Beacon Boatyard is a separate moorings, dry dock and full-service boatyard business at the downstream edge of the marina.

Beyond Medway Bridge marina, the river runs beneath the Medway Crossing, which carries the M2 motorway and the Channel Tunnel Rail Link across the river. If moving near LW, beware unmarked shallows on the W side once through the bridge.

RIVER MEDWAY
Rochester to Cuxton

Depths in Metres

Above The long pontoons of Medway Bridge Marina

Left Medway Bridge Marina fuel berth

Medway Crossing to Aylesford

Still heading generally SW, two more marinas swiftly come up on the starboard side, the first of which is Port Medway with moorings, engineering and electrical facilities, plus two dry docks. There is a train station just outside the gate.

PORT MEDWAY MARINA   ME2 1AB

Contact
☎ 01634 720033
www.portmedwaymarina.co.uk
Email enquiries@portmedwaymarina.co.uk
Access 24hr on outside pontoons
Facilities WC, showers, launderette
Water On pontoons
Electricity On pontoons
Gas Calor
Boat repairs 20-T and 85-T hoist, dry docks (one roofed), slipway
Provisions In Cuxton, 10 minutes walk
Pub/Restaurant In Cuxton
Trains To Maidstone and Strood
Transport Trains to Maidstone and Strood; buses
Taxi ☎ 01634 515253.

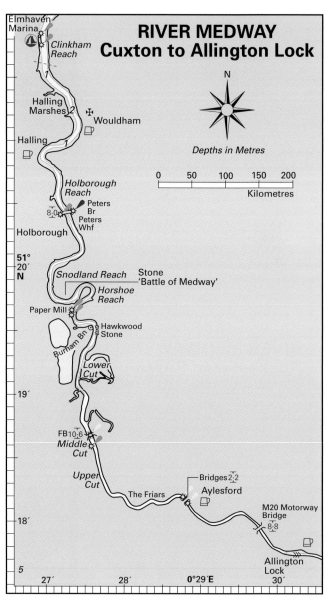

RIVER MEDWAY
Cuxton to Allington Lock

N

Depths in Metres

Elmhaven Marina
Clinkham Reach
Halling Marshes
Wouldham
Halling
Holborough Reach
Peters Br
Peters Whf
Holborough
51° 20′ N
Snodland Reach
Stone 'Battle of Medway'
Horshoe Reach
Paper Mill
Hawkwood Stone
Burham Bn
Lower Cut
19′
FB10.6
Middle Cut
Upper Cut
The Friars
Bridges 2.2
Aylesford
M20 Motorway Bridge
8.8
18′
Allington Lock
5
27′   28′   0°29′E   30′

Immediately upstream from Port Medway, with the same road access, is Cuxton Marina, with full- and half-tide moorings, a slipway and hoist.

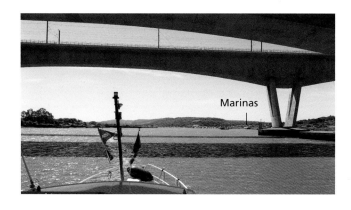

Marinas

Port Medway and Cuxton Marinas lie on the W bank, beyond the Medway Crossing bridges

Port Medway Marina

Cuxton Marina

Looking downstream at Elmhaven Marina

CUXTON MARINA   ME2 1AB

Contact
① 01634 721941
www.cuxtonmarina.com
Email enquiries@cuxtonmarina.co.uk
Access HW+/-4
Facilities WC, showers, laundrette, slipway,
12-T hoist
Provisions Restaurant, transport As Port Medway, above

ELMHAVEN MARINA   ME2 1AQ

Contact
① 01634 240489
www.elmhaven-marina.co.uk
Email elmhaven@btconnect.com
Facilities WC, showers, slipway
Provisions Shops at Halling, 10 minutes
Taxi ① 01634 420134

Above Cuxton there is a de-restricted stretch of the river used for waterskiing by the local club, whose clubhouse and short jetty are a few yards beyond the marina's pontoon.

The river runs on through open country with a chalk escarpment rising to starboard and, at Cuxton Point, the river bends to port. Here to starboard is the peaceful and

small Elmhaven Marina, last before Allington, close to the village of Halling and set at the foot of a chalk cliff. Visitors are advised to phone at least 24hr in advance.

Beyond Elmhaven, the village of Wouldham with its prominent church tower sits on the left bank; buried here is Walter Burke, who was purser on board HMS *Victory* at the Battle of Trafalgar and in whose arms Lord Nelson

Wouldham Church, resting place of Nelson's purser

The pontoon at Halling, agility needed to get ashore!

Approaching Peter's Bridge

A challenge for water inlet filters

died. The river curves round sharply to starboard and modern housing in Halling stands on the river bank ahead with a short, modern promenade on the river's edge. In the centre of the wall beneath this promenade there is a small modern pontoon landing stage at the foot of a ladder set in the high walls and there are also stone steps at the upstream end of the wall. A short shopping stop in Halling village is therefore possible, although the promenade railing's low gates accessing the ladder and the steps are both usually kept locked. Unfortunately it seems there is nobody on hand to unlock them, but the reasonably nimble can climb over them if need be.

The river runs on through a contrast of rural scenery and the remains of the industries that once lined the banks. There are numerous old wharves, many rotting and overgrown, and although there are one or two more modern-looking docksides by the paper mills there is currently no traffic using them. Many of the reed covered bends have beacons on them, needed because in flood the edges of the main channel may be covered. Some charts may still show lights on wharves along sections of the river, but it seems these have now all gone.

In between the dereliction there are delightful stretches where one could be miles from anywhere, each bend bringing a surprise. Sometimes the banks are lined with very tall reeds and many wild birds are to be seen, especially grey herons.

Beyond Halling in Holborough Reach, a new road bridge crosses the river (air draught 8m) which connects a large housing development called Peters Village on the E bank to the main road opposite. Note that the bridge is variously called 'Holborough Bridge' and 'Peters Bridge'.

Beyond the bridge the river snakes west, then east, and on the N shore here you may spot a large stone commemorating the so-called Battle of the River Medway in 43AD - following the Roman invasion the Catuvellauni tribes led by Togodumnus and Caratacus are said to have been defeated somewhere near here.

The depth steadily reduces and we stress the need to continue to match boat speed with the flood tide to ensure adequate depth but still sufficient clearance to get

The historic Hawkwood Stone

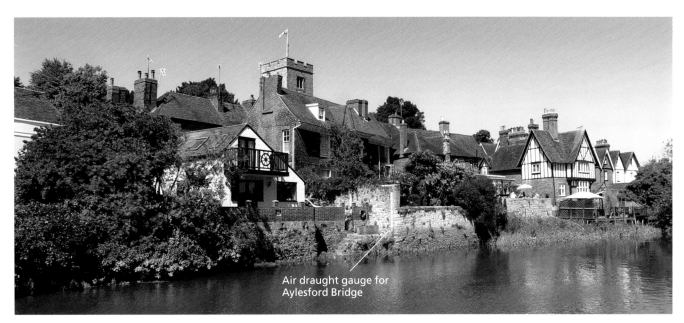

Air draught gauge for
Aylesford Bridge

Reaching the village of Aylesford

Passing Aylesford Priory

under the bridge at Aylesford and to reach the lock at Allington within locking hours.

A result of the plentiful reed beds is that there can be a fair amount of floating dead reed debris at some times of the year, which can wrap around and disguise more significant floating hazards, and of course clog engine cooling inlet filters.

Once past Snodland, the river snakes round a tight S-bend past Burham Marshes, reaching the Hawkwood Stone on your port side where the chart warns mariners to stay clear of the banks from here to Allington, because of piles and other obstructions. The Hawkwood Stone marks the southern limit of the Rochester Oyster Fishery, founded in 1728 and still ruling over fishing rights in the Medway between here and Garrison Point, Sheerness.

An inlet opens up to port a little further upstream, which the chart suggests was once the original course of the river, now drying up as an 'oxbow lake'. The shallowest patch you are likely to encounter on the passage is opposite this inlet.

Passing under a high (10·6m) disused footbridge, the river runs past New Hythe alongside a long wharf from more modern times. Beyond some untidy scrapyards, there is a recent housing development to starboard above a high stone wall, then after several more bends the river swings to port and passes the beautiful Aylesford Priory, now known as 'The Friars', a religious house of the Order of Carmelites and founded in 1242, but rebuilt much more recently.

The ancient Aylesford Bridge - blind bend beyond, make a sound signal!

Approaching Allington Lock

Around two more bends where great trees lean down to touch the water, the village of Aylesford comes into view on the left bank, a visual treat topped by its Norman church tower. More ancient history was made near here - in 455AD, Hengist and Horsa fought Vortigern in a defining battle between the Britons and the Saxon invaders, said to be centred around a ford where now stands an ancient stone road bridge with only 2·2m clearance at HWS.

A gauge on a wall on the port side about 50 yards below the bridge shows the air draught. There is a wharf on the starboard side just before you reach Aylesford where, if bound upstream on a falling tide, you could wait for sufficient clearance beneath the bridge. Do not dry out here, though, as the bottom is an unknown quantity. The 14th-century bridge stands on a blind right-hand bend, so approach with care and make a sound signal – normally the boat travelling against the tide should give way.

Allington Lock, close to HW

The village is a delight, but sadly (and very surprisingly) there is nowhere provided to welcome boating visitors.

Aylesford to Allington Lock

A more modern road bridge follows soon after the old bridge at Aylesford. After two more tree-lined bends, the M20 motorway bridge is seen ahead. Take special care along here to stay in the middle of the stream as collapsed wharves jut out a long way beneath the surface.

Beyond the bridge and soon after passing Gabriels Wharf boatyard on the starboard bank, you will reach Allington Lock, the head of the tidal navigation.

The lock is on the starboard side of the river with a large weir beyond to port. The chances are that you will be locking near to HW, when there are plenty of bollards within easy reach. Subject to space, short-term or overnight mooring may be possible within the lock cut – phone ahead to check with the helpful lock keeper. There are heated cabins for hire next to the lock keeper's cottage, and also a camping area.

The lock is managed by the Environment Agency (EA), which requires any boat using the river beyond the lock to be registered. Registration can be on a weekly or long-term basis. Compliance with the BSS (Boat Safety Scheme) is compulsory beyond the lock.

Half a mile upstream from the lock is the 100-berth Allington Marina, the first on the non-tidal navigation. A river bus runs between Allington and Maidstone.

Allington Marina, beyond Allington Lock

ALLINGTON LOCK ME16 0LU
Contact
01622 752864 www.allingtonlock.co.uk
Email allington.lock@environment-agency.gov.uk
Tides HW Sheerness +0100
Operating hours 0700–sunset (March–October) or 0800–1600 (November–February) and HW -3hr to HW +2hr. Locking may be available outside these hours on enquiry and with 24hr notice.
Max beam 6m
Facilities WC, showers, pump-out, electricity (limited), water, chemical toilet disposal
Slipway Above lock
River licence See www.gov.uk/register-a-boat/who-to-contact 03708 506506 *Email* boatreg@environment-agency.gov.uk
Pub/restaurant Malta Inn (just above lock on port side of river, at ME14 3AS) 01622 717251

ALLINGTON MARINA ME16 0NH
Contact
01622 752057
www.allingtonmarina.com
Email sales@allingtonmarina.com
Facilities WC, showers
Boatyard Repairs, engineer, 35T crane
Chandler On site
Water On pontoons
Electricity On pontoons
Fuel Diesel
Gas Calor
Taxi 01622 750000

17. THE SWALE

⊕ **Landfall waypoint**
51°24'·10N 001°01'·73E Immediately E of line between Whitstable
Street PHB and Columbine SHB
Charts
Imray 2100
Admiralty SC5606; 2571, 2572
Tides
Tides HW Sheerness
Harbour authority
Peel Ports Medway VHF Ch 74
Callsign *Medway VTS*
Honorary Port Pilots
Conyer and The Swale
Simon Smedley ✆ 01795 521562 *Email* conyer@eastcoastpilot.com

For any additional leisure boating information, contact the Medway &
Swale Boating Association, www.msba.org.uk

Main hazards

Tides

The Swale is not a river but a tidal waterway between the
Isle of Sheppey and the mainland, and the tide floods and
ebbs at both ends but not in a logical fashion. The stream
runs E for much longer than it runs W, which can be put
to good use on a passage E.

At HW Sheerness, the whole Swale is slack. The ebb
then begins to run E throughout the Swale for the first
hour or so. After that it splits between Queenborough
and Kingsferry Bridge with the W Swale ebbing into the
Medway and the E Swale into the Thames Estuary. The
separation point gradually moves E towards Elmley and
all flows stop at LW with the exception of a back eddy
along the W shore opposite Queenborough.

When the flood starts, it comes in from both ends, the
streams meeting at about Elmley. Later, the meeting
point often moves E towards Fowley.

Although every day follows this general pattern,
predicted tide timing and heights can be greatly affected
by wind, weather and barometric pressure, especially in
the E Swale.

Wind over tide in the popular anchorage at Harty,
especially strong easterlies against the ebb, can raise a
very steep chop.

Shipping

Commercial shipping uses the W Swale, almost always
entering and leaving via the Medway, to reach docks just
E of the Kingsferry Bridge. On rare occasions, small
coasters may use the E Swale as a short cut on a good
tide.

Approaches to East Swale

From the E, make along the coast to the Whitstable
Street PHB (Fl.R.2s) as described in the North Kent
Coast chapter.

From the W Take the Four Fathoms Channel from the
Spile SHB (Fl.G.2·5s), making good about 105° to avoid
isolated shoals to the S. If draught allows, and on a rising
tide, alter course at the 001°E meridian to make 180°
and join the E Swale approach at the Columbine Spit

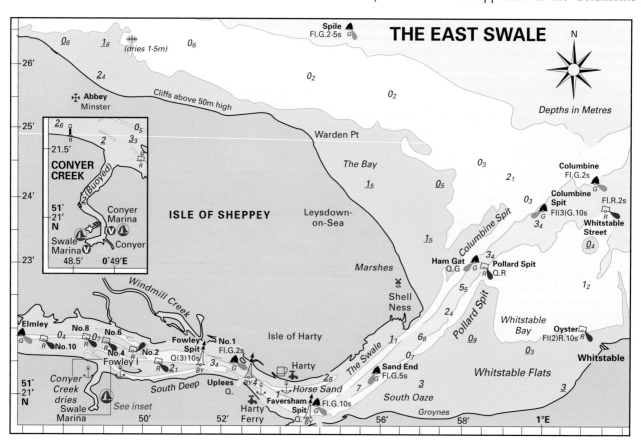

THE SWALE

When it was wider and had greater depth, the Swale was a main route from the English Channel to London, but the channel has narrowed and become shallower by silting and land reclamation to the point where the central section is barely navigable at LWS Sheerness.

With saltmarshes and mudflats on both sides, the Swale forms an area of international importance for breeding and wintering birds. Brent geese, widgeon, plover, oystercatcher and avocet and indeed all manner of wading birds are frequently seen, taking little heed of the hundreds of boats kept in the three main creeks – Faversham, Oare and Conyer – as well as at Queenborough.

At low water, the bones of many ships can be seen along the shores of these creeks and in the Swale itself, many of them relics of the hundreds of Thames barges that served the thriving local industries of brick, cement and gunpowder manufacturing, which are all now gone.

If you love the East Coast and the solitude it can offer, the Swale has considerable charm. It brings its own pilotage challenges, especially if you are on the move around low water, but if you run out of luck, the bottom is forgiving and there is plenty to look at while you wait for the water to return.

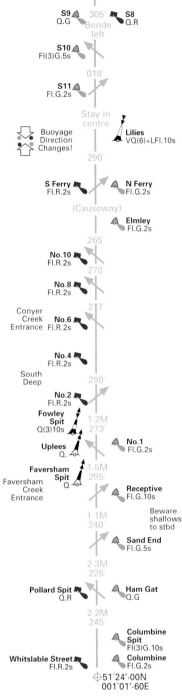

East Swale entrance to Kingsferry Bridge

SHB Fl(3)G.10s. With deeper draught (or less water) continue E to Columbine SHB (Fl.G.2s) for more depth.

Note The lights on these buoys and those further into the Swale have sometimes been used by Trinity House in experiments with sequencing.
Watch www.eastcoastpilot.com for any changes.

From the N Again if draught permits, follow the 001°E meridian past the Red Sand Tower and the Middle Sand SWM. For more water, once S of the Middle Sand, turn SE to enter the Swale at the Columbine buoy. If your draught makes it impractical to cross any of these flats, then a SE course through the Kentish Flats wind farm, two rows of turbines in from its western side, will keep you in more water; once through, then 225° will take you to the vicinity of the Columbine SHB (Fl.G.2s). Skippers may of course prefer to approach the East Swale from the NE, leaving the entire wind farm to starboard.

Enter the channel by passing between the Whitstable Street PHB (Fl.R.2s) and the Columbine SHB (Fl.G.2s).

East Swale

With a strong SW'ly blowing against the flood tide there is often a nasty chop in this area, only smoothing out at the Ham Gat SHB (Q.G) and the Pollard Spit PHB

The Ham Gat SHB, with Warden Point beyond, and Pollard Spit PHB mark the entrance to the East Swale

Approaching the East Swale from the E off Whitstable

The Ferry House Inn, on the Sheppey shore at Harty Ferry

(Q.R). Indeed, any kind of W'ly seems to funnel straight out of the East Swale.

In daylight, from out by the 'Street' (Whitstable Street), the small Pollard Spit and Ham Gat buoys are difficult to locate against the bright sand of Shell Ness, but their bearing is about 240°, range 2·1M from midway between the Street PHB and Columbine SHB. Making good that course just scrapes the S side of the deep water in the channel. In some conditions a clump of trees around a farmhouse on Sheppey appears as a single prominent feature on the approximate bearing, as shown in the photo on page 155.

With the Pollard Spit PHB close to port, a course made good of 225° will take you on another 2·3M to the Sand End SHB (Fl.G.5s), which is again hard to see against the background clutter. In daylight, a good indication that you are heading in the right general direction is the pair of unusually tall electricity pylons each side of Faversham Creek, 4M from the Pollard.

From Shell Ness westwards, most of the Swale has an 8kn speed limit enforced by the Port Authority.

Passing the prominent Shell Ness, its bright beach (often covered with thousands of oystercatchers) and collection of remote houses, the W bank of the deep water channel is very steep to, while the E side remains a fairly gentle shelf. Avoid grounding on the charted shellfish beds in the area and, if tacking in, note there is a substantial mound on the E side of the channel, SSE of the Sand End SHB.

From the Sand End SHB there is a shallow route WSW passing N of the Horse Sand, otherwise follow the main channel SW to the Receptive SHB (Fl.G.10s), which also marks a wreck. Follow a slight curve to port of the rhumb line from the Sand End to the Receptive, to avoid the edge of the Horse Sand, where seals are often hauled out. On the S side of the channel is the Faversham Spit NCB (Q), at the entrance to Faversham Creek.

HARTY FERRY

From the Receptive SHB, the Swale turns NW, passing through the anchorage known as Harty or Harty Ferry. The Isle of Harty, no longer an island but part of the Isle of Sheppey, stands on the N side of the anchorage with an ancient Saxon church on the skyline and the white Ferry House Inn nestling on the S side of the hill.
Ferry House Inn ME12 4BQ ☎ 01795 510214
www.theferryhouseinn.co.uk

The pub is named for the ferry that once ran between here and the mainland. A public causeway provides landing for visitors to the pub, which has accommodation and a restaurant. The landing is a little muddy, but the causeway is hard. It does not extend as far as LWS, but the mud beyond is quite firm. The pub runs clay pigeon shooting several times a month, which can be quite a disturbance on an otherwise peaceful day. As visiting by boat requires some effort, check opening hours beforehand as we have found that they can be 'variable'.

The S shore, also known as Harty Ferry, has a hard causeway, marked by substantial posts, which extends right across the mudflats.

The village of Oare is a pleasant walk away, just over a mile along the lane from the mainland causeway, with

The south shore at Harty Ferry

Faversham Creek   Hollowshore   Oare Creek

Southern Causeway

Moorings at Harty, and the causeway on the S shore

two pubs but no shop. Or a dinghy trip can take you to the Shipwright's Arms at the junction of Faversham and Oare Creeks (see details for Oare Creek).

A dark-roofed building owned by the Kent Wildlife Trust peers over the S sea wall and just across the road from it is a useful fresh water spring, unusual on marshland and once a supply for the long-gone widespread munitions factories that stretched westwards from here.

There are a few moorings on the N shore and many more to the S of the channel, most of them E of the causeway. These are a mixture of club and private moorings, where the usual rule applies that they may be used unless the owner or a club member appears; the private ones occasionally attract a charge levied by the local moorings manager. The club moorings are marked 'HCC' or 'CCC', and Club members obviously have priority. Anchoring clear of the moorings either side of the main channel generally finds good holding in soft mud.

The Harty anchorage is exposed to strong E winds, when it should be avoided if possible. With some N in the wind, you may find shelter under the N shore about a ½M W of the causeway, although it is much shallower and you must avoid charted wrecks on the mudflats. Note the Uplees NCB (Q) a few hundred yards W of Harty, which marks a large wreck close to the surface.

Harty is a classic East Coast anchorage, but the tide can run hard here and this must be considered when going ashore by dinghy, especially with wind over tide. The area teems with bird life that may wake you early on a peaceful summer morning.

The hard causeway on the S shore at Harty

FAVERSHAM

The Faversham area is served by two drying creeks: Faversham Creek which ends close to the town centre, and Oare Creek. Initial entry is into Faversham Creek, and Oare Creek branches off it to starboard at Hollowshore.

Faversham Creek initially runs SW from the Swale at the Faversham Spit NCB (Q). Speed limit in the creek is 6kn and careful progress on a rising tide is advisable. There is no commercial traffic, but quite large leisure vessels including Thames barges use Faversham Creek. If you are hoping for a berth at Faversham at Iron Wharf, Front Brents or Town Quay, it would be best to phone ahead. Iron Wharf, the first berthing point in Faversham Creek, is about 2¼M away.

In Oare Creek there are several moorings operators, the creek ending at the village of Oare on the outskirts of Faversham itself.

THE SWALE

Entry to Faversham Creek at LW

Faversham Creek entrance from the Faversham Spit cardinal buoy

Entry to Faversham Creek

Leave the NCB to starboard and follow the line of unlit PHBs, and a single SHB, until the creek bends to port opposite an SHM post marking a wreck. (The authors found this wreck to be a useful tide gauge – if its ribs are completely covered then there is sufficient depth in Oare Creek for a 1·5m draught boat to reach the head of the

Entering Faversham Creek, initially SW then swinging S towards Hollowshore at the No.8 buoy

creek.) Give the PHBs room; in some wind and tide conditions they lie over the shallows (see photo above).

Once past the final PHB, follow the centre of the channel S towards the buildings ahead at Hollowshore. Leave moored boats to starboard and be aware that sometimes there are ropes trailing in the water from laid-up derelict fishing boats. Overhead is a high tension electricity line with a charted safe air draught of 32m.

The larger of the buildings at Hollowshore is a boatyard shed and the smaller white building is the Shipwright's Arms pub. These are at the junction of Faversham and Oare Creeks where Oare Creek splits off to starboard (see below).

Faversham Creek, from Hollowshore to Iron Wharf

The general rule for going up Faversham Creek, unless you know it well, is to start at half flood or soon after, before the saltings are covered. The notes that follow are detailed, but in general the channel follows the outside of bends – quite extremely, in some cases, so don't be afraid to get close in to the bank. Don't just buoy hop – weave gently to stay with the best depth on your echosounder. The upper stretches of the creek have about 2·5m in the gutway at HW.

Enter Faversham Creek proper with the pub to starboard and, passing PHBs 10 and 12, follow the line

Faversham Creek swings SE off Hollowshore

Shipwright's Arms

Approaching Iron Wharf. Any berths are likely to be near the crane

FAVERSHAM

Tides Sheerness
Access HW-2hrs to HW+1½hr
Boatyard Iron Wharf Boatyard ME13 7BY
① 01795 536296 www.ironwharf.co.uk
Email manager@ironwharf.co.uk
Boat repairs 14-T crane, dry dock up to 90ft
Fuel Garage in town, ¾M
Gas Calor and Gaz from chandler
Facilities WC, showers, launderette
Chandler (at Iron Wharf) Faversham Chandlery ① 01795 531777
www.favershamchandlery.co.uk Open Thurs-Mon.
Email mark@favershamchandlery.co.uk
Shipwright (Next to Iron Wharf) Alan Staley ① 01795 530668
www.alanstaleyboatbuilders.co.uk
Sailmaker (In town) Wilkinson Sails ① 01795 521503
www.wilkinsonsails.co.uk
Other moorings Front Brents Jetty, Town Quay – see text for contact
Provisions, pub/restaurant Many in the town
Town information www.visitfaversham.org
① 01795 503286
Transport Buses; Trains to London, or to Ramsgate and Dover via Canterbury
Taxi ① 01795 536666, 591066

of the starboard bank until abeam the section of stone sea wall. Turn to port to bring the nearby pylon fine on the port bow to pass PHB 12A, getting close to the left bank N of SHB 3, before turning SE towards SHBs 5 and then 5A. Stay roughly mid-channel from here to pass SHB 7, then 7A, before crossing to starboard to pass PHB 14. From here, aim for two private pontoon moorings beyond some houses on the left bank (a boat may be moored there), opposite SHB 9, and then generally follow the outside of the right hand bend. SHB 11 follows, then a left hand bend around PHB 16. Keep in the middle of the stream until you reach PHB 18, when you'll see Iron Wharf ahead to port.

Faversham Creek, Iron Wharf to the head of navigation

Iron Wharf | Staley's Boatyard | Standard Quay | Town Quay

Front Brents Jetty

THE SWALE

Front Brents Jetty to starboard

A patriotic RIB lies at Faversham Town Quay, near HW

Iron Wharf is a large friendly DIY boatyard with a well stocked chandlery. There are no pontoons, and any spare drying berths for visitors (on previous enquiry) will be in perhaps 2m (at HW) against a wall or possibly rafted out from it.

Iron Wharf to Town Quay

Immediately above Iron Wharf and also to port are Chambers Wharf and Alan Staley's boatbuilding and restoration yard. Then you will see a tall brick building with an ancient sign saying 'United Fertiliser' followed by Standard Quay, opposite the start of some modern housing on the north bank. The best water tends to be along the starboard side of the creek in front of the housing, and ahead are some private pontoon moorings in a small inlet. Rounding a slight left-hand bend and resuming your passage in the centre of the creek, the Front Brents foreshore is on the starboard side a few hundred yards ahead, with a fixed road bridge beyond it.

In recent years the Front Brents Jetty, owned and run by the Town Council, stood here parallel to the creek bank and provided moorings with security, power and water. There was a tide gauge at the downstream end, showing the depth in feet, and the tidal height above LAT in metres. However, during 2018 the Jetty was closed indefinitely, needing repair or replacement, possibly by pontoons. Any progress will be reported on the East Coast Pilot website, and also prospective visitors may of course wish to contact the Town Council (*Email* adrienne.begent@favershamtc.co.uk, ☏ 01795 503286).

Alternative alongside moorings lie slightly further up the creek, on the port side just before the fixed road bridge, at the small Town Quay, a length of wall that usually has room alongside for two 10m boats, plus perhaps one more rafted alongside. Fender boards are recommended. A drawback if boats are moored end to end is that the only ladder is at the centre of the wall. Depth is perhaps 1·75m at HW, and the area dries to soft mud and is quite flat. There is reported to be a narrow ledge low down on the wall, covered by mud, and bilge-keeler skippers should perhaps fender out away from the wall a little more than usual to avoid catching a keel on it.

A very high HWS can reach the top of the wall. There is no security, nor any facilities, so visiting boats will need to be self-sufficient. Town Quay is run by the borough council, which sets a maximum stay of two nights, and fees may be paid by phone ☏ 01795 417850, or at a local office – details are on a notice on the nearby wall.

There are plans for the road bridge to be rebuilt as a swing or lifting bridge and restore access to the basin beyond, but at the time of writing sufficient funding had not been raised.

Faversham is an interesting historic town to visit with more than 475 listed buildings and what is said to be the country's best preserved mediaeval street, Abbey Street, which is a few steps away from the E side of the creek. Front Brents and the Town Quay are very close to the centre with its good mix of shops, pubs and facilities including restaurants. Shepherd Neame, the country's oldest and largest independent brewery, is across the road from the Town Quay.

HOLLOWSHORE

Hollowshore is the old name given to the small area at the junction of Faversham and Oare Creeks. It has one ancient pub, a boatyard and one private house. It is remote and there is no public transport.

The boatyard, where traditional wooden working boats are restored and repaired, is one of the many sites where Thames barges were built. With permission, a spare mud berth near the yard may be available, otherwise anchor off to the N and dinghy ashore.

The Shipwright's Arms has its own ghost, reputed to be a barge skipper shipwrecked one stormy night out in the Swale, who managed to get ashore and stagger to the pub door, but who could make nobody hear and was found dead there next morning.

HOLLOWSHORE   ME13 7TU

Boatyard/moorings Hollowshore Moorings
☏ 01795 529033
www.hollowshoremoorings.co.uk
Services Moorings, water, electricity, covered slip, crane, full repairs
Sailmaker Paul Martin ☏ 01795 537936 or
07792 579210 www.paulmartinsailmaker.co.uk
Pub/restaurant The Shipwright's Arms ☏ 01795 590088
www.theshipwrightsathollowshore.co.uk
Transport Taxi ☏ 01795 536666, 591066

Approaching the mouth of Oare Creek, to the right of the boatyard buildings

Oare Creek

If going far up Oare Creek, start at about HWN - 1½hr or HWS -2hr. The tide ebbs from the creek faster than it floods and it dries entirely after about half ebb. Watch the depth constantly as the gutway described below wanders from time to time.

Once past the craft moored in the first part of Faversham Creek, keep heading straight towards the pub (white building to left of large boatshed) and look for the end of a low fence that comes down to the shore from the sea wall to port. Look also for a very small R buoy in the entrance to Oare Creek, N of the boatshed. When you judge you are between the fence and the buoy, turn towards the R buoy and pass close N of it. About 20m further on, leave a larger orange buoy close to port. It marks the end of a slipway from the boatshed.

For its first ½M, the port shore is lined with boats moored on wooden jetties and some pontoons, all privately owned. The channel is unmarked. Stand about 10m off the sterns of the moored boats, keeping to the port side of the channel around the right hand bend where you may find a large floating dry dock and moored barges. Pass as close to these as you dare for the best water, then resume a distance of about 10m off the moored boats until about 200m before a left hand bend whose right bank has an ancient wooden wharf. Reach mid-channel opposite the beginning of the wharf and continue mid-channel around the bend.

Around the left hand bend there's an old gunpowder dock to port and the channel moves across close to the pontoons of Cylinder House Moorings by the old red-roofed shed (known locally as the Cylinder House, once a saltpetre store). At these moorings a spare berth may be available if requested in advance. Power (uses tokens)

OARE CREEK   ME13 7TX

Access HW±1½hr
Boatyard Youngboats (Terry Young)
☎ 01795 536176
(Closed Sun-Mon)
www.youngboats.co.uk
Email info@youngboats.co.uk
Services 8-T crane, berthing, storage
Water On pontoons
Electricity On pontoons (tokens from yard)
Scrubbing berth Max length 9m
Facilities WC, shower
Café on site opening mid-2019, open most days
Club Hollowshore Cruising Club
www.hollowshore.wordpress.com
Pubs/restaurants The Castle ☎ 01795 533674
The Three Mariners ☎ 01795 533633
www.thethreemarinersoare.co.uk
Transport Buses
Taxi ☎ 01795 536666, 591066

and water is available here, but the nearest available toilets are at Youngboats, a short walk away at the head of the creek (see below). Boats of up to 1·3m draught should reach these berths on most tides and should sit reasonably upright on soft mud.

Cylinder House Moorings ☎ 07905 106236
Email thecylinderhouse@yahoo.com

There are many more pontoon moorings at the head of the creek at Youngboats' yard. From the Cylinder House onwards, the channel meanders, gets shallower and is marked by pairs of withies although these are not constantly maintained. Halfway along this final stretch the channel veers all the way to the S shore then back to the middle. Keep to stbd of a line of vacant posts as you

The lower section of Oare Creek, the Thames barge yard ahead on the right-hand bend. Stay close to the moorings

Cylinder House Moorings; Youngboats yard is in the distance at the head of the creek

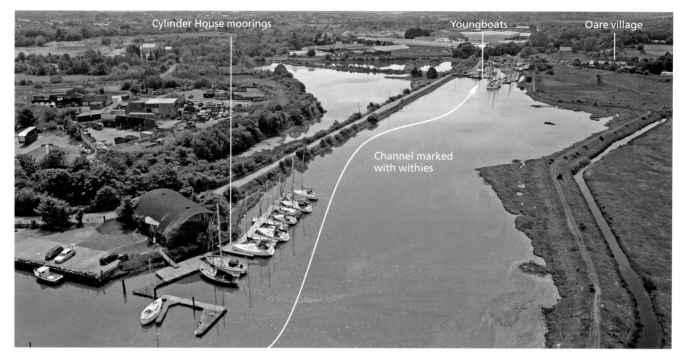

The upper reaches of Oare Creek at HW

reach the first berths. Boats much over 10m LOA will be tricky to turn at the head of the creek. If in doubt, phone Youngboats for advice.

Also in Youngboats' yard is the HQ of Hollowshore Cruising Club, a small, welcoming club for the many boat owners in these creeks. It's open on Sundays at lunchtime, usually with snacks available.

Oare village at the head of the creek has two pubs, both of which serve food. There is an occasional bus service from Oare; the bus stop is by The Castle pub. Faversham itself is perhaps a 30-minute walk away.

THE SWALE – HARTY TO CONYER

Continuing NW from Harty, the deep water channel runs past the Uplees NCB (Q) which marks a large wreck lying athwart the current, close beneath the surface. Reaching the Swale No.1 SHB (Fl.G.2s), opposite on the S shore are some scrubbing posts, although these have not been seen used for a while.

The Swale now opens up into a much broader stretch of water, a row of narrow chimneys at a paper mill prominent 4M W, but at LW much of the water disappears.

On the N shore, beyond the No.1 buoy, is Windmill Creek, which generally dries although a very shallow draught boat might stay afloat in a hole near the junction with Bells Creek.

The Fowley Spit ECB (Q(3)10s) guards the end of Fowley Island and marks the entrance to South Deep, with Conyer Creek beyond.

South Deep

South Deep, particularly towards its W end inside Fowley Island, is a delightfully quiet and sheltered spot for an overnight stop and is also the main route from the E to the entrance to Conyer Creek.

Start close to port of the Fowley Spit ECB and aim for an unlit SHB off the E end of Fowley Island. Keep an eye on the depth - the channel tends to follow a curve closing on the S shore. Two cables beyond the SHB there are several large white waiting buoys laid by moorings operators at Conyer. Carry on past the charted sluice (R.Bn) on the S shore and after about 100m you should find a hole with 1·5m at LWS. Fowley Island is low lying, little more than saltings that virtually cover at HWS, and is a wildlife reserve where landing is prohibited. Beyond this secluded anchorage, the route W leads to an unlit PHB, then SW via a channel marked with small red and green buoys to an equally small ECB just inside the mouth of Conyer Creek.

NW of Harty, the scrubbing posts and Uplees NCB. Kingsferry road bridge is in the far distance

Conyer Creek from the North, near LW

Fowley Spit Westwards

After Fowley Spit ECB the channel W narrows considerably and is marked with lit PHBs (Fl.R.2s) as far as Elmley.

Boats drawing up to 1m can pass through this shallowest section of the Swale after LWS+1hr, provided the PHBs are followed meticulously. The No.8 PHB marks the last chance to turn S into Conyer or South Deep. At night, constantly check that you are heading for the next PHB in the sequence – with their identical light characteristics, it is possible to be misled.

CONYER CREEK

Conyer, which dries from half tide, can be approached from the E via South Deep (see above), the deeper route, or from the W via the Swale No.8 PHB. If routing via the No. 8, look for the charted islet of Little Fowley, N of the creek entrance. Little Fowley is marked with a small buoy but has eroded away in recent years, so that it's still fully covered long after HW. Near HW you should find 2m all the way from No.8 to a point S of the islet, although depths change suddenly as you cross the gutways that meander across the flats.

There are two well marked routes for the final approach to the creek entrance. Either continue SE to the start of the E channel (30m W of the unlit PHB in South Deep), then following between the red and green buoys (you may find it shallow along this short stretch), or use a deeper W channel called the Butterfly.

If using the Butterfly Channel, find the first pair of marker posts for this about 300m NNW of the creek entrance, then follow between the posts, heading directly SW towards the sea wall, turning abruptly to port very close to the wall before meeting the E channel at the small ECB. This is clearly seen in the photo above.

From the ECB, the channel is marked by more small buoys leading first of all close to two wrecks on the E shore, then gradually moving out between a mix of buoys and posts to the W side of the creek approaching a sharp left hand bend. Around the bend, where buoyage ends but posts continue at intervals, the channel is nearer to the centre and the village of Conyer comes into view.

The very small Conyer Creek Marina on the E bank is reached first; it's the base of builders and repairers North Quay Marine. There may be drying berths available for visitors (see Conyer details). Use the centre of the right-hand bend as you approach.

The E route into Conyer Creek from South Deep

Conyer entrance at half tide, the deeper Butterfly Channel in the foreground, the E channel coming in the from the left, and South Deep beyond

Arriving at the small Conyer Creek Marina

Once past this marina and the housing on the port bank, Blackden Moorings' drying pontoon berths lie directly ahead of you to port in Conyer Dock. They can only occasionally accommodate visitors, so phone ahead to check availability ① 01795 522833.

Turn to starboard opposite Blackden Moorings into the large Swale Marina, providing 200 drying mud berths alongside pontoons and extending all the way to the head of the creek. Access all the way to the marina is about HW±2hr – phone the harbour office for advice. The well kept marina has a boatyard, and a modern clubhouse for berth holders which is also the base for Conyer Cruising Club.

CONYER

Tides Sheerness
Access HW±2hr
Pub/restaurant Ship Inn on Conyer Quay (including breakfasts at weekends) ① 01795 520881
Provisions Teynham village (bus or taxi)
Transport Buses (infrequent) to Teynham and trains from there to Ramsgate and Dover or London
Taxi ① 01795 426600, 444444.

CONYER CREEK MARINA   ME9 9HL

Contact
① 01795 521711 ① 07971 641129
Email info@northquaymarine.co.uk
www.conyercreekmarina.co.uk
Facilities WC, showers
Water and Electricity On pontoons
Boat repairs North Quay Marine on site ① 01795 521711 www.northquaymarine.co.uk
10-T crane, engineer, shipwrights on site

SWALE MARINA   ME9 9HN

Contact
Office ① 01795 521562
Email enquiries@swalemarina.co.uk
www.swalemarina.co.uk
Facilities WC, showers
Water and Electricity On pontoons
Fuel Diesel
Gas Calor and Gaz
Boat repairs 30-T travel hoist, 25-T slipway, Coppercoat agent, shipwright on site
Club Conyer CC www.conyercc.org.uk

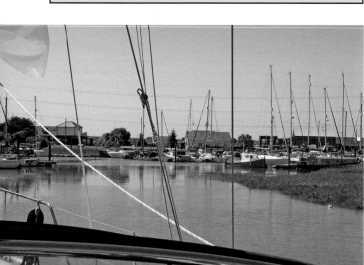

Final approach to Blackden moorings to port and Swale Marina at the head of the creek

Swale Marina at HW. Blackden Moorings on the far left

THE SWALE – CONYER CREEK TO KINGSFERRY

Heading W from the Swale No.8 PHB (Fl.R.2s), past No.10 PHB (Fl.R.2s) and the Elmley SHB (Fl.G.2s) near LW, the next feature is the disused ferry causeway at Elmley. (King James II is said to have fled the country from around here, hence the local name, Kingsferry.) The deepest water can be found slightly N of centre in the gap between two pairs of posts on the causeway. A buried gas pipe runs N-S just E of the causeway, so care should be taken not to anchor in the vicinity.

The Lilies buoy, where the Swale curves northwards into Clay Reach

From the causeway, steer between the North Ferry PHB (Fl.G.2s) and the South Ferry SHB (Fl.R.2s). Depth will increase as you head for the Lilies SCB (VQ(6)+LFl.10s).

Milton Creek branches away S here. Once a busy trading waterway, it leads to Sittingbourne town centre, but a low-level road bridge (air draught 4·2m) now bars access in its lower reach.

Note At this point in the Swale, the direction of lateral buoyage reverses.

Beyond the Lilies, on the W side of the channel, is the Grovehurst Jetty frequently used by ships delivering bulk cargo. N of this jetty the channel is marked by lit SHBs (to be left to port when heading N), S11 (Fl.G.2s) then S10 (Fl(3)G.5s) in Clay Reach. At S9 (Q.G) it turns NW past S8 (Q.R) and widens into Ferry Reach with the Kingsferry lifting bridge in view less than a mile away. From here to Long Point, beyond the bridge, the speed limit does not apply and the stretch is used by fast powerboats.

In Ferry Reach there is a busy dock on the S shore, Ridham Dock, which takes frequent coaster traffic – you should learn of any imminent traffic by monitoring the channel for Kingsferry Bridge, VHF Ch 10.

Heading E at the Elmley causeway soon after LW, where there is more depth towards the N end

Kingsferry Bridge lifted for a ship heading E towards Ridham Dock

Kingsferry Bridge and Sheppey Crossing

Kingsferry Bridge carries rail traffic and some local road traffic across a lifting span between two pairs of towers; the high level fixed road bridge (Sheppey Crossing) just W carries the bulk of road traffic between Sheppey and the mainland. If you need Kingsferry Bridge to lift (air draught when lowered is 3·35m at MHWS), it is best to call on VHF Ch 10 when you are an hour away, to ensure that the bridge keeper knows you are coming well in advance, and monitor Ch 10 thereafter.

The bridge is operated by Network Rail and does not open to a timetable, but it is required to lift on request if circumstances allow. In practice, although the bridge is manned continuously, the duty bridge keeper cannot open the bridge without permission from the railway signalman at Sittingbourne.

KINGSFERRY BRIDGE

Contact
VHF Ch 10
Callsign *Kingsferry Bridge*
☎ 01795 423627
Lights Alt Q R/G bridge lifting
F.G bridge open (28m MHWS)
Q.R bridge lowering, keep clear
Q.Y bridge out of action
No lights – bridge down (3·35m MHWS)

Waiting for a bridge lift on the NW side of Kingsferry

The train timetable allows for two lifts per hour, Monday to Saturday, at about H+10 and H+40 in 2018. On Sundays there is a lift just once per hour, usually around H+15. The bridge is, however, said to be restricted to three lifts in two hours to allow the machinery to cool. In warmer weather, even on weekdays the bridge keeper may advise that only one lift per hour is possible, to avoid overheating the elderly machinery whose replacement is long overdue. Normal courtesy and reasonableness when requesting a lift will probably ease your way through. Commercial shipping takes priority, but you will usually be allowed through immediately before or after a ship, as advised on Ch 10. In this situation do not assume anything – ensure that the bridge keeper tells the ship's pilot that you are waiting and that agreement is reached as to whether you lead or follow the ship through. The pilot will also be monitoring Ch 10.

If the lift is just for you and perhaps other leisure craft, help the bridge keeper reduce delays by keeping station close to the bridge at the time advised to you. The lift sequence starts with flashing R/G lights. Wait until a fixed G light is displayed before passing through. A loud horn is sometimes sounded with the G light.

When planning a passage through the bridge, bear in mind that there can be circumstances when the bridge cannot be lifted. In very hot weather it is sometimes not lifted at all for fear of unequal expansion jamming the mechanism. Such failures, and also periods of scheduled maintenance, are usually advised in the MSI broadcasts by HMCG.

Note The stretch between Kingsferry and the Medway is described in the next section, starting from the Medway.

THE SWALE - QUEENBOROUGH TO KINGSFERRY

WEST SWALE

⊕**Entry waypoint**
51°25'·84N 000°44'·00E Immediately NE of Queenborough Spit ECB (Q(3)10s)
Tides Sheerness

Main Hazards
Ruins on E shore marked by dolphins. Some commercial traffic.

Approaches
Approaches to the W Swale will be from seaward or down river from the Medway.

From seaward, follow directions for entering the Medway (see chapter 15) then, watching for commercial traffic, make for the W Swale entrance marked by the Queenborough Spit ECB (Q(3)10s).

Heading E down the Medway, the Queenborough Spit ECB can be hard to locate against the Sheerness shore and can be obscured by large tugs on moorings W of it. These tugs are active during shipping movements. Huge wind turbines stand on the shore behind.

Entering the west Swale at the Queenborough Spit buoy

Heading S in the Swale, leave the Queenborough Spit ECB to starboard and pass two large lit dolphins on the E shore (Q.R and Fl.R.4s) guarding dangerous remains of an old ferry terminal, which once hosted the 'Flushing Ferry' service to and from Vlissingen.

Queenborough

Queenborough town is on the Isle of Sheppey at the entrance to the West Swale, a little under 2M S of Garrison Point at the mouth of the Medway. It offers a safe and, except in strong N through NW'lies, sheltered anchorage and almost always has visitor moorings available. The harbour is run by the Queenborough Harbour Trust.

Immediately S of the second dolphin, lines of moorings begin on both shores. Beyond the moorings on the E side, a long pontoon (2F.R) carrying the harbour office lies parallel to the shore, connected at its S end by a bridge to the hammerhead of the all-tide landing (ATL) floating jetty, which stretches across the mudflats from the E shore. Call *Sheppey One* on VHF Ch 08 for mooring instructions.

Two dolphins guard the dangerous remains of an old ferry terminal

QUEENBOROUGH   ME11 5AA

Tides Sheerness
Contact
VHF Ch 08
Callsign *Sheppey One*
Harbour office ☎ 01795 662051 or 07456 459754
Email info@queenborough-harbour.co.uk
www.queenborough-harbour.co.uk
Access 24hr ATL (pontoons) and public Town Hard (dinghies only)
Facilities Trot-boat; WC & showers in club, if open, or public facilities nearby, key from Queenborough Stores in the main street.
Water On ATL
Electricity None
Fuel From petrol station ½M in Queenborough Rd
Repairs Jim Brett's yard in Queenborough Creek, with 8-T crane ☎ 01795 668263
Gas Calor and Gaz from petrol station
Provisions Up the main street 100 yards, also large supermarket 20 mins walk
Pub/Restaurant Flying Dutchman ☎ 01795 667189
Old House at Home ☎ 01795 662463
Others in town, ask in harbour office
Club Queenborough YC ☎ 01795 663955
Transport Buses; Trains to Sittingbourne for connections to London, Dover and Ramsgate
Taxi ☎ 01795 252525

The Harbour Trust is constantly developing the facilities when funds allow. Check the ECP website, Swale updates section, where we will show any significant changes.

Moorings that may be offered include alongside (possibly rafted) berths on the pontoon by the harbour office, and large multiple-occupancy buoys nearby.

SW of the ATL on the W side of the channel, a large concrete barge used to be available as a mooring and was popular for groups of boats cruising together. Unfortunately it was declared unsafe in 2018 - any replacement is likely to be another barge or a pontoon in the same position.

Do not anchor in the fairway, because commercial traffic operates 24hr through the Kingsferry Bridge, but you may find a place to bring up under the N shore of Loden Hope.

Queenborough and the All-Tide Landing

Town Hard   Kingsferry Bridge   Loden Hope   Long Point

All Tide Landing   HM Office

Harbour office

Approaching the pontoon and hammerhead of the All-Tide Landing

The Harbour Trust runs a trot-boat service for those who are on buoyed moorings, trot-boat hours varying with season, price included in the mooring fee. If using your own dinghy to get ashore, be aware that the tides run strongly here.

The ATL has a gate at its shore end, which lets you ashore, but requires a code or purchased token to pass seawards again. The code is provided free by the harbour staff, or tokens to open the gate can be purchased from the two nearby pubs and from the Queenborough Stores in the High Street.

Queenborough YC welcomes visitors who may use its facilities when it's open. When the club is closed, there is a public toilet/shower block on the small green just behind the sea wall (see info panel).

To the S of the ATL is the long, sloping concrete Town Hard, usable by dinghy, which allows free access to and from the shore but is not clean.

Queenborough Creek

Along the south side of the town is the drying Queenborough Creek. Access (HW+/-1½) is across the mudflats closely following the small markers from the S1 PHB (Fl.R.3s) off the end of the concrete hard, then through the floodgate (usually open). The Town Quay on the N side of the creek can be crowded, but the bottom is flat and free from obstructions; the Harbour

Office manages some of these spaces along the quayside. Also ask about use (at a small charge) of the scrubbing berth in the Creek, at the far end of the open quayside, where the bottom is a large concrete slab.

Flood gate activity is indicated by Control Lights as follows: 3F.R(vert) barrier closed; 3Fl.R(vert) closure imminent.

Queenborough to Kingsferry Bridge

The passage from Queenborough to the bridge is straightforward with good depth in the channel, plenty of lights at night and no unmarked obstructions. To help ships navigate at night, the channel is covered by sectored lights and leading lights.

Call the bridge keeper (Ch 10, Kingsferry Bridge) before leaving the moorings at Queenborough to find out when the next lift will be. See bridge details on page 167.

The channel runs round a right hand bend into Loden Hope, past S2 (Q.G) and S3 (Fl.G.2·5s) SHBs. To port is an old wharf with cranes.

At the end of Loden Hope is a hairpin bend to port with best water midway between the banks all the way round. Do not cut this corner. There is a PHB (Fl.R.3s) off Long Point and two sectored lights (Q.WG) on the outside of the bend.

Once round Long Pt, Long Reach runs past S4 (Q.R) PHB and S5 (Fl.G.5s) SHB to S6 (Fl.R.5s) PHB where the channel bends to port past S7 (Q.R) PHB. Do not cut this corner either.

From S7, Horse Reach leads past S7A (Oc.G) SHB and lit beacons on either hand before the final stretch to the bridge on about 140°. There is a WRG sectored light located E of the bridge to guide shipping through and the port authority specifically warns against looking directly at this bright light.

The waters each side of the bridge are the only areas in the Swale without an 8kn speed limit and powerboats and PWCs are active there, especially at weekends. This stretch can be crowded in summer with yachts waiting for a bridge lift and sharing a fairly small area with much faster boats. Skippers may find it easier to wait NW of the fixed road bridge rather than between the two bridges, especially when the stream is running SE.

Looking upstream along the Town Quay in Queenborough Creek

18. THE NORTH KENT COAST

This chapter describes the coastal pilotage from Ramsgate to the Swale and Medway, including the ports of Broadstairs, Margate, Herne Bay and Whitstable.

BROADSTAIRS AND MARGATE HARBOURS

Contact
Ramsgate Harbour office ✆ 01843 572100
Facilities Ad hoc berthing only

Ramsgate to North Foreland

On passage from Ramsgate N towards the Foreland, you can safely keep as close as ½M from the shore unless you have exceptional draught and it's LWS. Beware pot markers in the whole area. Apart from the very obvious steel dolphin (Fl.R.2·5s) ½M N of Ramsgate harbour, there are no charted individual hazards and you can enjoy the scenery of Thanet's chalk cliffs, soon giving way to the tiny haven of Broadstairs.

Broadstairs is a pretty little place and a bustling seaside resort in summer. The harbour, formed by a short stone arm at the N end of the bay, provides little shelter and dries completely to hard sand, but is perhaps not a proposition for a prolonged visit unless you have a sense of adventure, a suitable craft and the weather is settled. A lunchtime anchorage stop for a swim a few hundred yards off or a row ashore for an ice cream is something you might consider. The harbour is managed out of the Ramsgate Harbour office, where you can find advice if needed. Broadstairs SC runs dinghy races just offshore and occasionally hosts large events, which are best avoided by heading a little further out round them.

North of Broadstairs, the cliffs quickly rise again, surmounted by houses most of the way to the N Foreland lighthouse (Fl(5)WR.20s57m19-15M), which was notable for being the last in the country to be manned before it, too, became fully automated.

The cliffs reduce in height as you round the N Foreland and are punctuated by sandy bays. Off the Foreland itself, strong winds can produce very rough conditions – it's the meeting place of two tidal streams, where the waters of the Thames Estuary meet the English Channel. In a strong SW'ly, however, it's usually sheltered inshore, but be aware of the charted chalk ledges and also badly marked pots.

Approaching Broadstairs from the S near LW. Enter between the two beacons

Broadstairs Harbour at half-tide; note the beacons each side of the entrance

North Foreland light – beware of the chalk ledges that run out to sea

Stay outside the steel dolphin on the NE side of the Foreland. Margate in view in the distance

North Foreland westwards

Boats heading W have a choice here: to keep along the coast inshore of the mass of sandbanks that fills the Estuary (the 'overland' route) or to make N, turning NNW in the vicinity of the East Margate buoy (Fl.R.2·5s) for the Queens Channel (if heading for the Swale) or the Princes Channel if going to the Medway or Thames. Although the inshore route is the shortest, without local knowledge it should be treated with great caution in strong onshore winds and especially around LW, particularly through the shallows off Reculver.

The Princes Channel is a main shipping route and should be treated accordingly. Skippers of leisure craft should generally follow its S side taking care to avoid the significant shallows of the Ridge and the Pan Sand.

The Queens Channel, too, avoids the Reculver area if the shallows there are a concern in your passage plan. Neither route adds much distance to the passage to the Medway.

When following the inshore route along the Kent shore, head NW from the Foreland, rounding Foreness Point between the large steel dolphin marking an outfall (lit FL.R) and the unlit Longnose PHB three cables to the NE, and then on W through the South Channel.

Margate

A little less than two miles W of the Longnose is the small drying harbour of Margate. If planning to take a closer look at it, be sure to avoid the hidden remains of the pier just E, which was destroyed in a storm and is marked by a very large NCM (Q.3M). The harbour itself, with its single stone arm and stone lighthouse (F.R.4M) on its outer end, is sheltered from N through E but is totally open to the W, and dries at least 2m to mostly hard sand. From a distance, the harbour location is obvious from the N, but less so from the NW. HW is at about Sheerness -0035.

The Turner Contemporary gallery is close E of the harbour and a trip ashore to visit it, or perhaps the seafront delights of Margate, may be the only reasons to enter, although a suitable craft could certainly take shelter from winds in the sector from N through E to S. There is a broad slipway in the SE corner of the harbour and another narrower one outside, close E – do not obstruct these as they may be needed by the Margate lifeboat. Fender boards are advisable against

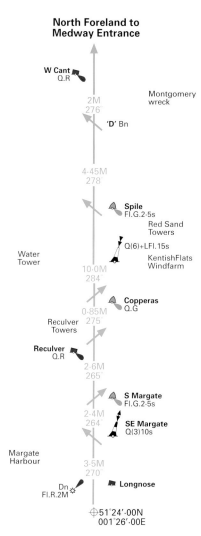

North Foreland to
Medway Entrance

W Cant
Q.R

Montgomery
wreck

2M
276

'D' Bn

4·45M
278

Spile
Fl.G.2·5s

Red Sand
Towers

Q(6)+LFl.15s

Water
Tower

KentishFlats
Windfarm

10·0M
284

Copperas
Q.G

0·85M
Reculver 275
Towers

Reculver
Q.R

2·6M
265

S Margate
Fl.G.2·5s

2·4M
264

SE Margate
Q(3)10s

Margate
Harbour

3·5M
270

Dn
Fl.R.2M

Longnose

⊕51°24'·00N
001°26'·00E

Turner Contemporary ⎜ NCM ⎜ Pierhead

Approaching Margate from the E, stay outside the N Cardinal post near the harbour

Slipway

Turner
Contemporary

Slipway

RNLI Station

Margate YC

Margate Harbour from the west, at LW

the wall – the best stretch of wall is perhaps between the first and second bends in, where there is more timber to lean on.

Like Broadstairs, this harbour is also managed out of the Ramsgate Harbour office if needed. Margate YC, mainly a dinghy sailing club, is just across the road at the foot of the hill.

Dried out alongside Margate's harbour arm

Margate westwards

Heading on W, the shore beyond Margate rises again as a low chalk cliff, which finally peters out again at Minnis Bay. The N side of the route on through the Gore Channel is marked by the SE Margate ECB (Q(3)10s), then S Margate SHB (Fl.G.2·5s); along here the deep channel is sheltered from the N by the Margate Hook Sand. Keep well S of the area around the S Margate buoy near LW as it's quite shallow in the vicinity. Beyond Minnis, the coastline sinks to barely more than a sea wall, blocking off the sea from what was once the Wantsum Channel which separated the Isle of Thanet from the mainland.

Reculver Towers are seen ahead. These two rectangular towers, linked together, are part of an ancient ruined church that stands inside the Roman 'Saxon Shore' fort of Regulbium, whose garrison guarded the N end of the Wantsum.

The old church at Reculver was built using materials from the Roman fort, but was largely demolished and moved a mile inland in the 19th century when it became clear that the sea would take it if unchecked. That the original Towers still stand today, on a low promontory, protected just yards from the waves by a sea wall, is due in part to their importance as a landmark for mariners. From time to time the towers are floodlit until midnight.

Steering about 265° from the S Margate SHB, the Reculver PHB (Q.R) marking the start of the Copperas Channel is some 2·4M distant. The Margate Hook beacon is a prominent, unlit SCM on the sandbank to starboard and once housed a refuge for shipwrecked sailors.

Off Reculver Towers, pass well outside the Reculver PHB

Be aware that near LW the Copperas Channel route is suitable only for shoal draught boats. The Channel itself has good depth, but its approaches from the E seem to be progressively shallowing with perhaps only 1m at LW in 2018. The troublesome area is the last mile before the Reculver buoy, best approached in 2018 on about a WSW heading. Leave the Reculver buoy itself at least 100m to port, then follow 275° for the Copperas SHB (Q.G). When about 250m past the Copperas, turn NW for the best water, watching the depth closely as you cross the tail of the Last Sand, and continue for at least ½M before resuming a W'ly heading across the Kentish Flats. Note particularly the unmarked Black Rock, SW of the Copperas buoy, which dries at LWS.

Incidentally, copperas, or iron pyrites, used in dyeing and tanning, was the basis of a major industry in the area.

Conspicuous to the NW are the turbines of the Kentish Flats wind farm, just over 4M off the Kent shore at its nearest point.

Reculver westwards

Having skirted the shallows W of the Copperas SHB, Herne Bay lies WSW, across a generally flat area of further shallows.

If going to Whitstable or the Swale, make for the Whitstable Street PHB (Fl.R.2s), about 6M W. If you plan to go to the Medway instead, the Spile buoy will be your target, just over 10M away bearing about 280° via the Overland Passage.

APPROACHES TO HERNE BAY FROM EAST

Main hazards

Entire approach is across flat shoals.
Disused pierhead (Q.18m4M) 0·6M NNW.
Steel dolphin (Fl.Y 5s) 0·95M ENE.
Area used by fast powerboats and PWCs.
Very soft mud in harbour.

HERNE BAY   CT6 5JG

⊕ **Landfall waypoint**
51°22'·70N 001°07'·20E
Charts
Imray 2100, C1
Admiralty SC5606, 1607
Tides
HW Sheerness -0025
Contact
Foreshore manager ☎ 01227 266719 (out of hours ☎ 01227 862000)
Email foreshore.services@canterbury.gov.uk

Access HW±2hr

About ½M N of Herne Bay SC (the dinghy club at the eastern end of the town) there's a substantial steel dolphin, lit Fl.Y 5s. On high ground inland, due S of the club, there is a prominent water tower in the shape of a cocktail glass. Out at sea NNW of the town is the

The sad remains of Herne Bay Pier,
¾ mile from shore

Herne Bay harbour looking E from the old pier platform that shuts off its W side

Approach into the harbour, by the E side of the stump of the old pier which has fairground items on it in season

Herne Bay harbour near LW

massive abandoned timber pierhead, once busy with paddle-steamer traffic to and from London and Southend. The pier, second longest in the country, was demolished after collapsing in storms in the 1980s.

The Council-owned harbour dries completely and is open to the W, although sheltered in part by the pier structure and a stone groyne beyond. It is formed by a rough stone arm (its root at the E end) that acts as a sea defence for the town. The harbour has no provision for visitors at all, but does represent a possible emergency haven or an adventurous short visit for shoal draught

craft that can take the ground. In strong N'lies at HWS the place should be avoided if at all possible, because waves will overtop the harbour arm.

Approach to the harbour is not dictated by any particular deeper route - the bottom is hard flat sand from some distance out and the harbour entrance is close to a conspicuous block of flats. Yellow buoys in the area define an 8kn inshore speed limit. The entrance is about 50m wide, the W side being a flat platform on piles carrying fairground items (like a helter-skelter) from time to time, and is the shore end of the old pier, lit 2FG(vert).

The W end of the arm, on your port side, is also lit, 2FR(vert). Turn E as soon as you pass the end of this arm to find the deepest water, which follows close to the arm.

The harbour dries completely to very soft deep mud over clay. A number of local fishing boats and other craft are moored here and it would be wise to buoy your anchor. Note there are no moorings provided, although you might find a spare one. If anchoring, it could be best to choose a spot at the W end.

Use the contact number when you arrive if you have not already got in touch.

Around HW you could lie briefly in at least 2m alongside the S edge of the broad public slipway inside the E end of the harbour which, in season, can be busy with powerboat launching and recovery. Until perhaps HW+3 you can land by dinghy on this slipway or on the beach, but do not even think of trying to wade ashore through the mud. Its treacherous nature is such that HM Coastguard uses the harbour for national training in mud rescue!

Herne Bay Westwards to Whitstable

Between the old Herne Bay pierhead and Whitstable is a popular area for pots, not all of which are properly marked.

The Whitstable Street shingle bank bars the way W and dries for 1M from shore at LWS. The Whitstable Street PHB (Fl.R.2s) at its N end, 2M from the shore, is the normal turning point for craft approaching the town.

WHITSTABLE

Main hazards

Shallows in approach.
'The Street' shingle bank to E.
Some commercial traffic.

Whitstable is the third refuge harbour along this stretch of coast, but is again not commonly visited. The town is very much an East Coast place, much more like the coastal towns of Essex and Suffolk than its neighbours in Kent and can be worth a visit if you are prepared to anchor or moor offshore and use the dinghy; the beach immediately E of the harbour has two slipways – one public, the other belongs to Whitstable YC, but stay off the RNLI launching area between the two. The town has become fashionable in recent years and local prices can

WHITSTABLE — CT5 1AB

⊕ **Landfall waypoint**
51°22'·70N 001°01'·20E

Charts
Imray 2100, C1
Admiralty SC5606, 1607

Tides
HW Sheerness -0010

Contact
VHF Ch 09 (monitored only during shipping movements)
Callsign *Whitstable Harbour Radio*
Harbourmaster Whitstable Harbour Office ① 01227 274086
(out of hours, ① 01227 862000)

Access HW±3hr

Slipway Timber ramp between YC and W arm of harbour

Club Whitstable YC ① 01227 272942 (Mon-Fri, 1000-1400)
www.wyc.org.uk

Chandler and outboard engineer ① 01227 274168/262525
www.whitstablemarine.co.uk

Rigger At chandler above

Whitstable harbour entrance, beyond the Oyster buoy

Whitstable harbour from the W at half-tide

reflect this. There are many small specialist shops and art galleries and a number of good restaurants. There is also a fish market on the S quay of the harbour.

It's very much a working port, home to the local fishing fleet and coasters carrying aggregates or timber frequently call. The harbour dries to soft mud at LWS and is not a yacht-friendly place. In an emergency it would be available, but try to contact the HM before attempting to enter. The walls are high and unforgiving and fender boards are needed, unless you can raft alongside. There is a pontoon in the NE corner but this is normally fully booked for regular day-trip traffic. In onshore winds there can be a considerable swell in all parts of the harbour.

The harbour entrance is difficult to make out even in clear weather. It is lit at night, but in daylight the town behind is fairly featureless. Look for a long low roof (visible well out to sea) and a tall silo, both just E of the harbour.

The harbour approach is across shallows. At night, locate the lit Oyster PHB (Fl(2)R.10s) and a SHM dolphin (Fl.G·5s) close to the West Quay head. The two pierheads display 2F.R(vert) and 2F.G(vert) respectively.

The yacht club is just W of the harbour and, although predominantly a dinghy club, it has a small cruising section and may have a spare mooring on enquiry from the secretary. The beach in front of the club and for 150m W is firm, flat shingle compacted on mud (it was a Thames barge hard) and is an ideal spot for a scrub or below waterline maintenance in quiet weather – as a guideline, a boat with 1·2m draught will ground at about half tide. There is a public slipway and close by there is a

chandler where help may be available for rigging or outboard problems. A few hundred yards further west there is a large and expanding area of flags, posts and buoys guarding numerous metal trestles for raising shellfish. The area is extremely hazardous and must be avoided.

Further southwest in Whitstable Bay are more charted oyster beds, again limiting anchoring possibilities.

There is no shelter in Whitstable Bay in strong SW through N winds, when a far better option is to make for the Swale. A NW'ly in particular can make life very uncomfortable with a vicious, steep chop quickly building up across the shallows.

RECULVER TO THE MEDWAY

On passage from the Copperas Channel to the Medway, passing outside the Isle of Sheppey, shape a course of about 280° to the Spile SHB (Fl.G.2·5s) at the W end of the Four Fathoms Channel, just over 10M distant.

This takes you along the Overland Passage, an ancient name still shown on charts and referring to the shallow water where least charted depth is around 2·5m. Just N of the rhumb line from the Copperas SHB to the Spile SHB, note the charted buoyed exclusion area marking shallows (0·9m at LAT) where wind farm export cables cross each other on the sea bed and are protected by piles of rock armour. Three of the four buoys are lit Fl.(4)Y.10s, while the fourth and southernmost is a SCB lit Q(6)+LFl.15s. It is possible that this area will grow in future years as more cables are added.

The Richard Montgomery wreck, in its exclusion zone, seen from the south

Off Whitstable, another old name takes over, the Four Fathoms Channel, which on some charts has the legend 'at HWS' wisely added after it. If passing through at less than half tide, avoid going too close inshore off NE Sheppey where there are several shallow patches only highlighted on large scale charts.

W of the Spile, the route crosses an area of continuing shallows called the Cant. The chart warns of '*numerous pieces of wreckage, some of which dry at LWS*' across the Cant, but despite this there is much fishing and trawling activity and the area is heavily used by small craft without problems.

The Cant has various substantial charted posts dotted across it, but these do not mark hazards. Obstructions stretch N from the shore towards the old Mid Cant post but these stop three cables short of the post itself.

If depth is not an issue, head 278° from the Spile to the Mid Cant post and then 275° towards the West Cant PHB (Q.R) on the SE side of the Medway approach channel. Otherwise stay further out to round the Cheyney Spit, which extends to the N of the unlit 'D' beacon, which is topped with an orange diamond.

The infamous wreck of the *Richard Montgomery* lies on the Sheerness Middle Sand, NW of the approach channel, with her masts still visible. A Liberty Ship on her maiden voyage in 1944 with a cargo of munitions bound for Normandy, she was at anchor when she swung onto the sands and broke her back; she was partly unloaded soon afterwards, but a huge quantity of bombs and other munitions still lie there. The wreck is regularly surveyed, but the cargo has always been considered too dangerous to touch and the wreck is surrounded by an exclusion zone defined by lit yellow buoys.

When approaching the Medway, listen on Ch 74 to Medway VTS for shipping movements and maintain a good lookout astern. Note that smaller ships do use the buoyed secondary channel that runs along the S edge of the main Medway Channel. There is a charted Recommended Yacht Track for entering or leaving the Medway, which runs along the western edge of the entrance – it is safer to use this rather than enter close to Garrison Point where you may meet an outbound ship. For full details of the Medway entrance, see Chapter 16.

NORTH KENT COAST

The Medway entrance near the W Cant buoy

The D Beacon, 3 miles E of Garrison Point

19. RAMSGATE

⊕ **Landfall waypoint**
51°19'·53N 001°30'·27E (Immediately S of 'RA' SCB)
Charts
Imray 2100, C1, C8
Admiralty SC5606, 5605; 323, 1828, 1827
Tides
HW Dover +0030
Contact
Ramsgate Port Control VHF Ch 14
Call sign *Ramsgate Port Control*
☎ 01843 572112
www.portoframsgate.co.uk

Main hazards

The N section of the Goodwin Sands lies only 4M from the harbour entrance and any passage N of this area, heading E or W, must be undertaken with extreme caution, particularly on the flood tide, which sweeps SW onto the sands.

Shallows lie S of the harbour entrance, the Quern Bank being closest, and the Cross Ledge further S. To the N, the shallows shelve gently with no uncharted hazards, but stand well off the North Foreland in strong E winds because confused seas build up inshore.

Ramsgate has become a busy base for wind farm construction and maintenance, which has added to existing fishing boat and fast pilot boat traffic. Cross-Channel car-ferry traffic ceased in 2013, with no sign of it starting up again at the time of writing.

There is a dredged approach channel running E-W but small craft should use the Recommended Yacht Track that lies parallel to the S side of the channel.

Ramsgate's outer breakwaters are low lying, built of rubble and can be difficult to make out from the E. The N pier head has a G beacon (Q.G 5M); the S has a R beacon (VQ.R 5M).

The tide sweeps across the entrance at up to 2kn, roughly NE-SW, between local HW-1¼ and HW+4hr.

A long-standing local byelaw, which prohibited animals on board or anywhere in the harbour, is being rescinded and pets are currently allowed, provided they have arrived directly from a UK location.

Approaches

From N Follow the coast S from North Foreland keeping ½-1M offshore. There is a Small Craft Holding Area a short distance N of the approach channel No.3 SHB (Fl.G.2·5s) and a track S from there crosses the channel just W of No.3 SHB and No.4 PHB (Q.R) to join the E–W Recommended Yacht Track.

Exercise great care crossing the approach channel and if in doubt, check with Port Control before doing so. Alternatively, with care, small craft can arrive close N of the No.5 NCB (closest to the entrance) before calling Port Control (see 'Entry' below).

From E In daylight, first sighting will be the chalk cliffs of the Foreland, N of the harbour. By night, North Foreland light (W sector) should be identified. Approach the 'RA' SCB (Q(6)+LFl.15s) then join the Yacht Track on the S side of the channel. Keep a sharp lookout for commercial traffic.

Ramsgate harbour entrance from the NE. Entry is between the pierheads, signals are displayed on the cream-painted Port Control building – permission must be requested for entry and departure

Once through the pierheads, head for the Harbour SHB

Final approach to the Royal Harbour

From SE Approach outside the Goodwins, keeping clear of the Goodwin Knoll, to arrive at the 'RA' buoy. Do not risk turning NW across the N end of the Knoll, especially when the flood tide is setting hard onto the bank. Every year, unwary skippers are caught out here and provide work for the local RNLI crew.

From S From the S, either follow the Gull Stream NE from Deal Pier, turning N towards the No.4 approach channel buoy once past the Brake PHB (Fl(4)R.15s) or stay close inshore through Ramsgate Channel to W of the Brake and Cross Ledge banks.

The inshore route requires extreme caution, especially close to the B2 SHB (Fl(2)G.5s), which is small and difficult to locate. It guards the Cross Ledge bank, which shifts frequently and must be left well to starboard. Once past, continue in a wide arc W to pass well W of the West Quern WCB (Q(9)15s) to arrive close S of the harbour entrance. This route is not advised at night, nor near LW.

There is a Small Craft Holding Area immediately off the S breakwater.

Entry

Note that sails should be dropped before entering the harbour - if you cannot do this for some reason, seek permission from Port Control first.

From the No.4 channel PHB, follow the charted Recommended Yacht Track. Pass close N of the North Quern NCB (Q) to clear shallows.

It is essential that skippers call Ramsgate Port Control on Ch 14 and ask for permission to enter the harbour.

Ramsgate's Royal Harbour

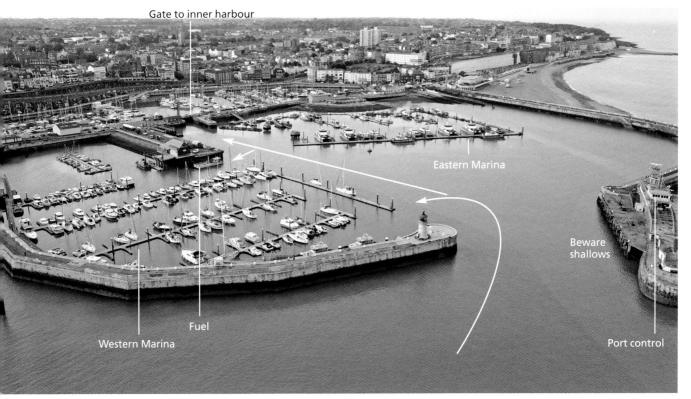

Gate to inner harbour

Eastern Marina

Beware shallows

Fuel

Western Marina

Port control

Control lights are displayed (3.vert.G clear to enter; 3.vert.R no entry) on the cream painted Port Control building at the root of the N breakwater. They can be difficult to identify against town lights at night. When a light (Fl.Or) is displayed there, it means a ship is manoeuvring and you must not enter or leave harbour.

On receiving permission to enter, proceed under power through the outer entrance. If required to wait, use one of the charted holding areas.

Ramsgate Entrance to Ramsgate Marina

Maintain a listening watch on Ch 14. From the outer harbour, the marina lies to the N in the Royal Harbour behind high stone walls. Leave the Harbour SHB (Q.G) to starboard and light (F.R) on end of W Pier close to port. There may be a seasonal PHB (Fl.R.2s) paired with the Harbour buoy. Beware the drying bank on starboard (E) side and watch out for boats leaving. They may appear suddenly round the pierhead in contravention of Port Control's instructions. Once round the pierhead, call Ramsgate Marina on Ch 80 to request a berth (0600-2200H in summer). Outside hours, Port Control may advise.

Ramsgate Marina

There are actually three parts to the marina – West, East and Inner. Leisure craft use the West Marina, immediately to port inside the Royal Harbour entrance. The older part, the East Marina, lies N from the entrance and is entered between two lit dolphins at its W end. Beware the drying East Bank to starboard guarded by a SHB (Fl.G.5s), which is moored actually over the bank. The East Marina is mainly used by commercial craft.

Visitors' berths in the West Marina are usually plentiful, except during large events, like Ramsgate Week. By day in summer, you may be allocated a specific berth, but generally you will be advised to find an empty one on a choice of pontoons, where no 'Reserved' notice is displayed. The W Marina is usually dredged to about 2·5m.

In strong winds from N through E and S or even SW, the harbour can be affected by swell, the E Marina more so than the W, but you will normally be in the W Marina anyway. The further into the marina you go, the less this is likely to affect you.

For long term stays only, and only by previous arrangement, you may be able to berth in the Inner Harbour. This is entered through a lifting bridge and gate, NW beyond the W Marina, and open free-flow approx HW±2hr. A red and yellow flag by day and a

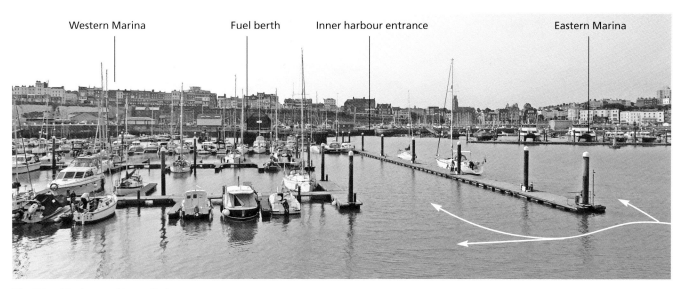

Western Marina · Fuel berth · Inner harbour entrance · Eastern Marina

The West Marina, and Inner Harbour entrance

single green light by night indicate if the gate is open, but always call *Dock Office* on Ch 14 for clearance to proceed.

The main Marina Office is a wooden building immediately W of the lifting bridge, and there is a secondary office at the top of the NW ramp out of the W Marina. Access to the pontoons and toilet buildings is protected by key codes issued on payment of berthing fees. There is also a small unsecured toilet block on the W Marina pontoons.

Remember to call Port Control on Ch 14 for permission before leaving your berth.

The Royal Temple YC overlooks the harbour with fine views and is friendly and welcoming to visiting yachtsmen. Ramsgate is not only a busy stopover for leisure craft, it has excellent eating, shopping and provisioning, 'probably' Britain's largest pub (the Royal Victoria Pavilion), an interesting maritime museum, and is a short bus ride away from historic Canterbury, Sandwich, and Broadstairs. Aircraft enthusiasts will enjoy the famous Spitfire Museum at Manston (☎ 01843 821940 www.spitfiremuseum.org.uk).

The friendly Royal Temple YC, overlooking the harbour and immediately above a row of restaurants

RAMSGATE MARINA CT11 9LQ

Contact
VHF Ch 80
Call sign *Ramsgate Marina*
Marina berthing office ☎ 01843 572110
Harbourmaster ☎ 01843 572100 or 07919 211143
Email portoframsgate@thanet.gov.uk
www.portoframsgate.co.uk

Access 24hr

Fuel Red & white diesel and petrol from fuel barge by Commercial Jetty pierhead at N side of W Marina

Facilities WC, showers, launderette, WiFi, pump-out (inner harbour), 40-T boat hoist

Water On pontoons

Electricity On pontoons

Gas Calor and Gaz at Marlec Marine (see below)

Chandler, engines and spares Marlec Marine ☎ 01843 852452 www.marlecmarine.com

Engineer M-Sea Marine ☎ 01843 410045 or 07784 104861 Ramsgate Marine ☎ 07772 003385

Rigger, sailmakers Northrop Sails ☎ 01843 851665 www.northropsails.com

Paint and materials Bowman ☎ 01843 447300 or 07900 562111 (All above businesses are in the 'arches' behind the inner harbour)

Slipways Two – one in inner harbour near chandler, the other by the E Marina. Both 5T limit. Use by prior arrangement only – contact marina berthing office (see above).
Larger slipways, repairs and maintenance behind E Marina – Ramsgate Harbour Slipways ☎ 01843 593140 www.eap-ltd.co.uk/ramsgate/

Provisions In town

Post Office, banks In town

Pubs/restaurants Royal Temple YC (lunchtime bar food). Many others in town

Yacht club Royal Temple YC ☎ 01843 591766
Email info@rtyc.com www.rtyc.com

Transport Trains – mainline station with frequent services to London and Dover. Buses – useful frequent 'Thanet Loop' service stops opposite Inner Marina

Taxi ☎ 01843 601601, 581581

20. THAMES ESTUARY PASSAGES

Introduction

In this chapter we suggest routes for some typical passages around and across the Thames Estuary, and discuss the factors that can affect them.

HAZARDS

Tides

Tides can run hard in the estuary, approaching 3kn in some areas during springs – see tidal stream diagrams on pages 5-7. There's also a kind of 'roundabout' effect in the area of the Shingles banks, SW of the Long Sand.

The Estuary is, in effect, a bottleneck and this topography, combined with wind speed and direction and barometric pressure, can significantly affect predicted tidal times and heights. These factors must be taken into account when planning a passage, especially if short cuts across some of the banks are to be used.

Timings for passages will often have to be a compromise. For example, a bank may need to be crossed on the flood near local HW, which may mean having to fight the ebb on the final leg up river to a planned destination.

Charted buoys and sand banks

Although the shores of the Estuary are mostly soft mud, the offshore banks are certainly not. They tend to be extremely hard sand and grounding a small craft here on the ebb in rough seas can be very dangerous. Even being stranded on a rising tide in deteriorating weather can be an alarming situation.

Despite their hard nature, however, the sands are also constantly shifting and the UK Hydrographic Office publishes frequent corrections to the charts of the Estuary. Indeed, many of the charts are re-published as often as every two years to take account of all the changes. Note, however, that new surveys almost certainly do not look at areas that leisure sailors are most interested in, such as swatchways across sandbanks. These may not have been surveyed for many years.

Our advice is to keep up to date with corrections and buy the new chart versions when they are published. Chart suppliers Imray can supply corrections by post or

The Princes Channel is the main shipping route through the Estuary, and is not a straight line which can make planning to dodge the traffic difficult

The WWII Maunsell Forts at Red Sand, shown here, and Shivering Sand stand sentinel beside the shipping lane

from their own website, www.imray.com, while corrections to Admiralty charts can be obtained from Notices to Mariners at www.nmwebsearch.com.

In the same vein, published lists of the positions of navigation marks should be treated with caution. Buoys may be moved and occasionally removed altogether or relocated and given new names, as has happened several times in the Estuary in recent years. A chart corrected up to date should be the primary source of waypoints. The positions published in the nautical almanacs each year are probably the most regularly updated, but these books are printed well in advance of publication and, unless thoroughly corrected as well, should only be used as a 'reality check' for your own waypoints derived from the chart.

Altered or updated waypoints must also be corrected in the ship's GPS set and on any electronic plotters.

Wind and weather

The NE-SW tidal streams, coupled with prevailing SW winds and frequent NE winds over the area, mean that rough seas and wind against tide conditions will often be met in the Estuary. The 'Thames Estuary chop' can be as unpleasant a sea as you can find anywhere, even in as little breeze as a F4. Many yachtsmen have a rule of not setting off if there's a '6' in the forecast and that is probably an excellent general rule to follow in the Estuary, especially for windward passages across very shallow areas, such as the Kentish Flats, and in fast-running channels like the Swin and the Wallet. Not for nothing is the Wallet sometimes referred to as 'Vomit Alley'!

Traffic

The whole Estuary is busy with commercial shipping, some of it very large and fast moving and almost invariably 'Constrained by Draught'. A good lookout is essential, as is a listening watch on VHF Ch 16 and 69 (the Port of London Authority (PLA) channel for the outer Thames). Be aware of the charted 'Precautionary Areas'. The Oaze area in particular can be tricky to cross N/S because it contains the junction of several channels – ships approaching in the distance will probably not hold the fixed course you see at any point in time on radar or AIS, so beware of making assumptions based on such information.

Tidal heights

When navigating the Thames Estuary it's worth remembering that current tidal heights at gauges at Walton, Margate, Shivering Sands and Southend are broadcast every half hour (H+15 and H+45) by London VTS on VHF Ch 69. This information can help you make routing decisions if you are considering taking a shortcut. Tide tables only contain predictions - tidal heights and timings can be dramatically affected by the weather.

Wind farms

The Scroby Sands, Gunfleet, Kentish Flats, Thanet, and London Array wind farms are now fully operational. The Kentish Flats farm has been expanded south and west, further development of the Thanet is planned, and it is entirely possible that others will be expanded and new ones constructed. Further development will have an increasing effect on passage-making across the Estuary, as is discussed on page 3. Cable laying during construction, in some cases across long distances, is another typical modern hazard we have to contend with, together with continuous ongoing maintenance.

Before planning a passage across the area, it would be wise to get the most up-to-date information about the wind farms and to plan accordingly.

General advice

Work up a comprehensive passage plan before you start, including detailed tidal information for points on your journey. The *Admiralty Tidal Atlas* can be a great help in doing this.

Do not attempt shortcuts in bad weather. Shortcuts across sandbanks will, by their nature, offer little water under the keel and in rough seas there will be increased danger of grounding in the troughs. Unless certain of adequate depth, the prudent navigator will take the long way round and have contingency plans for using an alternative route or even abandoning the passage.

The estuary is littered with old beacons – the Cant, the Whitaker and the Blacktail to name just three – that are

The Maplin Edge buoy at the S end of the Middle Deep, the Gunfleet Sands and Essex shore beyond

useful reference points, but are reaching the end of their lives. Most were erected long ago by an Admiralty Hydrographic Training Unit, possibly to aid surveys of the estuary, but they are not maintained and they are not being marked when they collapse. There are other marks usually visible in good weather, such as the WWII forts at Red Sand, Shivering Sand, Knock John and Roughs, all of which can be useful position fixing aids. The towering chimney on the Isle of Grain, on the W side of the Medway entrance, was visible at quite extraordinary distances, but has now gone.

Use every opportunity and device to maintain an up-to-date position on the chart. During a passage across the Estuary, decisions and course changes will come up very frequently and each will demand precise knowledge of the vessel's position. Such position fixing has been made considerably easier for most navigators with the widespread use of GPS and electronic plotters, but nevertheless maintain the log, as often as every 15 minutes in poor visibility, recording each buoy or beacon identified and passed. Do not ignore the chance to confirm a GPS position by visual identification or hand-bearing fixes. Everything will be of use should the electronics fail.

ROUTES

Along the coast

Passages between the area of the Medway and Swale in the S and the Essex and Suffolk rivers in the N will follow the 'coastal' route and be able to take advantage of the tide.

A passage from the E Swale to the Blackwater or beyond, for example, might start from Harty just before local HW, push the last of the flood down to the Columbine or Columbine Spit buoys, then head N (with an appropriate W component to allow for tide) to pass the Middle Sand SWM and the Red Sand Towers and across shipping lanes before entering the SW entrance to the W Swin at the SW Barrow WCB as the ebb gathers pace.

From the Medway the passage to this point is straightforward, albeit needing similar close attention when crossing shipping channels to reach the Essex shore.

The route would then pass the Maplin SHB, cross into the Middle Deep between the Maplin Edge SHB and Maplin Bank PHB, and continue NE to pass the E

Once in the Estuary in their hundreds, Thames barges are still to be seen but these days plying a leisure trade – here *Greta* is taking sightseers to a wind farm

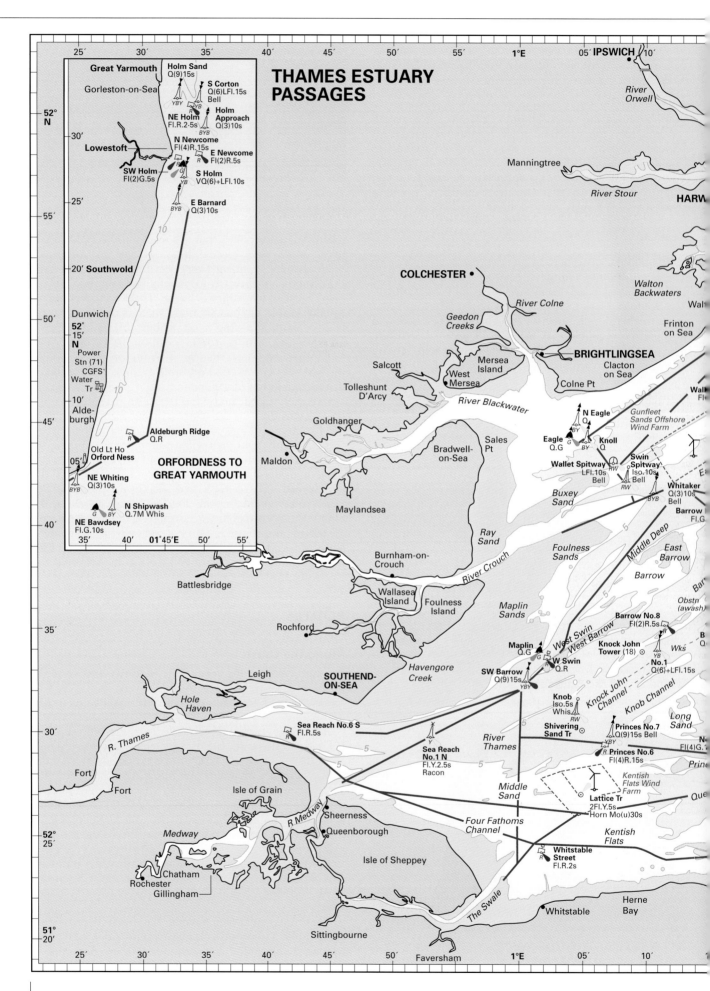

THAMES ESTUARY PASSAGES

52° N — 25′ — **30′** — 35′ — 40′ — 45′ — 50′ — 55′ — **1°E** — 05′ **IPSWICH** 10′

River Orwell

Great Yarmouth
Gorleston-on-Sea

Holm Sand
Q(9)15s

S Corton
Q(6)LFl.15s
Bell
YB

NE Holm
Fl.R.2·5s
BYB

Holm Approach
Q(3)10s

Lowestoft

N Newcome
Fl(4)R.15s
BY

E Newcome
Fl(2)R.5s

SW Holm
Fl(2)G.5s

S Holm
VQ(6)+LFl.10s
YB

E Barnard
Q(3)10s
BYB

Manningtree

River Stour

HARW

52° 30′ N

Southwold 20′

Dunwich
52° 15′ N
Power Stn (71)
CGFS
Water Tr
52° 10′
Alde-burgh
Old Lt Ho
Orford Ness 05′

Aldeburgh Ridge
Q.R

ORFORDNESS TO GREAT YARMOUTH

NE Whiting
Q(3)10s
BYB

N Shipwash
Q.7M Whis
G BY

NE Bawdsey
Fl.G.10s

35′ 40′ **01°45′E** 50′ 55′

COLCHESTER •

River Colne

Geedon Creeks

BRIGHTLINGSEA

Walton Backwaters

Wal

Frinton on Sea

Clacton on Sea

Colne Pt

Wal
Fl

Salcott

Mersea Island

West Mersea

Tolleshunt D'Arcy

River Blackwater

Goldhanger

Sales Pt

Bradwell-on-Sea

Buxey Sand

N Eagle
Q.
BY

Eagle
Q.G G

Knoll
BY Q

Gunfleet Sands Offshore Wind Farm

Wallet Spitway
LFl.10s
Bell
RW

Swin Spitway
Iso.10s
Bell

Whitaker
Q(3)10s
Bell
BYB

Barrow
Fl.G

Maldon

Maylandsea

Ray Sand

Foulness Sands

Middle Deep

East Barrow

Barrow

Barr

Obstn (awash)

Burnham-on-Crouch

Battlesbridge

River Crouch

Wallasea Island

Foulness Island

Maplin Sands

West Swin *West Barrow*

Barrow No.8
Fl(2)R.5s

B
Q

35′

Maplin
Q.G G

W Swin
Q.R R

SW Barrow
Q(9)15s
YBY

Knock John Tower (18) ⊙

No.1
Q(6)+LFl.15s
YB

Wks

Rochford

Leigh

Hole Haven

SOUTHEND-ON-SEA

Havengore Creek

Knob
Iso.5s
Whis
RW

Shivering Sand Tr ⊙

Princes No.7
Q(9)15s Bell
YBY

Knock John Channel

Knob Channel

Long Sand

Princes No.6
Fl(4)R.15s

30′

Sea Reach No.6 S
Fl.R.5s

Sea Reach No.1 N
Fl.Y.2.5s
Racon

River Thames

Kentish Flats Wind Farm

Lattice Tr
2Fl.Y.5s
Horn Mo(u)30s

Fl(4)G.

Prin

Que

Fort
Fort

Isle of Grain

Middle Sand

Four Fathoms Channel

Kentish Flats

52° 25′

Medway

Sheerness

Queenborough

R Medway

Chatham
Rochester
Gillingham

Isle of Sheppey

Whitstable Street
Fl.R.2s R

Herne Bay

51° 20′

25′ **30′** 35′ 40′ **45′** 50′ Faversham **1°E** 05′ 10′

Sittingbourne

The Swale • Whitstable

E. Swale to Wallet

Wallet Spitv
LFI.10s
1·2M
325°

Swin Spitwa
Iso.10s
2·5M
347°

Beware
shallows over
Whitaker Spi

Maplin
Approach
FI(2)G.10s

3·7M
040°

Maplin Middle
FI.G.5s

1·9M
038°

Maplin Edge
FI.G.2.5s

Maplin
Q.G
Bell
3·6M
032°

SW Barrow
Q(9)15s

Red
Sand
Tower

Middle
Sand Bn
8·4M
000°

Columbine Spit
FI(3)G.10s

51°23'·8N
001°00'·00E

North Foreland to W Swin

SW Barrow
Q(9)15s

Shivering
Sand
Towers
5·0M
303°

Princes No.7
Q(9)15s

Cross shipping lane

Princes No.2
FI(2)R.5s
7·0M
275°

But staying out
of shipping lane

Princes S
Q.R
5·4M
290°

E. Margate
FI.R.2.5s
4·5M
350°

N. Foreland
Light

51°22'·60N
001°28'·00E

North Foreland to Harwich Approach

Landguard
Q.
2·1M
355°

Stone Banks
FI.R.5s
3·6M
302°

S Cork
Q(6)+LFI.15s
10·0M
290°

Long Sand Head
VQ
9·5M
356°

Kentish Knock
Q(3)10s
17·5M
025°

N. Foreland
Light

51°22'·60N
001°28'·00E

The Wallet Spitway buoy marks the N end of the Spitway, between the Buxey and Gunfleet Sands

while the streams in the Wallet are weaker.

This inner northern Estuary route is readily reversible, timing a departure S from the Whitaker area to ensure enough depth at the planned destination. Due care must be taken with timing at the Spitway, as you may well be around there near LW.

Skippers on passage SW on this inner route from the Ore, Deben or Orwell areas are recommended to time their departure to reach the Whitaker as suggested above. They will be at sea during most of one ebb and one flood tide and it is preferable to fight the ebb in the Wallet and carry the flood in the Swin. If bound for the N Foreland via this inshore route, perhaps because of poor weather, time your departure to arrive at the SW end of the Swin near HW Sheerness, then cross to the Kent coast and carry the ebb down towards Margate – the Kent sector being described in detail in Chapter 18.

Round the outside

Between N Foreland and Harwich, given a favourable wind, the simplest route is one that goes around the outside of most of the banks.

Leave N Foreland at around HW Dover -1hr and head for the Long Sand Head. You can sail down the Knock Deep, passing through the London Array wind farm, or go outside the Kentish Knock Sand. On this outside route, note that the 'Long Sand Head Two-Way Route' runs E of a line joining the Kentish Knock ECB and the Long Sand Head NCB. Stay W of this line, turning just inside the Long Sand Head buoy to track NW across the SW portion of the Sunk Inner Gyratory System, making either for the Medusa Channel or the Roughs Tower and the Cork Sand Yacht Bn, and then on into Harwich. You should be able to carry a favourable tidal component until about HW Dover -6hr which should then mean entry to the Orwell in the first hours of the flood.

In reverse, a departure from the Orwell on the last of the ebb would give about 6hr of SW-going stream, but the ebb from the English Channel starts heading N off the Foreland at about HW Dover -1hr.

Maplin PHB and Maplin Approach SHB. This buoy is some 18M from the Columbine and the passage will have used at least 3hr, perhaps 4hr, of ebb out of a total of little more than 5hr of ebb tide available on this down tide route. Note that sections of the East Swin fall within the Shoeburyness Firing Danger Area, which is the reason for the buoyage being moved to the Middle Deep.

From the Maplin Approach, if the Crouch is your destination, head NW towards the Inner Whitaker SCB (being careful of the depth over the Whitaker Spit), then SW into the Crouch. Otherwise, this coastal route heads NNW to the Swin Spitway SWB, crossing the Buxey Sand to the Wallet Spitway SWB before heading NW for the Blackwater. If your destination is the Orwell area or beyond, then the Wallet is the best route, even if you have to cross the Spitway near local LW, because the early flood runs hard SW on the S side of the Gunfleet,

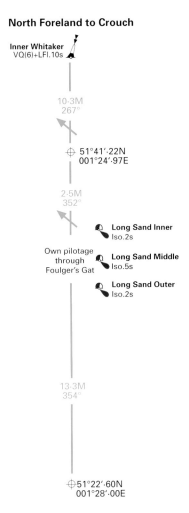

North Foreland to Crouch

Inner Whitaker
VQ(6)+LFl.10s

10·3M
267°

⊕ 51°41'·22N
001°24'·97E

2·5M
352°

🔴 **Long Sand Inner**
Iso.2s

Own pilotage
through
Foulger's Gat

🔴 **Long Sand Middle**
Iso.5s

🔴 **Long Sand Outer**
Iso.2s

13·3M
354°

⊕51°22'·60N
001°28'·00E

Across the middle

Between the N Foreland and the Crouch or the Blackwater, typical routing has in the past used the N Edinburgh Channel or Fisherman's Gat to cross the Long Sand, and shortcuts across the Sunk Sand. However, shipping route changes and the demise of beacons on the Sunk Sands have altered some of the options. Note also that craft of less than 6m draught are now discouraged by the PLA from using the Knock John Channel and Black Deep.

The N Edinburgh Channel across the Long Sand is no longer buoyed and has been replaced as a shipping route by Fisherman's Gat, to the NE. Fisherman's Gat was once the preferred route for small craft, but in recent years yachts have also used Foulger's Gat, even further to the NE.

Despite the availability of Foulger's Gat, consider use of the unbuoyed N Edinburgh Channel, although this requires careful navigation. Better still is Fisherman's Gat, which offers an easier passage, but keep outside the buoyed shipping channel – although it's not busy, remember it is a confined space where ships will be constrained by their draught. There is plenty of room for leisure craft outside the buoyed channel, especially on its N side, and passage through it is generally less stressful, and barely further, than using Foulger's.

Although Foulger's Gat is now enclosed within the boundaries of the London Array wind farm, the developers left a route open through it marked by the Long Sand Inner, Middle and Outer SWBs. However,

The huge landmark of Grain Tower at the Medway entrance has gone, once visible right across the Estuary but now replaced by a few short chimneys

there may be occasional short-term closures during maintenance and when wide exclusion zones are enforced around towers. Refer to www.eastcoastpilot.com for the latest information. Beware of strong cross-tides at each end of the Gat, be aware that the SWBs can be hard to make out from a distance, and because the route is a dogleg, you may not be able to see the next buoy hidden behind turbines. It is possible, too, to become disorientated with so many identical turbines around you, unless you pay special attention to maintaining your heading. We do think that Fisherman's Gat is worth considering instead.

There are now no helpful marks for crossing the Sunk Sand between the Black Deep and Barrow Deep channels. Crossing in the right conditions of weather and tide is still possible, but the navigator must be particularly careful. One possible crossing point from the Black Deep is roughly due N from No.8 ECB (at the NW end of Fisherman's Gat), taking care to keep clear of the unmarked sunken wreckage of the Sunk Bn. A second lies SW of Black Deep No.3 SHB, on a heading WNW towards the Barrow No.2 PHB, and a third uses a route not far from the submerged ruin of the SW Sunk beacon.

If using the first of these, note that special care is needed over the extending NE end of the E Barrow Sand.

Again, the navigator must exercise due caution if using any of these crossing points and especially see our comments about the book *Crossing the Thames Estuary* (Imray) below.

To avoid navigating across the Sunk Sand, you may choose to make NE to the Sunk Head Tower NCB and from there NW to pick up the Medusa Channel towards Harwich and the rivers further N.

On a passage from the N Foreland towards Essex, the timing is difficult overall, because the need for sufficient water at the Sunk may require fighting the start of the ebb in the Crouch or Blackwater on arrival. Equally, when departing from either of these rivers you may again be faced with arriving at the Sunk on a falling tide. Shallow draught certainly increases your options and with good weather the trip from the Foreland to the Crouch may be better accomplished by starting at around HW Dover +2½hr, reaching the Barrow Deep at LW Dover, nicely positioned to carry the new flood to your destination.

An alternative is not to take the shortcuts at all, but to use the Middle Deep and W Swin and the Princes Channel, cutting across the shipping lanes between the SW Barrow WCB and the Princes No.7 WCB. This route is longer (but not that much longer if going from or to the Crouch or the Blackwater) and carries its own tidal considerations, but in poor conditions it would probably be the best option.

Crossing the Thames Estuary

Crossing the Thames Estuary (Imray) by Roger Gaspar is designed to help with all of these tidal and passage planning decisions in much greater detail than we can cover here and is thoroughly recommended as a companion to ECP at your chart table. Roger's book has a very useful supporting website www.crossingthethamesestuary.com which often carries current information about using uncharted routes across the banks.

INDEX

abbreviations, vii
Abraham's Bosum, 25
Ada Point, 97
Admiralty Tidal Atlas, 183
Aldboro Point, 73
Alde River, 22, 25, 26, 27 29
Aldeburgh, 24, 27-28
Aldeburgh Boatyard, 27
Aldeburgh YC, 27, 28
Allhallows, 118
Allington Lock, 134, 145, 147, 153
Allington Marina, 147, 153
Alresford Creek, 73
Althorne Creek, 96-98
Anglia One wind farm, 8
apps, iv, v
Associated British Ports, 49
AW Marine 'The Marina', 113
Aylesford, 151-153
Aylesford Bridge, 145

Ballast Hill (Stour), 46-47
Ballast Quay (Fingringhoe), 73
Baltic Wharf (Crouch), 96
Baltic Wharf (Stour), 46, 47
Barking Reach, 123
Barling Ness, 108, 109
Barling Quay, 109
Barlinghall Creek, 108
Barrow Deep, 187
Barrow Sand, 187
Barthorp's Creek, 24, 25
Bartlett Creek, 138
Bartonhall Creek, 109
Bass' Dock, 36
Batchelor Spit, 76
Bateman's Tower, 68
Bathside Bay, 42
Battle of the River Medway, 150
Battlesbridge, 101
Bawdsey (Deben), 31, 32-33
Bawdsey Cliffs (Ore), 23
BBC World Service radio masts, 26
Beacon Boatyard, 147
HMS Beagle, 105
bearings, 1
Beaufort scale, 4
Beaumont Quay & Cut, 65
Bedlams Bottom, 136
Bedwell's Boatyard, 62
Bee Ness, 138
Bell Wharf (Leigh), 111
Bells Creek (Swale), 162
Bench Head Shoal, 66, 67, 68, 77, 78
Benfleet Creek, 110, 112, 113-115
Benfleet MB & YC, 115
Benfleet YC, 110, 113, 114, 115
Besom Fleet, 79
Bishop Spit, 138

Black Deep, 187
Black Point, 97
Black Rock, 173
Blackden Moorings, 164, 165
Blackedge Point, 109
Blackman's Breakwater, 38
Blacktail, 106, 183
Blackwall Basin, 126, 127
Blackwall Point, 125
Blackwall Reach, 125-127
Blackwater & Chelmer Navigation, 89
Blackwater Marina, 85, 86-87
Blackwater River, 76-91, 183, 186, 187
Blackwater SC, 88, 89
Blyth (Thames), 117, 118
Blyth River (Southwold), 18-21
Boyton Dock, 25
Bradwell, 82-84
Bradwell Beacon, 82
Bradwell CC, 83
Bradwell Creek, 82-84
Bradwell Marina, 82, 83-84
Bradwell Power Station, 78, 82, 84
Bradwell Quay, 84
Bradwell Quay YC, 83, 84
Bradwell Waterside, 84
Bradwell-on-Sea, 84
Brake, 179
Bramble Creek & Island, 65
Brandy Hole, 100-101
Brandy Hole Moorings, 100-101
Branklet 'preferred channel', 93, 102
Breydon Bridge, 11
Breydon Water, 8, 10
Bridge Reach (Medway), 145
Bridgemarsh Creek, 98
Bridgemarsh Island, 97, 98
Bridgemarsh Marina, 97-98
Brightlingsea SC, 69, 71
Brightlingsea, 68-71
Brightlingsea Spit, 68, 69
Brinkman's Wharf, 113
British Waterways Marinas Ltd, 127, 130
Broads access, 8, 10, 11, 17
Broads Authority, 17
Broadstairs, 170, 181
Broadstairs SC, 170
Broomway, 102, 105, 106
Bugsby's Reach, 125
Bullman's Wharf, 107
HMS Bulwark (wreck), 138
Burham Marshes, 151
Burnham SC, 94
Burnham Yacht Harbour, 94, 95, 96
Burnham-on-Crouch, 93, 94-96
Burntwick Island, 136
Butley River, 25

Butt & Oyster, 51, 52
Butterfly Channel, 163
Butterman's Bay, 51
Buxey Sand, 66, 76, 92, 93, 186

Camber Dock, 134
Canal & River Trust, 127
Canary Wharf, 126
Canewdon, 98
Cant, 134, 177, 183
Canterbury, 181
Canvey Island, 110-115, 117, 119
Carlton (Road) Rail Bridge, 16, 17
Cathouse Reach, 52, 53
Chainrock Jetty, 115
Chambers Wharf (Faversham), 160
Channel Tunnel Rail Link, 147
chart datum, 1
chart plotters, iv
chart symbols (keys to), vi, vii
charts, iv, 1, 182
Chatham, 134, 143-145
Chatham Maritime Marina, 139, 143-144
Chatham Naval Dockyards, 144
Chatham Ness & Shoal, 145
Chelmer River, 90
Chelmondiston, 52
Chelmsford, 89
Cheyney Spit, 177
Church End, 104
Cindery Island, 70, 71
Clacton, 3
Clamp House, 51
Clay Reach, 165
Clementsgreen Creek, 100
Cliff Foot Rocks, 38, 58
Cliff Quay (Orwell), 54, 56
Cliff Reach (Crouch), 96-97
Cliffe Fleet, 119
Coalhouse Point, 119
Coastguard, 2, 116, 118
Coastwatch (NCI), 2, 115
Cob Island, 28, 29
Cobmarsh Island, 79
Cockham Reach, 142
Cocum Hills, 68, 78
Colchester, 71, 73
Colchester Oyster Fishery, 72, 73
Collier's Reach (Alde), 28
Colliers Reach (Blackwater), 89, 90
Collimer Point, 50
Colne Bar, 66, 67, 68, 77
Colne Deep Water Channel, 67, 68
Colne River, 66-75, 76, 77
Colne Smack Preservation Society, 70
Colne YC, 70, 71

ColRegs, 3
Colton Creek, 51
Columbine & Spit, 154-155, 156, 183
Constable country, 47
Conyer (village), 163
Conyer CC, 157, 164
Conyer Creek, 154, 155, 162, 163-164
Conyer Creek Marina, 163, 164
Conyer Dock, 164
Cook's Boatyard (Maldon), 91
Copperas Bay (Stour), 45
Copperas Channel (N Kent), 172-173, 176
Cork Sand, 40, 41, 186
Coryton, 115, 117
courses & bearings, 1
Crab Knoll, 60
Crayford Ness, 122
Creeksea, 96
Cross Ledge, 178, 179
Cross Ness, 123
Crouch River, 76, 92-102, 107, 186, 187
CRS Marine, 90
Cruising Association, 129, 130
Cuckolds Point, 130
Cutty Sark, 127
Cuxton Marina, 148, 149
Cuxton Point, 149
Cylinder House Moorings, 161

Dabchicks SC, 79
Dagenham, 122, 123
Damhead Creek, 138
dangers & hazards, 2, 3
Darnet Ness, 138-139
Dartford Creek Tidal Barrier, 122
Dauntless Yacht Centre, 113, 114
Deal Pier, 179
Debbage Yachting, 57
Deben River, 30-37, 44, 186
Deben YC, 35
Decoy Point, 84, 88
Dedham Vale, 47
Deer Park Lodge, 53
Dengie Flats, 92
Devil's Reach, 103, 104
Dickens, Charles, 115, 134
distances, 1
distress calls (Thames), 118
Docklands, 126-127
Doctor Flats, 87
Dogger Bank wind farm, 3
Doubles buoys, 88
Dover Coastguard, 2
Dovercourt Bay, 41
Dovercourt Beach, 38, 58
Downham Reach, 53

Eagle, 66, 77
East Barrow Sand, 187

East Haven Creek, 115
East Hoo Creek, 138
East Mersea Stone, 68, 70, 71, 72
East Suffolk Water Ski Club, 32
East Swale, 154-167
Easter Reach, 98
Eastwood's Wharf, 137
Edith May (barge), 137
electronic charts, iv, 1
Elmhaven Marina, 149
Elmley, 154, 165
Embankment Marina
   (Gravesend), 117, 119, 120
emergency medical help, 2
Erith, 122-123
Erith YC, 122-123
Erwarton Ness & Bay, 38, 45
Essex Marina, 94, 96
Essex Marina YC, 96
Essex Marine, 113
Essex YC, 111-112
Everson's Boatyard, 35
ExCeL Exhibition Centre, 124
Exchem, 64, 65

Fagbury, 38, 49
Falkenham Marsh, 33
Fambridge, 98-100
Fambridge Yacht Haven (Stow
   Creek), 98, 99-100

Faversham Creek, 155, 156,
   157-160
Felixstowe Container Port, 3, 38,
   39, 58, 60
Felixstowe Ferry, 30, 31-33
Felixstowe Ferry Boatyard, 32
Felixstowe Ferry SC, 31, 32, 33
*Fellowship Afloat Charitable
   Trust*, 81
Fenn Creek, 101
Ferry Reach (Swale), 165
Fiddler's Reach, 122
Fingringhoe Creek, 74
Fingringhoe Firing Range, 73
Fingringhoe Nature Reserve, 73
Fisherman's Gat, 187
Folly Point, 138, 140
Foreness Point, 171
Foulger's Gat, 187
Foulness Island, 102-104
Foulness Sand, 92, 93
Foundry Reach, 61
Four Fathoms Channel, 154,
   176, 177
Fowley Spit & Island, 154,
   162-163
Fox's Marina & Boatyard, 54, 55
Fox's Marina YC, 55
Frank Halls Boatyard, 62
Freston Tower, 53-54
Frinton, 63
Front Brents Jetty, 157, 160
fuel suuplies, 118, 131
Fullbridge, 90, 91
Funton Reach, 136

Gabbards wind farms, 3, 8
Gabriel's Wharf, 153
Gallions Point Marina, 118, 121,
   123-124

Gallions Reach, 123-124
Galloper Bank, 40
Ganges Cliff & Jetty, 45
Garnham's Island, 65
Garrison Point, 134, 135, 177
Gashouse Creek, 42
Gedgrave Cliffs, 25
Geedon Channels, 73
Gillingham, 118, 140-142
Gillingham gas holder, 138, 139,
   140
Gillingham Marina, 139, 140-
   141
Gillingham Pier, 141-142
Gipping River, 57
Goldhanger Creek, 84-85, 88
Goldhanger SC, 84-85
Goodwin Knoll, 179
Goodwin Sands, 178
Gore Channel, 172
Gorleston, 8, 10
GPS, 183
Grain, Isle of, 118, 134-135,
   183, 187
Grain Edge, 118, 134
Grain Hard, 118, 135
Grain Spit, 134
Grain Tower Fort, 135
Granary Reach (Deben), 35
Gravesend, 117, 119-122
Gravesend Pontoon, 121
Gravesend SC, 119, 120, 121
Great Cob Island, 80
Great Oakley Dock, 65
Great Wakering, 107
Great Yarmouth, 3, 8-11, 184
Greater Gabbard wind farm, 3
Green Point (Deben), 33
Greenhithe, 122
Greenland Dock, 128
Greenland Pier, 127
Greenwich, 125-128
Greenwich Meridian, 125
Greenwich YC, 125
The Grindle (Pin Mill), 51
Grovehurst Jetty, 165
Gull Stream, 179
Gulliver wind generator, 12-13
Gunfleet Sands & wind farm, 3,
   66, 76, 183, 186
The Gut (W Mersea), 79

Hadleigh Ray, 110, 111, 112-114
Half Acre Creek, 136, 138
Halfpenny Pier (Harwich), 41-42
Hall Point, 52
Halliday Flats, 58
Halling, 149, 150
Halls (Frank) Boatyard, 62
Halstow Creek, 137
Ham Gat, 155-156
Ham Ooze, 136
Hamford Water, 61, 64-65
Hamilton Dock (Lowestoft), 15
The Hams, 35
Harlow (Blackwater) SC, 85, 86
Harty, Isle of, 156
Harty (Ferry), 154, 156-157,
   162, 183
Harwich, 3, 12, 38-43, 58, 186,
   187

Harwich & Dovercourt SC, 42
Harwich International Port
   (Parkeston Quay), 41, 45
Harwich Shelf, 38
Harwich Town SC, 42
Haven Bridge (Great Yarmouth),
   8, 10, 11
Haven Marina (Ipswich), 56
Haven Marina (Lowestoft), 16,
   17
Haven Point (Roach), 107
Haven Ports YC, 50
Havengore Bridge, 102, 105-107
Havengore Creek, 106-107
Havergate Island, 24
Hawkwood Stone, 151
hazards & dangers, 2, 3
Hedge End Island, 63, 64
Hedgecock's, 90
Heiko (Thames fuel barge), 118,
   131
Hengist & Horsa, 152
*Hermitage Community
   Moorings*, 130-131
Herne Bay, 173-175
Herne Bay SC, 173
Herring Point, 88, 90
Heybridge, 86, 89-90
High Hill, 60
Hilly Pool Point, 88
*Historic Dockyard Museum
   (Chatham)*, 144
Holborough Reach, 150
Holbrook Creek, 45-46
'The Hole', 113
Holehaven Creek, 115, 117, 118-
   119
Hollesley Bay, 23, 25
Holliwell Point, 93
Hollowshore, 157, 158, 160
Hollowshore CC, 157, 161, 162
Hollowshore Moorings, 160
Holm Channel, 10
Holm Sand, 10, 13-14
Honey Island, 65
Honorary Port Pilots (HPP), v
Hoo Island, 139, 140, 142
Hoo Marina, 142
Hoo Ness, 142
Hoo Ness YC, 142
Hook Sand (Margate), 172
Horrid Hill, 138
Horse Reach (Swale), 169
Horse Sand (Deben), 32, 33
Horse Sand (Swale), 156
Horse Shoal (Crouch), 94, 102
Horseshoe Point, 135
Horsey Island, 61, 64, 65
Horsey Mere, 61, 63, 64, 65
Humber Coastguard, 2
Hundred of Hoo SC, 139
Hythe Quay (Maldon), 90, 91

Iken Cliffs, 28
Inner Bench Head, 66-67, 68,
   77-78
Ipswich, 36, 48, 55, 56
Ipswich Haven Marina, 56
Ipswich River *see* Orwell River
Ipswich Wet Dock, 48, 55
Iron Wharf, 157, 159-160

Island Point (Hamford Water),
   60, 61
Island YC, 112-113
Isle of Grain, 118, 134-135, 183,
   187
Isle of Harty, 156
Isle of Sheppey, 154, 156, 168-
   169, 176
Isle of Thanet, 172

James Lawrence (Sailmakers),
   70, 71
Jenningtree Point, 123

Kentish Flats & wind farm, 3,
   155, 173, 182, 183
Kentish Knock Sand, 186
Kethole Reach, 136, 138
King Edward Quay (Colchester),
   75
King's Boatyard, 51, 52
Kingsferry Bridge, 154, 165, 167-
   169
Kingsnorth Power Station, 138
Kirby Creek, 64, 65
Kirby-le-Soken, 65
Kirton Creek, 33
Knock Deep, 186
Knock John Channel, 187
Knock John Tower, 183
Knoll, 66, 68, 76, 77, 92
Kyson Point, 35

Lake Lothing, 16, 17
Landermere Creek & Quay, 65
landfall waypoints, 1
Landguard Beach, 42
Landguard Point, 38, 39, 40
Larkman's Boatyard, 36, 37
Last Sand, 173
Lawling Creek, 85-87
Lawrence, James (Sailmakers),
   70, 71
The Leavings, 80-81
Leigh Creek, 110-112
Leigh Marina, 111
Leigh Middle, 117
Leigh MBC, 111, 112
Leigh SC, 111-112
Leigh-on-Sea, 110-112
Levington Creek, 50, 51
life-saving signals, vii
lights, 3
Lilies, 165
Limehouse Marina, 118, 121,
   129-130
Limehouse Reach (Medway), 145
Limehouse Reach (Thames),
   127-130
Little Fowley, 163
Little Wakering, 108
Loden Hope, 168, 169
Loder's Cut, 35
London (Thames River), 116-133
London Array wind farm, 3, 183,
   186, 187
London Coastguard, 2, 116, 118
London Gateway Port, 3, 115,
   116, 117, 118
*London natural gas (LNG)
   terminal*, 134, 135

London Thamesport container terminal, 134, 135, 138
London VTS, 116, 118, 123, 124, 125
Long Point (Swale), 165, 169
Long Reach (Medway), 138-139
Long Reach (Orwell), 51
Long Reach (Swale), 169
Long Reach (Thames), 122
Long Sand, 182, 186, 187
Long Sand Head Two Way Route, 185, 186
Longnose, 171
Lower Halstow, 137
Lower Halstow YC, 137
Lower Hope Reach (Thames), 117, 119
Lower Pool (Thames), 130
Lowestoft, 3, 12-17, 184
Lowestoft CC, 16
Lowestoft Harbour Bridge, 15-16
Lowestoft Haven Marina, 16, 17
Lowestoft Marina, 16, 17

Maidstone, 153
Maldon, 90-91
Maldon Little Ship Club, 90, 91
Maldon YC, 90
Manningtree, 47
Manston, 181
Maplin Sands, 102, 105-106, 183-186
Marconi SC, 85
Margaret Ness, 123
Margate, 170, 171-172, 186
Margate Hook Sand, 172
Margate YC, 172
Mariner's Farm Boatyard, 138
Marinestore Chandlers, 91
Maritime Safety Information, 2
Marsh End Sand, 110
Martlesham Creek, 35
Martlesham Creek Boatyard, 35
Mayland Creek, 85
Mayland Spit, 85
Maylandsea, 85
Maylandsea Bay SC, 87
medical help, 2
Medusa Channel, 40, 41, 60, 186, 187
Medway & Swale Boating Association, 154
Medway Bridge Marina, 147-148
Medway CC, 140
Medway Channel, 177
Medway Crossing, 147-148
Medway Queen, 142
Medway Recommended Yacht Track, 177
Medway River, 134-154, 167-168, 176-177, 183
Medway Towns regeneration scheme, 134, 145
Medway YC, 142
Melton, 33, 35
Melton Boatyard, 36, 37
Mersea Flats, 66, 67, 68
Mersea Fleet, 79
Mersea Island, 72, 79
Mersea Quarters, 78-79, 80
Methersgate, 35

Middle Creek (Medway), 139, 142
Middle Deep, 183, 186, 187
Middle Sand, 155, 177, 183
Middleway (Roach), 107
Mike's Boatyard, 111
Mill Beach, 88
Millwall Docks, 126
Milton Creek, 165
Minnis Bay, 172
Mistley Marine, 47
Mistley Quay, 46-47
Motney Hill, 138
Mucking, 109, 119
Mundon Stone Point, 85
Museum of Docklands, 127
Mussel Scarfe, 61
Mutford Lock, 17
Mutford Road Bridge, 17

Nacton, 51
Narrow Cuts (Roach), 107
Nase Point, 102
Nass Beacon, 78, 79, 80, 82
Nass Sand Bank, 80
National Coastwatch Institution (NCI), 2, 115
National Maritime Museum, 127
navigation (Thames Estuary passages), 182-187
Naze Tower, 58, 60
Neptune Marina (Ipswich), 56, 57
New Cut (Ipswich), 57
New England Creek, 107
New Hythe, 151
Newcome Sand, 14
Nor Marsh, 138
Nore Sand, 118
Nore Swatch, 117, 118, 134
Norfolk Broads access, 8, 10, 11, 17
North Edinburgh Channel, 187
North Fambridge Yacht Station, 98-99
North Fambridge YC, 98
North Foreland, 3, 170, 171, 178, 186, 187
North Quay Marine, 163, 164
Northey Island, 88
Northfleet Hope, 122
Notices to Mariners, iv, viii

O2 Dome & cable car, 125
Oakley Creek, 64-65
The Oaks, 28
Oare (village), 156-157, 162
Oare Creek, 155, 157, 158, 161-162
Oaze Deep, 182-183
HMS Ocelot, 144
Old Tree Point, 101
Oliver's Wharf, 69, 70
Onega Gate, 128
Ore River, 22-26, 30, 186
Orford, 24, 25-26
Orford SC, 26
Orfordness, 23, 25, 26, 184
Orinoco Channel, 139, 142
Orwell River, 38, 41, 44, 48-57, 186

Orwell Road Bridge, 51, 53, 54
Orwell YC, 54, 55
Osea Island, 84, 85, 88
Ostrich Creek, 54-55
Otterham Creek, 138
Otterham Creek Boatyard, 138
Oulton Broad, 17
Ovens, 119
Overland Passage, 173, 176
Oxley, 23, 24

Packing Marsh Island, 79
Paglesham, 102-108
Paglesham Reach, 104
Pan Sand, 171
Parkeston Quay, 41, 45
passage planning (Thames), 117-118, 183
Pelican CC Strood, 146
Peters Village, 150
Pewit Island (Colne), 72
Pewit Island (Oakley Creek), 65
Pigpail Sluice, 26
Pin Mill, 51-52
Pin Mill SC, 52
Pincushion Island, 71
Pinup Reach, 138, 139, 140
Pioneer Sailing Trust, 70
The Platters, 40
Point Clear, 68, 70, 71
Pollard Spit, 155-156
Poplar Dock Marina, 126
Port of London Authority (PLA), 3, 116, 117, 118, 182
Port of London Authority moorings, 121, 122
Port Medway Marina, 148, 149
Port Pilots, Honorary (HPP), vi
Port Werburgh, 139, 142
position fixing (Thames Estuary), 183
pot markers, 2
Potter Reach, 52
Potton Creek, 107-108
Potton Island, 104, 108
Potton Point, 104, 107
Potton swing bridge, 108
Precautionary Areas, 182-183
Princes Channel, 171, 187
Prior's Boatyard, 94
Priory Spit, 66
Pye Channel, 58, 60, 61, 64
Pye End, 39, 58, 60
Pye Sand, 58
Pyefleet, 68
The Pyefleet, 72-73, 79

QEII Road Bridge (Thames), 122
QR codes, v
Quarters Spit, 79, 80
Quay Reach (Paglesham), 102-104
Queenborough, 155, 166, 167-169
Queenborough Creek, 169
Queenborough Spit, 135, 166, 167-168
Queenborough YC, 168, 169
Queen's Channel, 171
Quern Bank, 178, 179

radio, vii, 2
Radio Caroline, 84
Rainham Creek, 138
Rainham Fairway, 138
Rainham Marshes, 123
Ramsgate, 170, 178-181
Ramsgate Channel, 179
Ramsgate Marina, 180-181
Ramsgate Recommended Yacht Track, 178, 179
Ramsholt, 33
Ransome, Arthur, 52, 60, 64
Rats Bay, 145
Ray Channel (Blackwater), 79
Ray Gut (Leigh), 110
Ray Sand (Rays'n) Channel (Crouch), 76, 92
Raypits Reach, 98
Receptive, 156
Reculver, 171, 172, 173
Reculver Towers, 172
Red Sand & Tower, 155, 183
Rice & Coles Boatyard, 94
Richard Montgomery (wreck), 134, 177
The Ridge, 171
Ridham Dock, 165
riding lights, 3
River Police (Thames), 130
Roach River, 93, 102-109
Roach Sailing Association, 102, 104, 107
Robertson's Boatyard, 36, 37
Rochester, 134, 145-146
Rochester Bridge, 134, 145, 145-146
Rochester CC, 146
Rochester Oyster Fishery, 151
Rochester Pier, 146
Rochford, 109
The Rocks, 33
Rolling Ground, 40
rolling roads, viii
Roman River, 74
Ross Revenge (pirate radio ship), 84
Rotherhithe, 127-129
Roughs Tower, 183, 186
route distances, 1
routes (Thames Estuary passages), 183-187
Rowhedge, 71, 74-75
Royal Burnham YC, 94
Royal Corinthian YC, 94, 95
Royal Engineers Museum, 134
Royal Engineers YC, 144
Royal Harbour (Ramsgate), 181-182
Royal Harwich YC, 52-53
Royal Naval College, 127
Royal Naval Dockyards, 134, 144
Royal Norfolk & Suffolk YC, 12, 15
Royal Temple YC, 181
Rushley Island, 107
Russia Dock Woodland, 128

St Clement's Reach, 122
St Katharine Docks, 117, 118, 130-133

St Lawrence Bay, 84
St Mary's Island, 142
St Osyth Boatyard, 71, 72
St Osyth Creek, 71-72
St Peter's Flats, 93
St Peter's on the Wall, 84
Salcott Channel, 79
Sales Point, 78, 93
Saltpan Reach, 134, 135, 138
Sand End (E Swale), 156
Sandwich, 181
Saunders Ness, 127
Scroby Sands & wind farm, 3, 10, 183
Sea Reach (Thames), 116-118
Secret Water (A. Ransome), 60, 64
Segas SC, 140, 141
The Shade, 136
The Shard, 130
Sharfleet Creek, 135-136, 138
Sheerness, 134, 167, 177
Sheerness Naval Dockyard, 134
Shelford Creek, 107
Shell Ness, 156
Sheppey, Isle of, 154, 156, 168-169, 176
Sheppey Crossing, 167
Shingle Street, 23
Shingles banks, 182
Shipways Boatyard, 90, 91
Shivering Sand Tower, 183
shoal draught, iv
Shoeburyness Firing Danger Areas, 93, 105-106, 186
Shore Ends (Crouch), 93
Short Bros seaplane factory, 146
Short Reach (Medway), 139, 142
Shortpole Reach, 98
Shotley Marina, 41, 42-43, 45, 49
Shotley Spit, 38, 41, 42, 45, 48
Shuttlewood's Boatyard, 104, 105
signals, vii, 3
Sirdar (barge), 136
Sittingbourne, 165
Skipper's Island, 65
Slaughden Quay, 24, 27-28
Slaughden SC, 27
Slaughterhouse Point, 136
small craft symbols (charts), vii
Smallgains Creek, 110, 112-113, 114
Smith Shoal, 46
Snape (& Maltings), 25, 28, 29
Snodland, 151
South Channel (N Kent), 171
South Deep (Swale), 162, 163
South Dock Marina, 118, 121, 127-128
South Woodham Ferrers YC, 101
South Yantlet Creek, 138, 140
Southend Pier, 110
Southey Creek, 88
Southwold, 18-21
Southwold SC, 21
Spile, 134, 154, 173, 176, 177
Spit NCB (Walton Backwaters), 61, 63
Spitfire Museum, 181
Spitway, 76, 92
Staley's Boayard, 159, 160

Stambridge Mills, 109
Standard Quay, 160
Stanford Channel, 13-14
Stangate Creek, 117, 135-137
Stansgate, 85
Stebbens Boatyard, 89
Stoke Creek, 138
Stoke Saltings, 138
Stoke SC, 53
Stone, 84-85
Stone Banks, 40, 60
Stone Heaps, 49
Stone Point, 60, 61
Stone SC, 84
Stonner Island, 35
Stour River, 38, 41, 44-47
Stour SC, 47
Stow Creek, 99-100
Stratton, 50
Strood, 120, 145-146
Strood Channel, 79
Strood Pelican CC, 146
Strood Pier, 145
Strood YC, 146
The Stumble, 84, 88
Stutton Ness & Bay, 46
Suffolk Yacht Harbour, 50, 51
Sun Pier, 145
Sunk DW Route, 185
Sunk Gyratory System (TSS), 40-41, 185, 186
Sunk Head Tower, 187
Sunk Sand, 187
Sunken Buxey, 93
Sunken Island, 79
Sunken Pye, 58
Surrey Docks, 128
Sutton Hoo Viking burial site, 36
Sutton Wharf, 109
Sutton Wharf Boatyard, 109
The Swale, 154-169, 173, 176, 183
Swale Marina, 164, 165
Swallowtail Bank, 92, 93
Swatchway, 118
Swin Channel, 76, 182, 183-186, 186, 187
Swin Spitway, 92, 186
Swire Hole, 76, 92

Thames Barrier, 116, 117, 118, 121, 123, 124-125
Thames Estuary passages, 1, 3, 182-187
Thames Estuary wind farms, 3, 183, 184-185, 187
Thames fuel barge (Heiko), 118, 131
Thames Gateway container port *see* London Gateway Port
Thames & Medway Canal, 120
Thames River, 116-133
Thamesmead, 123
Thamesport container terminal, 134, 135, 138
Thanet, Isle of, 172
Thanet windfarm, 3, 183
Thirslet Creek, 84
Thirslet Spit, 84
Thorn Fleet, 79
Thunderbolt Pier, 144

Thurrock YC, 122
tidal differences on Dover & Sheerness, 4-7
Tide Mill Yacht Harbour, 35-37
tides & tidal streams, 1, 4-7, 182, 183
Tilbury, 119, 122
The Tips, 35
Titchmarsh Marina, 61, 63, 64
Tollesbury, 78, 80-82
Tollesbury CC, 81
Tollesbury Marina, 81-82
Tollesbury Pier, 84
Tollesbury Saltings, 82
Tollesbury SC, 81
Tower Bridge, 130, 131, 132
Town Quay (Faversham), 157, 160
traffic separation schemes (TSSs), 40-41, 184-185
Trawl Dock (Lowestoft), 15, 16
Trimley Bay & Marshes, 50
Trinity Buoy Wharf (Thames), 125
Trinity Quay (Harwich), 38, 48, 49
Troublesome Reach, 35
Twitter, viii
The Twizzle, 61, 63, 64
Two Tree Island, 112, 113, 114

U-boat wreck, 138
Ufford, 37
Up River YC, 101
updates, viii
Upnor Reach, 143
Upnor SC, 143
Upson's Boatyard, 27

Vange Creek, 115
Veronica (barge), 136
VHF radio, vii, 2, see also *London VTS*
Victoria Wharf (Leigh), 111
Victory Moorings, 144-145
The Violet, 108

Wadgate Ledge, 40
Wakering Boatyard, 107
Wakering YC, 109
Walberswick, 20, 21
Waldringfield, 34
Waldringfield Boatyard, 34
Waldringfield SC, 33, 34
Wallasea Bay, 94, 96
Wallasea Island, 94
Wallasea Ness, 93
Wallet Channel, 60, 76, 77, 182, 186
Wallet Spitway, 92, 186
Walton on the Naze, 58, 61-63
Walton Backwaters, 58-65
Walton Channel, 61, 63
Walton & Frinton YC, 61-62, 63
Walton Pier, 60
Walton Yacht Basin, 62-63
Wantsum Channel, 172
Warden Point, 155
Wat Tyler Country Park, 115
Waterside Marina (Brightlingsea), 70, 71

Waveney (Fish) Dock (Lowestoft), 12, 15
waypoints, 1, 182
weather, 182
Webb's Boatyard, 51, 52
websites, iv, v, viii, 30, 116
West India Docks & Visitor Moorings, 118, 126-127
West Mersea, 78-79
West Mersea YC, 79
West Swale, 135, 154, 166, 167-169
The West Water *see* Hamford Water
West Wick YC, 100
Westmarsh Point, 68
Westrow Point, 28
Wherstead Road Bridge, 57
Whisstock's Boatyard, 36
Whitaker Channel, 92, 93, 183, 186
Whitaker Spit, 93, 186
Whitstable, 173, 175-176
Whitstable Bay, 176
Whitstable Street, 154, 155, 156, 173, 175
Whitstable YC, 175, 176
Whitton Marine, 139
Wickham Point, 146
Wilford Bridge, 35, 37
Wilsonian SC, 142
Wilton (old minehunter), 111
wind, 182
wind farms, 3, 8, 183, 184-185, 187
Windmill Creek, 162
Wivenhoe, 71, 73-74
Wivenhoe SC, 73, 74
Wivenhoe Tidal Barrier, 73-74
Woodbridge, 35-37
Woodbridge Boatyard, 36
Woodbridge CC, 30
Woodbridge Haven, 30, 31
Woodrolfe Boatyard, 82
Woodrolfe Creek, 80, 81-82
Woolverstone, 48
Woolverstone Marina, 52-54
Woolwich, 116, 124
Woolwich Ferry, 124
Wouldham, 149-150
Wrabness, 46

Yantlet Channel, 117
Yantlet Creek, 118
Yantlet Flats, 118
Yantlet Secondary Channel, 117
Yokesfleet Creek, 104, 107
Youngboats, 161-162